STEP-BY-STEP

ASIAN COOKBOOK

STEP-BY-STEP

ASIAN COOKBOOK

RECIPES COMPILED BY ANNE McDOWALL

THUNDER BAY
P·R·E·S·S

San Diego, California

Thunder Bay Press
An imprint of the Advantage Publishers Group
5880 Oberlin Drive, San Diego, CA 92121-4794
www.advantagebooksonline.com

Copyright © Salamander Books Ltd, 2002

A member of **Chrysalis** Books plc

All notations of errors or omissions should be addressed to
Thunder Bay Press, editorial department, at the above address. All
other correspondence (author inquiries, permissions) concerning the
content of this book should be addressed to Salamander Books Ltd,
8 Blenheim Court, Brewery Road, London, N7 9NY, U.K.

ISBN 1-57145-845-X

Library of Congress Cataloging-in-Publication Data
available on request.

Printed in Spain

1 2 3 4 5 06 05 04 03 02

CONTENTS

THE FOOD OF ASIA

The various cuisines of Asia have much in common, particularly where geography and religion (the two main influences on diet) are similar, but there are also unique traits, between and within each country. Here we give a brief introduction to the food of each of the six countries whose recipes are featured in this book. In addition, each chapter opener indicates from which country the recipe comes (though some are obviously common to several). The order of recipes within each chapter follows the order given below, from west to east and south to north.

INDIA

Indian food encompasses the cooking of many different regions, and the foods are quite different in each region. In the north, where the climate is temperate, sheep are reared and the lamb dishes are generally cooked slowly in the oven. Traveling south through Delhi and the Punjab, the diet becomes much richer; here they cook mainly with ghee (clarified butter) and eat both goat and chicken. In these northern regions, instead of rice, the preference is for bread. To the east, around the Bay of Bengal, there is an abundance of fish from the many rivers and from the bay itself. Coconut palms grow in the hot and humid climate, so coconut features strongly in many recipes. On the west coast, in Gujarat, the people are mainly vegetarian, eating legumes and vegetables; likewise in Tamil Nadu in the far southeast. The humid tropical conditions of the southwest, in Goa and Malabar, encourage date and coconut palms and banana plants to flourish and there is an abundance of fish and shellfish. Southern Indians eat more rice than the northerners and they prefer to steam foods. The dishes are traditionally very hot, much more so than in the north.

Religion influences diet at least as much as geography. There are hundreds of different religions, each with their own customs and taboos. Muslims and Jews don't eat pork, while Hindus and Sikhs are prohibited from eating beef. Although many Hindus are strict vegetarians, others eat fish and shellfish.

The imaginative use of spices sets Indian cooking apart from other cuisines; it is by far the most aromatic of all types of cooking. The most commonly used spices are cumin, coriander, mustard, black pepper, turmeric, cinnamon, cardamom, and cloves.

CHINA

China is a vast country, extending from the subtropical regions of Hunan and Kwantung in the south, right up to the dry plains of Mongolia in the north, while the western borders go right into central Asia, reaching almost to the frontier of Afghanistan. Because it is such a vast country, there are dramatic contrasts in geography and climate across China. The great diversity of regional history, customs, life, and culture have caused a distinct cuisine to evolve in each of the four major provinces.

The cooking of Beijing and northern China is a fusion of three distinct influences, high-class court and mandarin dishes, rustic Mongolian and Manchurian fare, and the indigenous cooking of the cold, northerly climate. Here rice is less important than wheat and a variety of pancakes, noodles, and dumplings are found. Grilling, lacquer roasting, spit-roasting, slow-simmering, and deep-frying are the most common cooking techniques in the northern regions. Sauces are richly flavored with dark soy sauce, garlic, scallions, spices, and sesame oil. Lamb, generally disliked elsewhere in China, is common here.

The Szechuan cuisine of the western regions tends to be hearty rather than delicate, and is renowned for highly spiced foods, especially dishes containing chilies. Szechuan cooks have perfected a fascinating range of

Above: This bustling food market on the streets of Hong Kong is typical of many throughout Asia. As well as buying meat, fish, and vegetables, locals will buy snacks such as dim sum and spring rolls (see pages 34 and 41) to eat on the street.

hot-sour, savory-spiced, and sweet-hot-piquant dishes, many of which are characterized by the crunch and bite of pickles. Many dishes are relatively dry and more reminiscent of southern stir-fries than of the sauce-rich dishes of the east.

The cooking of the east is more starchy, and richer, not only in the amount of oil used in cooking, but also in the range of ingredients, the amount of soy sauce, and the number and combinations of spices. Rice is used a lot, not only plain as an accompaniment, but also combined with vegetables, and as a stuffing. With a long coastline and well-watered lands, there is a fine selection of seafood and plenty of freshwater fish, and a great range of vegetables is also available. Many people in Shanghai have a sweet tooth, and make savory dishes that are generally sweeter than elsewhere.

Southern cooking is probably the most inventive, rich, and colorful in China. It has been influenced by a steady stream of foreign traders and travelers, and is richly endowed with year-round produce from land and sea. Fruits flourish and are combined in meat and savory dishes more often than elsewhere. Vegetables are used in quantity, but meat sparsely. Stir-frying is the most popular cooking method, but steaming and roasting are also common and the use of oil in cooking is kept to a minimum. Every meal includes rice and dishes often contain thick but delicate sauces. The area produces some of the best soy sauce in the country and, because of this, specializes in "red cooking" (slowly baking or braising food in soy sauce).

MALAYSIA

Malaysian cuisine is a fusion of the different cooking styles and dishes of three nationalities: Indian, Chinese, and indigenous Malay. These have merged to make a unique, harmonious blend that is an identifying characteristic of the cuisine of this tropical peninsula.

The Indians contributed spices such as cumin, turmeric, and chilies, and their art of blending spices is reflected in the many Malaysian curries. Indian-style flatbreads, chutneys, and relishes frequently accompany meals. The Chinese influence is evident in the use of soy sauce, hoisin sauce, spring rolls, and stir-fries, and is particularly strong in the Nonya cooking of Singapore, which combines the Chinese emphasis on texture and balance of tastes with the Malaysian predilection for curries and chili dishes. A definite Thai flavor can be detected in the use of lemongrass, cilantro, and galangal. The many years of Portuguese, Dutch, and British occupation have also left their mark on Malaysian cooking.

Malaysian cuisine is a very healthy one. Chicken is the most widely eaten meat. With a large Muslim population and a significant number of Hindus, pork and beef are not used to any great extent. Besides, the climate is not conducive to rearing livestock for eating. Fish and seafood are plentiful and widely eaten. Rice is a staple in the diet, while noodles are also used to bulk up meat dishes, to thicken soups, and generally add substance to the diet. Both rice and noodles are also popular as snacks.

Desserts are light and refreshing. A Malaysian meal does not usually include a dessert beyond some of the tropical fruits, such as mangoes, lychees, pineapples, rambutans, and carambolas (star fruit), that grow in profusion. Coconut palms thrive, so coconut is a common ingredient. Coconut milk provides the liquid for many of the country's curries and the national soup, Laksa Lemak (see page 22). It is also the basis of desserts such as coconut custard.

THAILAND

Thai food is an original and rich amalgam of evocative aromas, subtle blends of herbs and spices, and contrasting textures and tastes, and contains flavors and techniques that are familiar from Chinese, Indian, and Japanese cooking. The dishes are light and fresh and characterized by flavors such as lime, cilantro, coconut milk, garlic, and chili. A fresh, sweet-sour taste is also typically Thai, derived from tangy lime or tamarind and palm sugar. Mild fish sauce provides the main savory flavoring.

Rice is a very important part of the diet. As well as being the foundation of many one-course dishes, rice plays a vital supporting role for other dishes, and balances highly spiced ones. Thai dishes are created to be mixed and eaten with rice. Thai curries can be searingly hot, though they are cooked quickly and do not have the rich heaviness that results from long, slow simmering. Coconut milk is used to soften the pungency of the spices and combines flavors to give a sophisticated subtlety to the finished dish.

Thailand has a long coastline and many inland rivers, which provide fish and shellfish that are both ubiquitous and varied. Meat is considered more of a luxury and is often "stretched" by being combined with vegetables, rice, noodles, fish or shellfish, or plenty of coconut-based sauce. Chicken is more abundant, but the birds are smaller than Western ones. Duck is popular, particularly for special occasions. Dairy products are not used in Thai cooking. Vegetables are important, but they are not often cooked on their own or served as a specific dish. Instead they are combined with meat, poultry, or fish, eaten as a salad, either hot or cold, or simply served with *nam prik* (see page 232).

VIETNAM

At first sight, there seems to be little difference between Vietnamese and Thai cooking, but on closer examination, you will discover that, partly because of their geographical proximity, the influence of Chinese cuisine is more strongly felt in Vietnam than in Thailand, while the latter seems to have absorbed more influences from the Indian subcontinent.

There is an amazing variety of regional cuisine in Vietnam. Apart from the extensive external influence of China, Vietnam also has a long-established vegetarian tradition derived from Mahayana Buddhism, which originated in India and was introduced into Vietnam by way of China and Thailand. In addition, there is still evidence of the more recent French colonial influence, not to mention the American influence of the 1960s.

Ho Chi Minh City in the south is the most cosmopolitan of all Vietnamese cities and the home of incredible tropical seafood and specialties from the Mekong River delta. With its hot, humid climate and fertile lands, this region also produces a great variety of vegetables, fruits, and meats. The French influence is particularly strong here. The small island of Phu Quoc, off the Vietnam/Cambodia border, is reputed to produce the best fish sauce (*nuoc mam*) in Vietnam.

Hue, the former Imperial capital in the center of the country, has the most sophisticated cuisine and, as the temperate climate is ideal for the cultivation of exotic vegetables, it specializes in vegetarian food. Ho An of the central coast was home of the most important ports in southwest Asia between the seventeenth and nineteenth centuries, and the Dutch, Portuguese, American, Japanese, and Chinese merchants all came here.

In Hanoi, the capital of Vietnam, which is in the north, close to the Chinese border, the food is less spicy and the Chinese influence particularly strong, with stir fried dishes and clay-pot cooking. The climate is milder here than in the south, and the Red River delta with the Gulf of Tongking produces a wealth of fish and shellfish, as well as vegetables and other foods.

JAPAN

Japan was an agricultural nation for thousands of years until after the Second World War. Houses were traditionally constructed mostly of wood, so wood was, and still is, a very valuable resource. With few other fuel resources, the Japanese had to find various ways of appreciating both their agricultural produce and the plentiful supply of fish caught in the surrounding seas without burning lots of wood and charcoal. Consequently, the Japanese developed ways of eating raw or nearly raw food.

In Japan, eating raw fish is considered the best, if not the only, way to appreciate the real flavor of fish, and sashimi (prepared raw fish) has pride of place in a Japanese meal. Fish for sashimi must be really fresh, refrigerated until ready to use, and handled as little as possible. Another Japanese specialty is sushi, based on boiled rice, flavored with a rice vinegar mixture while warm, then fanned to cool it quickly and give it a glossy sheen. There is a wide variety of sushi, such as sushi rolls made with vegetables or fish enclosed in sushi rice, wrapped in nori seaweed, then rolled up and sliced.

Due to Shintoism, the ancient mythological religion, and later Buddhism, which was introduced from China, the Japanese remained a noncarnivorous nation until the opening up of the country to Western influences toward the end of the nineteenth century. Today, despite Japan's economic growth and the pressure from overseas governments to open up the domestic market, Japan is still largely a nation of fish and vegetable eaters. When meat is used, it is sliced thickly and normally cooked with vegetables. As a result, Japanese cooking is naturally healthy without trying to be so.

GLOSSARY OF INGREDIENTS

Asafetida A pale brown resin made from the sap of a giant fennel-like plant native to India and Iran. It has a garlicky flavor and is used sparingly as a flavoring in Indian dishes. It is available in powder or lump form.

Bamboo shoots The young shoots of certain varieties of bamboo, these are pale yellow in color with a crunchy texture and fairly bland flavor. They are available in cans, whole or sliced; rinse in fresh water before use. Will keep a week if stored in fresh water in a covered container in the refrigerator.

Banana leaves Used to make containers for steamed foods. Aluminum foil can be used instead, but the food will not have the same delicate flavor.

Basil Thai (or "holy") basil leaves are darker and their flavor slightly deeper, more spicy, and less "fresh" than ordinary sweet basil, with a touch of lemony flavor. Bundles of leaves can be frozen whole in a polyethylene bag up to about two weeks; remove leaves when needed and add straight to dishes. Substitute Thai sweet basil or ordinary sweet basil if necessary.

Bean sprouts These are the sprouting shoots of the mung bean. They have a mild, watery taste and crisp texture and can be steamed, stir-fried, or eaten raw. Always use fresh sprouts in preference to canned ones. They will keep fresh in the refrigerator three or four days.

Black beans Small black soybeans, fermented in salt and spices, are available in cans or plastic packages, and also as a paste or a sauce.

Bok choy Also known as *pak choi* and, in Japan, as *hakusai*, this leafy vegetable has a slightly bulbous base and long leaves that have white stalks and ribs topped by dark green leaves. The stalks have a mild, refreshing flavor and the leaves taste pleasantly tangy and bitter. It is best cooked quickly to retain both the flavor and texture, but can also be served raw and is particularly good for making pickles. It stays fresh for a long time when stored in the refrigerator. Bok choy is widely available, but if you are unable to find it, use Chinese cabbage or spinach.

Candlenuts Cream-colored waxy nuts used to add thickness and texture to curries and casseroles. Raw macadamia nuts or cashews can be substituted.

Cardamom A member of the ginger family common in Indian dishes. Its long, light-green or brown pods contain seeds with a strong, lemony flavor and heady aroma. Ground cardamom is available, but it is better to grind the seeds as needed. Whole pods should be removed from the dish before eating.

Chili sauce A bright-red, hot sauce made from red chilies, vinegar, garlic, sugar, and salt. It can be used in cooking but is more often served as a dip. Vietnamese chili sauce is much more fiery than standard Chinese chili sauce or Western hot pepper sauce.

Chilies A very important feature of Asian cooking, and used in large amounts. Many different varieties of chilies are now readily available, and are often labeled to show the degree of hotness. As a rule, smaller varieties are hotter than large ones. Dried chilies, which are always red, have a more earthy, fruity flavor, and fresh green chilies have a "greener," less-rounded flavor than red ones, which are riper. Thais favor small and very fiery bird's-eye chilies. The seeds and white veins inside a chili are not only hotter than the flesh, but have less flavor and are generally removed before cooking. Chilies contain an oil that can irritate the eyes and skin, so avoid touching your face when preparing chilies, and wash your hands well afterward.

Chinese cabbage Similar to bok choy, but with paler leaves, Chinese cabbage has a stout, elongated head of tightly packed, firm, crinkly, pale yellow–green leaves with a thick, white center vein and a mild, delicate flavor. It can be lightly stir-fried, steamed, or eaten raw.

Cilantro Ideally, buy whole bunches and stand them in cold water in a cool place. Large cilantro bunches often include the roots, which have a more muted taste than the leaves. Fresh roots will keep several days if wrapped and stored in a cool place, or can be frozen. If unavailable, use cilantro stalks.

Cinnamon Whole cinnamon sticks are highly aromatic and pungent and should be broken into two or three pieces before use to release their flavor. Remove from the dish before serving. Ground cinnamon has a much milder flavor and should only be used as a substitute if very fresh.

Cloves A common spice in Indian cooking. Whole cloves keep their flavor better than the powder and can be ground as needed.

Coconut cream The layer that forms on the top of coconut milk when it is left to stand. It is usually added at the very end of preparing a dish.

Coconut milk This is not the liquid that comes from a coconut, but is made by soaking coconut flesh in hot water (see page 224). Once cool, coconut milk should be kept in the refrigerator. It may separate when left to stand; either spoon off the thick layer and use as coconut cream or stir it back into the milk. Ready-prepared coconut milk, sold in cans and plastic packages, sometimes has a thicker consistency than homemade coconut milk.

Creamed coconut Sold in hard white blocks, which should be kept in a cool place or in the refrigerator. Creamed coconut can be used to make coconut milk: grate or chop 3 oz. and dissolve in 1¼ cups hot water. Alternatively, it can be added, after grating or chopping, straight to the hot cooking liquid in a pan toward the end of cooking.

Cumin Commonly used in Indian cooking, these small seeds have a nutty flavor and aroma. Whole seeds will keep fresh longer than ground cumin.

Curry leaves A small, dark green leaf used in some southern Indian dishes.

Daikon Also known as *mooli* or *Chinese radish*, the daikon resembles a large parsnip. The white, crisp, and slightly pungent flesh is a staple of Japanese cooking, but is also used in Chinese dishes. It is eaten raw in salads (usually shredded), cooked in vegetable dishes, pickled, and used in sauces.

Dried shrimp Used throughout southeast Asia, these are sold in clear plastic packages (make sure the shrimp are a good pinkish color). They need to be soaked in hot water for 10 to 15 minutes and are usually ground before use. Keep them in a cool place in an airtight container. (See also *shrimp paste*.)

Fish sauce Used in southeast Asia much as soy sauce is used in China, fish sauce is a thick, salty, brown liquid made from salted shrimp or fish.

Five-spice powder A mix of ground star anise, Szechuan peppercorns, fennel, cloves, and cinnamon, which gives a fragrant, spicy, sweet flavor to Chinese dishes. Some brands include other spices such as ginger and coriander seeds.

Galangal Resembles fresh ginger (to which it is related), but the skin is thinner, paler, more translucent, and tinged with pink, and it is less hot. To use, peel and thinly slice or chop. The whole root will keep up to two weeks if wrapped in paper and kept in the vegetable crisper in the refrigerator, or it can be frozen. If frozen, allow to thaw just enough to enable the amount required to be sliced off, then return the root to the freezer. Galangal is also sold dried or in slices, but fresh ginger is the best substitute if fresh galangal is unavailable.

Ghee A form of clarified butter (after the moisture has evaporated, the milk solids are allowed to brown), this is a common cooking medium in India. It has a long shelf life, high smoke point, and a nutty, caramel-like flavor.

Ginger When buying fresh ginger, choose firm, heavy pieces that have a slight sheen. Keep it in a cool place up to a week or, for longer storage, wrap it in absorbent kitchen paper, place in a plastic bag, and store in the vegetable crisper in the refrigerator. Once peeled and chopped or sliced, it adds a sweet, spicy flavor to all kinds of sweet and savory dishes. Vinegared ginger is widely used in Japanese cooking and is available in packages.

Hoisin sauce A thick, dark reddish–brown sauce made from soybeans, vinegar, spices, garlic, and sugar, with a sweet flavor. Also known as *Chinese grill sauce*, it is very versatile. It can be used for dipping and marinating, as well as for cooking. Refrigerate after opening; it will keep for many months.

Kaffir lime leaves Dark green, highly aromatic leaves with a clean citrus-pine smell and flavor. Kaffir lime leaves freeze well, laid flat in a heavy-duty plastic bag. Use the grated peel of ordinary limes if kaffir leaves are not available, substituting 1½ teaspoons for each kaffir lime leaf.

Konbu (kelp) A giant seaweed sold in dried form in Asian markets. Full of vitamins and minerals, it is a healthy food best eaten simmered with other vegetables. It is also used for dashi (Japanese fish stock).

Konnyaku A gelatin-like cake made from yam flour, it has no taste or nutritional value but is eaten for its texture. It is available fresh in packages at Asian markets.

Lemongrass A deliciously fragrant, lemony herb that is indispensable to Far Eastern cooking. To use, cut off the root tip and top end to leave the lower 4 to 6 in., peel away the tough outer layers, then thinly slice the inner part. To prevent drying out, store with the end in a little cold water. Lemongrass also freezes well; to defrost, hold briefly under running hot water. The grated rind of half a lemon can be substituted for one lemongrass stalk.

Lily buds Also known as *golden needles* or *yellow flowers* in Chinese, these are the dried buds of the tiger lily flower. Soak in warm water for about 30 minutes, then rinse in fresh water and discard the hard tip before use.

Long beans Although these can grow to over 3 ft., it is best to use younger, smaller ones. Green beans can be substituted.

Lychees Available in cans, but fresh lychees are now becoming more readily available. The nobbly, brittle coating is easily cracked to reveal the delicious, crispy, fruity white flesh surrounding a smooth central pit.

Mango Select fruit that feels heavy for its size and is free of bruises or damage. A ripe mango yields to gentle pressure and should have an enticing, scented aroma. The flesh inside should have a wonderful, luxurious, and slightly exotic texture and flavor. If a mango is a little firm when bought, leave it in a warm, sunny place to finish ripening. The central pit is large and flat and usually difficult to separate from the flesh without using a knife.

Mint There are many varieties of mint in the Far East and it can be used at almost every meal. Thai mint has a spearmint flavor. If Thai mint leaves are not available, spearmint or garden mint are the best substitutes.

Mirin This is thick, sweet rice wine, which gives a very subtle, sweet flavor to dishes. If not available, sweet sherry can be substituted, but reduce the amount of sugar in the dish by half.

Miso A very salty paste made from fermented soybeans, miso is used in Japanese soup and salad dressings and is also good in marinades for fish and meat. The orangey-brown variety is slightly sweeter than the more salty, reddish-brown one.

Mushrooms Asian cooks generally use dried mushrooms, which have a much more intense fragrance and flavor than fresh ones. Dried mushrooms must be soaked before cooking: put them in a bowl, cover with boiling water, cover the bowl, leave about 30 minutes until swollen and pliable, then drain well and squeeze dry. Discard the hard stalks before use.
Chinese (dried) mushrooms Also known as *shiitake* or *black mushrooms*, they have a pronounced flavor. Dried mushrooms vary in quality and thickness; choose the thickest (usually the most expensive) ones.
Straw mushrooms These have a pleasant, delicate flavor with an interesting texture. They are available in cans and should be drained and rinsed before use, as well as dried.
Black fungus Also known as *wood fungus* or *cloud ears*, and always sold in dried form, these dried mushrooms have a crunchy texture with a subtle flavor.

From top to bottom: coconut milk, galangal, lemongrass, green chilies, fresh noodles, curry leaves, kaffir lime leaves, garlic, candlenuts, fresh noodles, red chilies, bok choy.

Mustard seeds White and yellow seeds have the mildest flavor, black the strongest. Brown seeds are moderately hot and generally have husks attached.

Noodles Most types are interchangeable, but rice vermicelli and bean thread noodles can also be crisp-fried. Egg noodles are rarely seen in Vietnam, where only rice flour noodles are used. Dried noodles are usually soaked in cold water for 10 to 20 minutes until softened before cooking. In general, the weight doubles after soaking. After draining, the cooking is usually quick.
Egg noodles In Asia both fresh and dried egg noodles, which are wheat-based, are used in a variety of different widths, but in the West fresh noodles can be quite difficult to find. They may be found packed in plastic bags in the refrigerated section of an Asian market. Fresh "nests" should be shaken loose before using. Some dried egg noodles are soaked before use; others are cooked like dried pasta by dropping them into a saucepan of boiling water. Some varieties cook quickly, so test for doneness frequently.
Rice noodles Also known as *rice sticks*, these semitransparent noodles come in three different widths and are sold in bundles. There are also very fine strands, known as *rice vermicelli*. The noodles are usually soaked for about 5 minutes in boiling water, then rinsed in cold water before cooking, but vermicelli rice noodles are sometimes served crisp. Fresh rice noodles are packaged cooked and wet in wide, pliable "hanks." To use, cut into ribbons without unwinding and stir into a dish just long enough to warm through.
Bean thread noodles Also called *glass, shining, mung bean* or *cellophane noodles*, these are fine noodles made from mung beans. Tough and semitransparent when raw, they need to be soaked before cooking.
Soba noodles Japanese thin, flat noodles made from buckwheat and wheat flour. They are grayish-brown in color.
Somen Japanese wheat flour noodles, fine, glossy, and white in appearance and usually sold dried. Various colors and flavors are available.
Udon These wide, flat, ribbonlike Japanese wheat-flour noodles are available dried, fresh, or precooked in a variety of widths.

Nori Dried seaweed available in wafer-thin sheets, it has a sweet, salty flavor and is used in Japanese cooking to wrap sushi, or as a garnish or flavoring.

Oils Vegetable oil is used when the taste is not a part of a recipe. Peanut oil is used for its characteristic flavor. Other oils, with a lower burning point, are used for flavorings.
Peanut oil A slightly sweet, mild oil that withstands heat very well. Use it in moderation as it has a high saturated fat content.
Sesame oil Asian sesame oil is made from roasted sesame seeds, so is dark in color and has a delicious, rich, nutty flavor. Because the flavor is quite pronounced, the oil is used only in small amounts, rather like a seasoning. Sesame oil is sold in small bottles that should be stored in a dark, cool place, but not the refrigerator as the oil will become cloudy.
Chili oil Hot, pungent oil that should be heated gently as it burns easily. It is best used as a flavoring rather than a cooking agent.

Oyster sauce A thick brown sauce made from concentrated oysters cooked in soy sauce, then mixed with seasonings. It is often added to Chinese stir-fried dishes, particularly beef. Its taste is not fishy, but richly meaty.

Palm sugar A delicious honey-colored, raw sugar with a slight caramelized flavor, widely used in Malaysia and Thailand. It is sold in lump and free-flowing forms in cans and plastic packages in Asian markets. Light brown sugar is an adequate substitute.

Papaya Also known as *paw-paw*. Use the unripe green papaya for salads or in cooking. When it turns yellow or red, it is eaten as a fruit.

Pea eggplants Very small eggplants about the size of a pea, and usually the same color, although they can be white, purple, or yellow. The fresh, slightly bitter taste is used raw in hot sauces and cooked in curries.

Plum sauce This thick, sweet condiment, made from plums, apricots, garlic, vinegar, and seasonings, is used in Chinese cooking or as a dip.

Rambutans A Malaysian variety of the lychee, but with a more acidic flavor.

Rice The staple food of Asia. A number of different types are used:
Fragrant long-grain rice Also known as *Thai fragrant rice* and *jasmine rice*, this is the rice most commonly used in southeast Asian cooking. Ordinary long-grain rice can be substituted if necessary.
Basmati rice This rice, with its long, slim grains and nutty flavor, is the rice most often used in Indian recipes. Long-grain rice can be substituted.
Sticky (or glutinous) rice An aptly named short, round-grain variety. It can be formed into balls and eaten with fingers, or used for desserts.
Ground, browned rice This is sometimes added to dishes to give texture. Dry-fry raw long-grain white rice until well browned, then grind finely.
Japanese rice Authentic Japanese rice is short grained and slightly sticky. California medium-grain rice is a suitable substitute.

Rice paper Made from rice flour, salt, and water, then dried in the sun on bamboo mats, rice paper is available in round or large square sheets and is used for wrapping spring rolls and other foods. The sheets must be dipped in warm water a few seconds before use.

Rice wine Made from glutinous rice, yeast, and spring water, this wine is used extensively in Asian cooking. Similar to sherry in color, bouquet, and alcohol content (18 percent), it has its own distinctive (rich and sweetish) flavor. Pale, dry sherry may be substituted or, if a sweet, spicy flavor is required, sweet sherry may be used. (See also *mirin* and *sake*.)

Saffron The dried yellow-orange stigma of a crocus's purple flower, saffron is used as a flavoring (it has a slightly bitter, honeylike flavor) and coloring agent in Indian cooking. Although expensive, only a few threads are needed in a recipe.

Sake A strong rice wine made from fermented rice and water. Along with tea, it is Japan's most famous drink and the one most frequently served with meals, usually lukewarm.

Sansho pepper A delicately pungent Japanese green pepper, which is not used for cooking but as a condiment at the table. It is available in bottles.

Sesame paste A flavoring often used in southeast Asian cooking made from toasted white sesame seeds.

Shallots The red variety commonly found in Asia is smaller than the Western type. It has quite a pronounced flavor that is fruity rather than pungent. Shallots are used in large amounts instead of onions, and are included as part of a spice paste. Ordinary shallots, or the white parts of scallions, can be substituted

Shrimp paste Known as *belaccan* in Malaysia but more often found elsewhere as *trasi* or *blachan* (the Indonesian and Burmese names). Shrimp paste is made from fermented shrimps, dried and pounded to a paste, and is used in small amounts. It is always cooked before use. It may be ground to a paste with other flavorings, or it may be toasted, broiled, or fried. Break off the amount you need and either hold it in tongs over a naked flame, turning it so it roasts evenly, or spread it onto a piece of foil and broil it. Alternatively, wrap it in foil and cook it in a dry frying pan until it is crumbly and smells fragrant. Raw shrimp paste has a strong smell, so keep it in a tightly covered jar; the smell disappears during cooking.

Soy sauce The essential ingredient in Chinese and Japanese cooking, soy sauce (*shoyu* in Japan) is made from soybeans, flour, and water, which are fermented and aged several months. Light soy sauce (sometimes known as thin soy sauce) is thinner, paler in color, and saltier than dark (thick) soy sauce, which is heavier, sweeter, and has a more rounded flavor. Light soy is used with vegetables, seafood, and soups; dark soy with dark meats and for dipping sauces. When soy sauce is used, additional salt is often unnecessary.

Star anise These attractive pods, in the shape of an eight-pointed star, have a mild licorice flavor. They should be removed from a dish before serving.

Star fruit Long, almost translucent yellow, ridged fruit, also known as *carambola*. The whole fruit is edible, and when cut across the width, the slices resemble five-pointed stars. Raw star fruit have a pleasant, juicy sharpness, but when poached the flavor is more distinctive.

Szechuan peppercorns These reddish colored, mildly spicy, aromatic dried berries should be toasted and crushed or ground before use. To toast, dry-fry in a wok for a few minutes. Crush in a mortar and pestle.

Tamarind This has a distinctive fruity/lemony sharpness. The sticky, brown-black "pulp" can be found in Asian markets, peeled, seeded, and wrapped as a block in a square package. To make tamarind water, break off a 1-oz. piece, pour over 1¼ cups boiling water, break up the lump with a spoon, then leave for about 30 minutes, stirring occasionally. Strain off the tamarind water, pressing on the pulp; discard the remaining debris. Keep the water in a jar in the refrigerator. Ready-to-use tamarind syrup can sometimes be bought—it is usually more concentrated, so less is used. To make tamarind paste, soak 4 oz. tamarind in 1 cup hot water for about 3 hours, then strain it through a cheesecloth to extract as much liquid as possible. Ready-prepared tamarind paste is also available.

Tofu Also known as *bean curd*, tofu is made from puréed yellow soybeans and has a distinctive soft texture and neutral flavor. It is low in fat and high in protein, and so is widely used in low-fat recipes. In Japan, tofu stores still make it every day and traditionally there are two kinds, silk or cotton, made from soya milk strained through silk or cotton cloth. You can buy fresh as well as prepacked tofu at Asian markets. The fresh tofu available outside Japan is normally a cotton tofu and the prepacked one is a silk tofu. Firm tofu, the type recommended for cooking, is sold in solid cakes, which are kept in water and drained and chopped before use. Handle and cook with care to keep the tofu from breaking up.

Turmeric A rhizome similar to ginger, though smaller and more delicate in appearance. It is usually used fresh in Asia, but in the West is more often used ground; ½ teaspoon ground turmeric is equivalent to 1 in. of fresh tumeric. Fresh turmeric needs to be peeled before use.

Vegetables chow-chow Also known as *Szechuan preserved vegetables*. Various vegetables, preserved in salt, are available in cans and plastic pouches, but the label "preserved vegetables" will invariably mean mustard greens. They have a crunchy texture and hot, spicy flavor, but are salty, so rinse before use. Once opened, jars should be covered and stored in the refrigerator and canned vegetables transferred to a glass or earthenware container.

Vinegars *Rice vinegar* is the mildest of all vinegars, with a sweet, delicate flavor and comes in several varieties. *White rice vinegar* is clear, with a mild, delicate flavor. *Red rice vinegar* is sweet and spicy. If possible, use a pale rice vinegar for light-colored sweet-and-sour dishes, and try a dark variety for dipping sauces. If unable to find either, use cider vinegar. *Chinese black vinegar* is thicker than most vinegars, made from grains other than rice, and aged to impart complex, smoky flavors with a light, pleasant bitterness. It is used sparingly as a seasoning. Substitute balsamic vinegar, sherry, or a good red wine vinegar if Chinese black vinegar is not available.

Wasabi This is hot, green horseradish used in Japanese raw fish dishes. It is sold as a paste in tubes or in powdered form. The latter needs to be mixed with an equal quantity of warm water before use.

Water chestnuts Round, white root vegetables about the size of a walnut, water chestnuts are crunchy with a mild, slightly sweet flavor. They are available fresh from Asian markets but are more commonly sold in cans. Rinse well before using. Once opened, store in fresh water in the refrigerator for up to a week.

Wonton wrappers Thin, pastry-like sheets made from eggs and flour. They can be bought fresh or frozen in squares or rounds. They can be kept in the refrigerator, wrapped, for about five days.

Yellow bean sauce A thick, spicy, aromatic sauce made from fermented yellow beans and quite salty. It is often used in sauces for fish and poultry. It may be chunky or smooth.

From top to bottom: galangal powder, tamarind, dried shrimp, turmeric, basmati rice, fragrant long-grain rice, shallots, palm sugar, soy sauce, mortar and pestle.

PREPARING, COOKING, AND SERVING FOOD

Cutting ingredients, particularly vegetables, is a very important part of Asian cooking. Indeed, more time is often spent preparing ingredients than cooking them, particularly for stir-frying, where it is important that ingredients are cut in equal-size pieces so that they cook evenly.

Roll cutting: Cut a diagonal slice from the vegetable. Make a one-quarter turn of the vegetable toward you and make a diagonal slice slightly above and partly across the face of the first slice. Continue cutting in this way.

Diagonal cutting: Hold a heavy chef's knife or Chinese cleaver at a 45° angle and move it along the length of the width of slice desired.

Shredding: Cut the sides and ends of the vegetables so that they are flat. Work the knife across the vegetables, just in front of the fingers. Cut the vegetable lengthwise across the slices to the width of a matchstick.

COOKING UTENSILS

Asian cooks use a small number of practical and versatile utensils designed to make the most efficient and economical use of heat. Many of these items will be found in a well-equipped Western kitchen, and for those specifically Asian utensils, a Western alternative will usually suffice.

Mortar and pestle Used during the preparation of the majority of savory dishes. A small blender or coffee grinder kept specifically for the purpose will take away the effort but will not produce quite the same results. When used for fibrous ingredients, such as galangal and lemongrass, the mortar and pestle crushes the fibers rather than cuts them and so releases the flavoring juices and oils more successfully.

Knives and cleavers Asian cooks generally use cleavers for all tasks that require a knife, but a selection of good-quality sharp knives will suffice.

Chopping board A large, heavy, wooden board is ideal.

Wok Used for frying, stir-frying, deep-frying, and steaming. A useful size to buy is one that is about 12 to 14 in. in diameter across the top. Choose one that has good, deep sides and some weight. Carbon steel is preferable to light stainless steel or aluminum, as these tend to develop hot spots which cause sticking, and do not withstand intense heat very well. Nonstick and electric woks do not reach sufficiently high temperatures. A skillet could be used for frying and stir-frying, a deep-fat frying pan for deep-frying, and a saucepan for steaming.

The wok may also have a lid, which is used when braising and red-cooking, and a metal ring or stand to hold the wok steady over the heat.

A wok rack may be used in the wok when steaming to support the steaming basket above the level of the water.

Steamer Bamboo steamers are used throughout the Far East. These are designed to sit over a wok and often two

Clockwise from top left: wok, Chinese hot pot, bamboo steamer, Chinese cleavers, chopsticks, wire ladle, clay pot, mortar and pestle.

or more are stacked on top of each other so that a number of dishes can be cooked at the same time. The steam is absorbed by the bamboo lid, keeping water from dripping onto the food. The food is often placed on a plate in the steamer and served directly from it so that all the nourishing juices and flavor are retained.

Rice cooker Because of the amount of rice eaten and the number of people cooked for, many households now use an electric rice cooker. A heavy saucepan with a tight-fitting lid will be adequate for Western needs.

Karahi or balti pan A deep, round-bottomed, traditional Indian vessel with two circular carrying handles. Food is cooked in this and, if used with a stand, it is brought to the table, where food is served directly from it.

Long-handled spatula Metal or wooden and curved and shaped like a shovel, these long spatulas are used for scooping and tossing food in the wok.

Strainers The best ones are wire baskets with bamboo handles, which are used to scoop noodles and other ingredients out of boiling water, stock, or oil while cooking or during a "pot-style" meal.

Fondue (hot pot) Traditionally, a charcoal- or spirit-burning Chinese hot pot (also known as a *Mongolian fire kettle*) is used for tabletop cooking. A fondue set is an acceptable substitute.

Chopsticks Used for cooking (stirring and mixing) as well as eating; the chopsticks used for stir-frying are longer.

When using chopsticks to eat, an equal amount of chopstick should protrude on each side of the hand and the tapered ends should point downward. The lower chopstick, which remains stationary, is held with the tips of the fourth and little finger, the upper part of the chopstick resting comfortably in the base of the thumb and the index finger. The upper one is held firmly with the thumb, index, and middle fingers as you would a pencil. Use the thumb to brace the stationary chopstick securely against the top of the fourth finger. There should be about a 1-in. space between the sticks. Press the upper chopstick down with the index and third finger so that it meets the stationary chopstick to pick up the food. Tap the ends of the chopsticks gently on the table to align them.

Clay pots Small earthenware pots are used as casseroles, especially in Vietnamese cooking. The Western versions are usually too large for Asian dishes, so try to find a set of small Asian clay pots.

Daikon grater Commonly used in Japanese cooking, which uses a lot of grated daikon and ginger, this differs from an ordinary cheese grater in having a curved base, which catches the juices from the ingredients.

Makisu A piece of bamboo blind the size of a place mat, which is used mainly for rolling sushi. Use any flexible place mat of a similar texture.

Molds A rectangular mold is used to make pressed sushis and flower-shaped ones for pretty pieces of sushi and hors d'oeuvres.

Whisk About 10 in. long and consisting of thin strips of bamboo tied together at the top, this is used for cleaning the wok.

COOKING METHODS

Whether food is being cooked for a family meal or formal banquet, it is generally lightly done. Stir-frying is the most common cooking method throughout most of the Far East, but the following methods are also popular ways of cooking food. Because of the importance of contrasts in texture as well as taste, several methods may be used to prepare a single meal.

Stir-frying For successful stir-frying, food should be finely sliced or shredded with every piece cut to the same size. Heat the wok over a high heat before pouring in a little oil. Once the oil is almost at smoking point, add the ingredients. Toss them, keeping them moving from the center to the sides.

Steaming A healthy cooking method, since few of the food's nutrients are lost, steaming also preserves the color and texture of ingredients. Steaming is far more popular in the East than in the West, and is a common way to cook meat, poultry, fish, dim sum, pastries, and desserts. It was developed as a fuel-saving measure, as several foods can be cooked at once in baskets stacked above each other. Foods that require the most cooking are put in first, and those needing less time are placed on top as cooking progresses.

Broiling Foods to be broiled benefit from being marinated before cooking. This adds flavor and helps to keep the foods moist when exposed to direct heat, which is particularly important when using little or no fat.

Braising Rich, slow-cooked dishes make a pleasant change to stir-fries. Foods are initially seared in a little oil, then further cooked in a liquid, such as stock thickened with cornstarch to form a sauce, or coconut milk. Cooking in this way ensures nutrients and flavor are retained in the sauce.

Deep-frying Done in a wok, this needs less oil. Foods are often marinated first, then sometimes coated in batter. Often the food if fried until almost cooked, then removed from the oil, the oil reheated, and the food added again to finish cooking and become really crisp.

Oven-cooking Few Asian cooks have ovens, but it is a method often used in restaurants. The most renowned oven-cooking method is Cantonese red-roasting, in which meat, fish, or root vegetables are cooked slowly in dark soy sauce, sometimes with other flavorings added. During the lengthy cooking, which may be as long as four hours, the soy imparts a fairly dark, reddish-brown color and a rich flavor to the food. Because soy sauce is very salty, sugar may be added as a counterbalance.

SERVING AND EATING

Throughout Asia, meals tend to be sociable times, particularly the main meal of the day, which is normally eaten in the evening. A traditional meal will usually comprise several dishes, served simultaneously, which everyone shares. Diners will often have their own bowl of soup and rice and will help themselves to other dishes. Importance is given to selecting dishes to provide a contrast of textures as well as flavors, so a soft, steamed dish may be served with a crisp, fried one, or a strongly spiced one with a bland one. Desserts are not usually served, except at formal banquets, but there is usually fresh fruit. Many of the sweets and starters featured in this book are commonly eaten as snacks during the day, often bought from street vendors. Food presentation is also important, and garnishes are common. A few simple ones are shown on the following page.

CARROT FLOWERS

1 long carrot, about 1 in. in diameter

Use a small, sharp knife to make a cut toward the pointed end of the carrot, forming a petal shape about ¼ in. wide. Repeat cuts around carrot to form a flower with four petals.

GARNISHES

2 small, firm tomatoes
6 to 8 radishes
4 scallions
4 small red or green chilies, seeded

To make tomato roses, use a small, sharp knife to peel off the skin, like an apple, in one piece. Curl the skin into a circle, then invert it to form a rose.

Angle knife in such a way that with a slight twist, the flower comes away from the carrot. Repeat this process along the length of the carrot.

To make radish flowers, cut thin petals all the way around each radish, starting at the root and finishing at the top. Plunge into iced water and leave for about 1 hour; petals will open up to form a flower. Drain and pat dry before use.

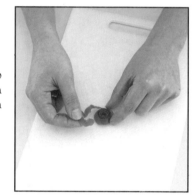

Drop carrot flowers into a pan of boiling salted water for about 1 minute to improve color. Drain and rinse in cold water. Dry well. Use as a garnish, singly or in clusters.

To make scallion and chili flowers, make fine cuts about halfway along the length of the vegetables to form fine petals. Place in a bowl of iced water and leave for 5 to 10 minutes; they will open up to form curly flowers. Dry well before using as garnishes.

SOUPS

CHINESE CHICKEN STOCK

2½-lb. chicken, giblets removed
2 slices fresh ginger
1 clove garlic
2 scallions
large pinch salt
large pinch ground white pepper

Skin chicken and trim away any visible fat. Wash and place in a large saucepan with ginger, garlic, scallions, salt, and pepper. Add 9 cups cold water.

Bring to a boil, skimming away surface scum using a large, flat ladle. Reduce heat, cover, and simmer 2 hours. Let cool slightly.

Line a strainer with a clean cheesecloth and place over a large bowl. Ladle stock through strainer and discard chicken and vegetables. Cover and chill. Before using, skim away any fat that forms on the surface. Store in the refrigerator up to 3 days or freeze up to 3 months.

Makes 7½ cups.

CHINESE BEEF STOCK

2-lb. lean stewing beef
1-in. piece fresh ginger, peeled
1 clove garlic
2 shallots
1 stalk celery
2 carrots
2 tablespoons dark soy sauce
large pinch salt
large pinch freshly ground black pepper

Trim any visible fat and silver skin from beef. Cut into 2-in. pieces. Wash and pat dry with absorbent paper towels.

Place beef in a large saucepan with ginger, garlic, shallots, celery, carrots, soy sauce, salt, and pepper, and add 9 cups cold water. Bring to a boil, skimming away surface scum using a large, flat ladle. Reduce heat, cover, and simmer 2 hours. Let cool slightly.

Line a strainer with clean cheesecloth and place over a large bowl. Ladle stock through strainer and discard beef and vegetables. Cover and chill. Before using, skim away any fat that forms on the surface. Store in the refrigerator up to 3 days or freeze up to 3 months.

Makes 7½ cups.

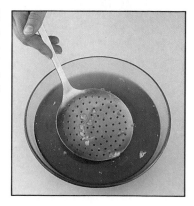

CHINESE VEGETABLE STOCK

1 stalk lemongrass
2 slices fresh ginger
1 clove garlic
2 scallions
1 large carrot, sliced
2 stalks celery
1 cup bean sprouts
large pinch salt
large pinch ground white pepper

Break lemongrass to release its flavor and place in a large saucepan with ginger, garlic, scallions, carrot, celery, bean sprouts, salt, pepper, and 9 cups cold water.

Bring to a boil, skimming away surface scum using a large, flat ladle. Reduce heat, cover, and simmer 45 minutes. Let cool slightly.

Line a strainer with clean cheesecloth and place over a large bowl. Ladle stock through strainer and discard vegetables. Cover and store in the refrigerator up to 3 days or freeze up to 3 months.

Makes 6 cups.

CHICKEN & ASPARAGUS SOUP

8 to 10 spears fresh asparagus
4 cups Chinese Chicken Stock (see page 16)
2 tablespoons light soy sauce
2 tablespoons dry sherry
2 teaspoons brown sugar
2 oz. rice vermicelli
½-in. piece fresh ginger, peeled and chopped
1½ cups lean, cooked, finely shredded chicken
salt and ground white pepper
2 scallions, finely chopped, to garnish

Trim ends from asparagus spears and slice spears into 1-in. pieces. Pour stock into a large saucepan along with soy sauce and sherry. Stir in brown sugar. Bring to a boil and add asparagus and noodles. Simmer, covered, 5 to 6 minutes.

Stir in chopped ginger and shredded chicken and season with salt and pepper. Simmer for 3 to 4 minutes to heat through. Garnish with chopped scallions and serve.

Makes 4 servings.

CHICKEN DUMPLING SOUP

1 cup lean ground chicken
1 tablespoons light soy sauce
3 tablespoons chopped, fresh chives
1 clove garlic, finely chopped
2 egg whites
1 teaspoon sugar
salt and freshly ground pepper
16 wonton skins
4 cups Chinese Chicken Stock (see page 16)
2 tablespoons rice wine

In a bowl, mix chicken, soy sauce, 1 tablespoon chives, and garlic. Bind together with 1 egg white and stir in sugar, salt, and pepper.

Place a little chicken mixture in center of each wonton skin, brush edges with egg white, and bring corners together, pinching edges to seal. Cook dumplings in a large pan of boiling water for 1 minute. Drain. Bring stock to a boil and stir in rice wine, dumplings, and remaining chives. Simmer for 2 minutes. Serve immediately.

Makes 4 servings.

HOT & SOUR TURKEY SOUP

½ cup lean ground turkey
1 oz. dried Chinese mushrooms, soaked in hot water for 20 minutes
4 oz. vegetables chow-chow, shredded
4 cups Chinese Chicken Stock (see page 16)
2 teaspoons brown sugar
2 tablespoons red rice vinegar
large pinch ground white pepper
1 tablespoon dark soy sauce
2 teaspoons cornstarch mixed with 4 teaspoons cold water
2 scallions, finely chopped
2 tablespoons chopped cilantro leaves

Cook turkey in a saucepan of boiling water for 3 minutes. Drain and set aside. Drain mushrooms and squeeze out excess water. Discard stems and slice caps.

Place ground turkey, mushrooms, vegetables chow-chow, stock, brown sugar, red rice vinegar, pepper, and soy sauce in a saucepan. Stir to combine. Bring to a boil and simmer 3 minutes. Add cornstarch mixture and cook, stirring, until thickened. Add chopped scallions and cilantro and serve.

Makes 4 servings.

BEEF & EGG DROP SOUP

1 tablespoon dark soy sauce
1 cup extra-lean ground beef
1 clove garlic, crushed
1 whole cinnamon stick, broken
2 tablespoons tomato paste
ground white pepper
4 cups Chinese Beef Stock (see page 16)
2 teaspoons cornstarch mixed with 4 teaspoons
  cold water
1 egg white, lightly beaten
2 tablespoons chopped cilantro leaves, to garnish

In a wok, heat soy sauce, then add the beef, garlic, and cinnamon stick, and stir-fry for 3 or 4 minutes or until beef is browned all over. Drain well on absorbent paper towels. Transfer beef mixture to a large saucepan and stir in tomato paste and white pepper. Pour in stock and bring to a boil, skimming away surface scum with a flat ladle. Cover and simmer for 20 minutes.

Discard cinnamon stick. Add cornstarch mixture and cook, stirring, until thickened. With soup still simmering, pour in the egg white in a thin stream, stirring until thin strands of egg form in the soup. Garnish with cilantro and serve.

Makes 4 servings.

CRAB & CORN SOUP

8 oz. baby corn
½-in. piece fresh ginger, peeled and finely chopped
1 clove garlic, finely chopped
6-oz. can crabmeat
2 tablespoons rice wine
1 tablespoon light soy sauce
4 cups Chinese Vegetable Stock (see page 17)
salt and ground white pepper
2 teaspoons cornstarch mixed with 4 teaspoons
  cold water
2 scallions, shredded, to garnish

Bring a small saucepan of water to a boil, add the baby corn, and cook 3 or 4 minutes or until just softened. Drain. In a bowl, mix together the ginger, garlic, crabmeat, rice wine, and soy sauce.

Pour the stock into a saucepan, bring to a boil, and add the corn and crab mixture. Simmer 5 minutes. Season with salt and pepper, add cornstarch mixture, and cook, stirring, until thickened. Garnish with scallions and serve.

Makes 4 servings.

THREE MUSHROOM SOUP

4 dried Chinese mushrooms, soaked in hot water
   for 20 minutes
2 oyster mushrooms
4 button mushrooms
4 cups Chinese Vegetable Stock (see page 17)
½-in. piece fresh ginger, peeled and finely chopped
1 clove garlic, finely chopped
2 tablespoons dry sherry
2 tablespoons dark soy sauce
4 oz. fresh tofu, drained and diced
2 teaspoons cornstarch mixed with 4 teaspoons
   cold water
2 tablespoons shredded basil leaves

Drain soaked mushrooms and squeeze out excess water. Discard stems and slice caps. Slice oyster mushrooms and cut button mushrooms in half.

Pour stock into a saucepan and add ginger, garlic, sherry, and soy sauce. Bring to a boil, reduce heat, and carefully stir in mushrooms and tofu. Simmer 5 minutes, then add cornstarch mixture and cook, stirring, another 2 minutes or until thickened. Stir in basil and serve.

Makes 4 servings.

BLACK-EYED PEA SOUP

1 cup black-eyed peas
1 large carrot
4 oz. daikon, peeled
1 bunch scallions
4 cups Chinese Vegetable Stock (see page 17)
2 tablespoons light soy sauce
2 cloves garlic, finely chopped
1 fresh red chili, seeded and finely chopped
salt and freshly ground pepper
carrot and daikon flowers (see page 14), to garnish

Place peas in a saucepan, add enough water to cover, and bring to a boil. Cover and simmer 45 minutes or until tender. Drain and rinse. Cut carrots and daikon into thin strips. Cut scallions into fine shreds.

Pour stock into a saucepan and stir in soy sauce. Bring to a boil and add prepared vegetables, garlic, and chili. Simmer 4 minutes, then add peas. Season with salt and pepper and cook 3 minutes. Skim surface, garnish, and serve.

Makes 4 servings.

WONTON SOUP

3 oz. boneless, skinless chicken
3 oz. lean pork
3 oz. Chinese sausage
3 oz. peeled shrimp
1 onion, chopped
1 carrot, chopped
1 stalk celery, chopped
6 canned water chestnuts
2 tablespoons soy sauce
1 tablespoon sesame oil
30 wonton skins
7½ cups chicken stock
2 oz. snow peas
1 carrot, cut into fine strips

CHICKEN & NOODLE SOUP

6 oz. rice vermicelli
8 oz. boneless, skinless chicken fillets
2½ cups chicken stock
2½ cups coconut milk
1 tablespoon tamarind paste (see page 11)
2 teaspoons grated, fresh ginger
1 stalk lemongrass, very finely chopped
3 tablespoons shrimp paste, toasted (see page 11)
7 oz. raw, peeled medium shrimp
¾ cup bean sprouts
½ small cucumber, peeled, seeded, and chopped
fried onion rings, sliced chilies, and cilantro leaves,
   to serve (optional)
Malaysian Spicy Sauce (see page 227), to serve
   (optional)

Dice one-quarter of the chicken, pork, sausage, and shrimp. Set aside. Put remaining chicken, pork, sausage, and shrimp in a food processor. Add onion, carrot, celery, water chestnuts, soy sauce, and sesame oil. Process to a smooth paste.

Cook the noodles in boiling water for 3 or 4 minutes. Drain and rinse under running cold water. Drain very well and set aside. Put chicken and stock in a saucepan. Bring to a simmer and poach 8 minutes. Lift chicken from stock (reserve stock). When cool enough to handle, shred and set aside. Add coconut milk to pan, along with tamarind, ginger, lemongrass, and shrimp paste. Bring to a boil, then simmer for 5 minutes.

Spoon a little of the meat paste onto the center of each wonton skin. Lightly moisten edges and draw them together to make small packets. In a large saucepan, bring stock to a boil. Add wontons in batches. Return to a boil and simmer 4 or 5 minutes. Add snow peas, carrot strips, and reserved meats and shrimp. Return to a boil and simmer an additional 4 or 5 minutes.

Makes 6 servings.

Add shrimp. Simmer for 3 or 4 minutes, then add bean sprouts and cucumber. Heat through for 1 or 2 minutes. Serve with small dishes of fried onion rings, sliced chilies, and cilantro leaves. Serve accompanied by spicy sauce (see page 227).

Makes 4 to 6 servings.

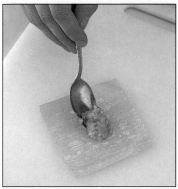

LAKSA LEMAK

3 dried red chilies, cored, seeded, and chopped
3 cloves garlic, crushed
6 shallots, chopped
2-in. piece fresh ginger, chopped
1 tablespoon ground coriander
1½ teaspoons ground turmeric
4 oz. rice vermicelli
2 tablespoons vegetable oil
1½ lbs. boneless, skinless chicken fillets, cubed
3 cups chicken stock
1 lb. raw, unpeeled medium shrimp
8 oz. tofu, cut into ½-in. cubes
2 cups bean sprouts
2 cups coconut milk
small bunch scallions

Soak chilies in 3 tablespoons hot water in a blender for 10 minutes. Add garlic, shallots, fresh ginger, coriander, and turmeric, and grind to a paste. Soak noodles in hot water for 3 to 5 minutes, stirring occasionally. Drain. In a wok or saucepan over medium heat, heat the oil. Stir in spice paste and cook for 3 or 4 minutes. Add chicken and cook, stirring, for 3 or 4 minutes. Add stock and simmer gently for 20 to 25 minutes.

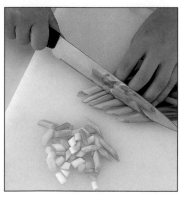

Add shrimp and simmer for 3 or 4 minutes, until they turn pink. Add tofu, bean sprouts, noodles, and coconut milk. Stir and simmer for 5 minutes. Thickly slice scallions, including some green, diagonally. Add half to pan and stir in. Serve garnished with remaining scallions.

Makes 6 servings.

PENANG HOT-SOUR SOUP

8 oz. whole fish, such as trout
5 cups fish or chicken stock
4 or 5 dried chilies, cored, seeded, and chopped
6 shallots, chopped
1 stalk lemongrass, chopped
3 slices galangal, chopped
1 teaspoon shrimp paste
1 tablespoon paprika
¼ teaspoon ground turmeric
15 fresh mint leaves
1 teaspoon brown sugar
1 teaspoon vegetable oil
3 tablespoons tamarind paste (see page 11)
8 oz. rice vermicelli
salt

In a saucepan, put fish and stock. Cover and simmer for 15 minutes. Lift fish from pan. When cool enough to handle, remove skin and bones from flesh. Return flesh to pan and simmer gently, uncovered, 15 minutes, then strain. Mash fish. Put chilies and ¼ cup hot water in a blender and soak for 10 minutes. Add shallots, lemongrass, galangal, shrimp paste, paprika, and turmeric. Mix to a smooth paste. Add to pan with strained stock.

Add mint, sugar, oil, tamarind, and 1 cup water. Simmer, uncovered, for 15 minutes. Add fish and simmer for 30 minutes. Soak noodles in hot water for 15 minutes until soft, then drain. Cook in boiling salted water for 1 minute, then drain. Put in warmed soup bowls.

Makes 3 or 4 servings.

SEAFOOD & COCONUT SOUP

3 stalks lemongrass, cut into 2-in. lengths
2-in. piece galangal, thinly sliced
1-in. piece fresh ginger, thinly sliced
2 teaspoons finely chopped red chili
4 cups coconut milk
10 kaffir lime leaves
7 oz. boneless, skinless chicken fillets, cut into
   1-in. cubes
⅓ cup fish sauce
juice of ½ lime
7 oz. raw large shrimp, peeled and deveined
7 oz. firm white fish fillets, cut into 1-in. cubes
small handful each cilantro and Thai basil leaves
cilantro sprigs, to garnish

TOFU SOUP

4 cups well-flavored vegetable stock
8 oz. tofu, cut into ½-in. cubes
1 fresh red chili, cored, seeded, and finely chopped
6 shallots, finely chopped
1 small carrot, finely chopped
2 scallions, sliced into rings
¼ cup light soy sauce
2 teaspoons light brown sugar
salt

Pour stock into a saucepan. Add tofu, chili, shallots, carrot, scallions, soy sauce, and sugar.

In a saucepan, put lemongrass, galangal, ginger, and chili. Add 1 cup water. Bring to a boil, then simmer for 5 minutes. Add coconut milk and lime leaves. Simmer for 10 minutes. Add chicken, fish sauce, and lime juice to pan. Poach for 5 minutes. Add shrimp and fish. Poach for an additional 2 or 3 minutes until shrimp turn pink.

Bring to a boil, uncovered. Stir briefly, then simmer for 2 or 3 minutes.

Add cilantro and basil to pan. Stir, then ladle into warm soup bowls. Remove and discard lemongrass and lime leaves before eating. Garnish with cilantro.

Makes 4 servings.

Add salt to taste. Ladle soup into warmed soup bowls. Serve as part of a main meal to counterbalance hot dishes.

Makes 4 servings.

VERMICELLI SOUP

5 cups chicken stock
1 small onion, chopped
2 stalks lemongrass, chopped and crushed
2 kaffir lime leaves, shredded
1 tablespoon lime juice
3 cloves garlic, chopped
2 fresh red chilies, seeded and chopped
1½-in. piece galangal, peeled and chopped
1½ tablespoons fish sauce
2 teaspoons crushed palm sugar
4 oz. clear vermicelli, soaked in cold water for
   10 minutes, then drained
2 tablespoons roughly chopped cilantro leaves
Thai holy basil leaves, to garnish

Put stock, onion, lemongrass, lime leaves, lime juice, garlic, chilies, and galangal into a saucepan and simmer 20 minutes.

Stir in fish sauce and sugar. When sugar has dissolved, add noodles and cook 1 minute. Stir in cilantro. Spoon into warmed bowls and garnish with basil leaves.

Makes 4 to 6 servings.

LEMONGRASS SOUP

6 to 8 oz. raw large shrimp
2 teaspoons vegetable oil
2½ cups light fish stock
2 thick stalks lemongrass, finely chopped
3 tablespoons lime juice
1 tablespoon fish sauce
3 kaffir lime leaves, chopped
½ fresh red chili, seeded and thinly sliced
½ fresh green chili, seeded and thinly sliced
½ teaspoon crushed palm sugar
cilantro leaves, to garnish

Peel shrimp and remove dark veins running down their backs; reserve shrimp and shells.

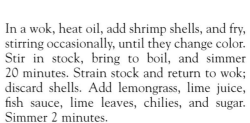

In a wok, heat oil, add shrimp shells, and fry, stirring occasionally, until they change color. Stir in stock, bring to boil, and simmer 20 minutes. Strain stock and return to wok; discard shells. Add lemongrass, lime juice, fish sauce, lime leaves, chilies, and sugar. Simmer 2 minutes.

Add shrimp and cook just below simmering point 2 or 3 minutes, until shrimp are cooked. Serve in warmed bowls garnished with cilantro.

Makes 4 servings.

PORK & PEANUT SOUP

CHICKEN & COCONUT SOUP

4 cilantro roots, chopped
2 cloves garlic, chopped
1 teaspoon black peppercorns, cracked
1 tablespoon vegetable oil
1 cup lean pork, finely chopped
4 scallions, chopped
3 cups veal stock
⅓ cup skinned peanuts
6 pieces dried Chinese black mushrooms, soaked for
   20 minutes, then drained and chopped
4 oz. bamboo shoots, roughly chopped
1 tablespoon fish sauce

Using a mortar and pestle, pound cilantro, garlic, and peppercorns to a paste.

In a wok, heat oil, add peppercorn paste, and cook 2 or 3 minutes, stirring occasionally. Add pork and scallions and stir 1½ minutes.

Stir stock, peanuts, and mushrooms into wok, then cook at just below boiling point for 7 minutes. Add bamboo shoots and fish sauce and continue to cook gently for 3 or 4 minutes.

Makes 3 or 4 servings.

3¾ cups coconut milk
4 oz. chicken fillets, cut into strips
2 stalks lemongrass, bruised and thickly sliced
2 scallions, thinly sliced
3 or 4 fresh red chilies, seeded and sliced
juice of 1½ limes
1 tablespoon fish sauce
1 tablespoon cilantro leaves, freshly torn into shreds
cilantro leaves, to garnish

Bring coconut milk to just below boiling point in a saucepan. Add chicken and lemongrass.

Adjust heat so liquid gives just an occasional bubble, then poach chicken, uncovered, for about 4 minutes until tender.

Add scallions and chilies. Heat briefly, then remove from heat and stir in lime juice, fish sauce, and shredded cilantro. Serve garnished with cilantro leaves.

Makes 4 servings.

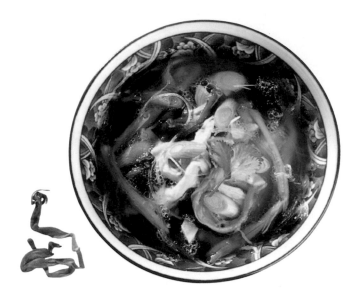

CHICKEN SOUP

1 tablespoon vegetable oil
½ teaspoon crushed garlic
2 shallots or 1 small onion, thinly sliced
3 cups chicken stock
1½ cups cooked, thinly shredded chicken meat
1 oz. bean thread vermicelli, soaked, then cut into
  short lengths
1 tablespoon black fungus, soaked and cut into
  small pieces
12 to 16 lily buds, soaked and trimmed
2 tablespoons fish sauce
salt and freshly ground black pepper
2 or 3 scallions, sliced
cilantro sprigs, to garnish

Heat oil in a wok or pan and stir-fry garlic and shallots or onion until aromatic; do not brown them. Add chicken stock and bring to a boil. Add chicken, vermicelli, fungus, lily buds, and fish sauce, bring back to a boil, and simmer about 3 minutes.

Taste and adjust seasoning, then add scallions. Serve soup hot, garnished with cilantro sprigs.

Makes 4 to 6 servings.

Variation: If ready-cooked chicken is not available, raw chicken fillets can be used instead, but increase cooking time by at least 2 minutes or until chicken is cooked.

VIETNAMESE FISH SOUP

1 tablespoon vegetable oil
2 cloves garlic, finely chopped
2 shallots or 1 small onion, chopped
1 tablespoon each chili sauce and tomato paste
2 medium tomatoes, chopped
3 tablespoons fish sauce
2 tablespoons sugar
3 cups chicken stock
2 tablespoons tamarind water or lime juice
8 oz. firm fish fillets, cut into small slices
4 oz. fresh scallops, sliced
4 oz. raw peeled shrimp
12 clams or mussels, scrubbed clean
2 or 3 tablespoons dry white wine or sherry
salt and freshly ground black pepper
cilantro sprigs, to garnish

Heat oil in a wok or pan and lightly brown garlic and shallots or onion. Add chili sauce, tomato paste, chopped tomato, fish sauce, and sugar. Blend well, then simmer for 2 or 3 minutes. Add stock with tamarind water or lime juice and bring to a boil.

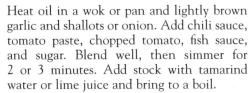

Just before serving, add seafood and wine or sherry to stock, bring back to boil, cover, and simmer 3 or 4 minutes until clam or mussel shells have opened; discard any that remain closed after cooking. Taste soup and adjust seasoning. Serve hot, garnished with cilantro sprigs.

Makes 4 to 6 servings.

Note: Take care not to overcook seafood. If using ready-shelled clams or mussels, reduce cooking time by half.

VIETNAMESE BEEF SOUP

6 to 8 oz. beefsteak, thinly sliced
¼ teaspoon freshly ground black pepper
½ teaspoon crushed garlic
½ teaspoon sugar
2 teaspoons soy sauce
1 tablespoon vegetable oil
1 teaspoon finely chopped lemongrass
2 shallots, thinly sliced
3 cups beef or chicken stock
1 tablespoon fish sauce
salt to taste
2 scallions, chopped
chopped cilantro leaves, to garnish

In a bowl, marinate beef slices with pepper, garlic, sugar, and soy sauce for at least 2 or 3 hours. Heat oil in a wok or pan and stir-fry chopped lemongrass and shallots for about 1 minute. Add beef or chicken stock and bring to a boil.

Add beef and fish sauce and bring back to a boil. Adjust seasoning and serve at once, garnished with chopped scallions and cilantro.

Makes 4 servings.

PAPAYA & PORK SOUP

4 cups stock or water
4 pork chops, each weighing about 3 oz.
1 small, unripe green papaya, peeled and cut into small cubes
2 tablespoons fish sauce
salt and freshly ground black pepper
1 tablespoon chopped scallions
cilantro sprigs, to garnish

Bring stock or water to a boil in a wok or pan and add pork. Bring back to a boil and skim off film from the surface, then reduce heat, cover, and simmer gently, 25 to 30 minutes.

Add papaya cubes and fish sauce, bring back to a boil, and cook soup for an additional 5 minutes.

To serve, place salt, pepper, and chopped scallions in a tureen. Pour boiling soup with its contents over it, garnish with cilantro sprigs, and serve at once. The meat should be so tender that one can easily tear it apart into small pieces for eating.

Makes 4 servings.

VERMICELLI & MUSHROOM SOUP

1 tablespoon vegetable oil
½ teaspoon crushed garlic
½ teaspoon finely chopped, fresh ginger
1 tablespoon chopped scallion
4 cups vegetable stock or water
2 tablespoons soy sauce
1 tablespoon sugar
2 oz. dried bean curd skins, soaked then cut into
    small pieces
2 oz. bean thread vermicelli, soaked then cut into
    short lengths
8 to 10 Chinese dried mushrooms, soaked and sliced
salt and freshly ground black pepper
cilantro sprigs, to garnish

Heat oil in a wok or pan and stir-fry garlic,
ginger, and scallions for 20 seconds or until
fragrant. Add stock or water and bring to a
rolling boil. Add soy sauce and sugar and
simmer about 30 seconds. (The soup can be
made in advance up to this point, then
brought back to a boil.)

Add bean curd skins, vermicelli, and
mushrooms, and cook for 2 or 3 minutes.
Adjust seasoning and garnish with cilantro
sprigs.

Makes 4 to 6 servings.

Variation: nonvegetarians can add a few
tablespoons of dried shrimp, soaked, if
desired. Chicken or meat stock can be used
instead of vegetable stock.

MIXED VEGETABLE SOUP

1 tablespoon vegetable oil
1 teaspoon crushed garlic
1 small onion, chopped
1 teaspoon chili sauce
1 tablespoon sugar
3 cups vegetable stock or water
2 tablespoons soy sauce
3 tablespoons tamarind water (see page 11) or
    2 tablespoons lime juice
9 oz. tofu, cut into small cubes
2 cups bok choy or spinach leaves, chopped
1½ cups bean sprouts
3 or 4 firm tomatoes, cut into thin wedges
salt and freshly ground black pepper
5 or 6 fresh basil leaves, coarsely chopped

Heat oil in a wok or pan and stir-fry garlic
and onion for about 30 seconds. Add chili
sauce and sugar and stir to make a smooth
paste. Add stock or water, bring to a boil,
then add soy sauce and tamarind water or
lime juice. Simmer 1 minute. (The soup can
be made in advance up to this point.)

Bring soup back to a rolling boil and add
tofu, bok choy, bean sprouts, and tomatoes.
Cook for about 2 minutes. Adjust seasoning
and serve soup piping hot, garnished with
chopped basil leaves.

Makes 4 to 6 servings.

DASHI

4-in. square dried konbu (kelp)
1½ oz. hana-katsuo (dried bonito flakes)

Wipe konbu with a damp cloth, place in a saucepan with 3 cups water, and let soak about 1 hour. Heat, uncovered, over medium heat for about 10 minutes, removing konbu just before reaching boiling point so it retains its subtle flavor. If the thickest part of the konbu is still hard, return it to the pan for a few more minutes, adding a little water to keep it from boiling. Reserve konbu.

Add 1 oz. hana-katsuo to the pan. Bring back to a boil (do not stir) and immediately remove from the heat. Using a tablespoon or ladle, remove foam from the surface and let stand a few minutes until the hana-katsuo settles down to the bottom of the pan. Strain liquid through a sieve lined with cheesecloth and reserve the hana-katsuo. This dashi (known as first dashi) is good for clear soups. However, for strongly flavored soups, noodle broths, and simmering, second dashi is used.

To make second dashi, put reserved konbu and hana-katsuo in a saucepan with 3 cups water and bring to a boil. Lower the heat and simmer, uncovered, 10 to 15 minutes, until dashi is reduced by one third. Add the last ½ oz. hana-katsuo and remove from the heat. Skim off foam, let stand, and strain as for first dashi.

Makes 4 servings.

Note: For instant dashi, mix dashi-no-moto (freeze-dried dashi powder) with water.

CLEAR SOUP WITH CHICKEN

3½-oz. chicken fillet
2 tablespoons cornstarch
12 snow peas
DASHI SOUP:
1 quantity dashi (opposite)
1 tablespoon soy sauce
½ teaspoon salt

Slice chicken fillet crosswise diagonally into eight pieces and pat lightly with cornstarch.

Bring a saucepan of water to a boil and drop in chicken pieces, one at a time so that they do not stick together. Cook a few minutes (do not overcook), then drain in a mesh bowl or colander. Keep them warm. Remove strings from snow peas, trim ends, and slice diagonally. Cook in boiling water for 1 or 2 minutes, until soft but still crunchy. Set aside.

Heat dashi and season with soy sauce and salt. Place two pieces of cooked chicken fillet and three snow peas in each of four individual soup bowls. Pour hot soup over them and serve at once.

Makes 4 servings.

CLEAR SOUP WITH SHRIMP

MISO SOUP WITH TOFU

4 raw jumbo shrimp or 8 medium shrimp
3 tablespoons sake or 6 tablespoons white wine
1½ oz. dried somen (very fine) noodles
watercress, to garnish
DASHI SOUP:
1 quantity dashi (see page 29)
1 tablespoon soy sauce
½ teaspoon salt

Make a slit lengthwise along the back of each shrimp and remove black vein-like intestine.

Place shrimp in a saucepan with sake and 3 tablespoons water, or with white wine only, and steam 2 or 3 minutes. Remove from heat and let cool in the saucepan. Peel shrimp, leaving tail shell on. Cook noodles in boiling water for about 3 minutes, then rinse in cold water, changing water several times. Divide noodles between four individual soup bowls. Place one large shrimp or two medium shrimp on each portion of noodles.

Heat dashi and season with soy sauce and salt. Pour hot soup gently over shrimp and noodles and garnish with a few sprigs of watercress.

Makes 4 servings.

2 tablespoons dried wakame (seaweed)
3 tablespoons miso
4 oz. firm tofu, cut into tiny dice
1 scallion, finely chopped
ground sansho pepper (optional)
STOCK:
2 cups second dashi (see page 29), or 2½ cups water
  and 1 or 2 teaspoons dashi-no-moto (freeze-dried
  dashi powder)

First make second dashi, following method on page 29, or add dashi-no-moto to boiling water and stir to dissolve.

Meanwhile, soak wakame in plenty of water, 10 to 15 minutes, until fully opened up. Drain and cut wakame into small pieces if necessary.

Put miso in a teacup and mix with a few spoonfuls of stock. Return stock to a low heat (do not boil) and add diluted miso. Add wakame and tofu to the pan and turn up the heat. Just before it reaches boiling point, add the finely chopped scallion and remove from the heat. Serve hot in individual soup bowls, sprinkled with a little ground sansho pepper if desired.

Makes 4 servings.

APPETIZERS

CHEESY STUFFED TOMATOES

8 tomatoes
2 tablespoons vegetable oil
1 small onion, finely chopped
1 clove garlic, crushed
1-in. piece fresh ginger, grated
1 teaspoon ground cumin
½ teaspoon turmeric
½ teaspoon cayenne pepper
2 teaspoons ground coriander
salt
½ cup fresh Indian cheese or natural fromage frais
¼ cup cheddar cheese, shredded
1 tablespoon chopped cilantro leaves

Cut a slice from the top of each tomato. Scoop out centers and discard seeds, then chop pulp and set aside. Turn tomatoes upside down on absorbent paper towels and let drain. Heat oil in a small skillet, add onion, and fry 5 minutes, stirring occasionally, until soft. Stir in garlic and ginger and fry 1 minute. Stir in cumin, turmeric, cayenne pepper, and ground coriander. Season with salt and fry for an additional minute.

Stir in tomato pulp and cook, uncovered, about 5 minutes, until thick. Preheat oven to 375°F. Stir fresh cheese or fromage frais and half the cheddar into spice mixture and spoon into tomato shells. Sprinkle remaining cheddar over the tops and place on a baking tray. Cook 10 to 15 minutes, until tops are golden brown and the tomatoes are soft. Sprinkle with chopped cilantro and serve hot.

Makes 4 servings.

ONION BHAJIS

¾ cup chickpea flour, sifted
1 tablespoon vegetable oil, plus extra for deep-frying
1 teaspoon ground coriander
1 teaspoon ground cumin
2 fresh green chilies, seeded and finely chopped
½ cup warm water
salt
2 onions, finely sliced
herb sprigs, to garnish

Put flour in a blender or food processor fitted with a metal blade.

Add oil, coriander, cumin, chilies, and water. Season with salt. Process until well blended and smooth, then pour batter into a bowl. Cover and leave in a warm place for 30 minutes. Stir in onions.

Half-fill a deep-fat fryer or deep pan with oil and heat to 375°F or until a cube of day-old bread browns in 40 seconds. Drop about five 2-tablespoon amounts into the oil and fry for 5 or 6 minutes, until golden. Drain on absorbent paper towels. Serve hot, garnished with sprigs of herbs.

Makes 4 servings.

Note: Make sure that the oil doesn't become too hot—the bhajis must fry slowly so that the centers cook through.

SHRIMP & MUSTARD SEEDS

1 lb. raw jumbo shrimp
1 tablespoon mixed black and yellow mustard seeds
½ teaspoon turmeric
½ teaspoon cayenne pepper
salt
2 tablespoons butter or ghee, melted
strips of orange and lime zest, to garnish

Peel shrimp, leaving tail shells on, then make a small incision along the spines and remove the black veins. Push two or three shrimp at a time onto short wooden skewers, then set aside.

Reserve 1 teaspoon mustard seeds and grind remainder in a mortar and pestle or coffee grinder. Transfer to a small bowl and mix in turmeric and cayenne pepper and season with salt. Add ⅓ cup water and blend until smooth. Add shrimp, turning to coat them in the marinade, and marinate in a cool place for 30 minutes.

Heat broiler. Drain skewered shrimp and place on a broiler rack, brush with butter, and sprinkle with reserved mustard seeds. Cook 3 to 5 minutes, turning over once and basting occasionally with any remaining marinade, until shrimp are just tender. Serve hot, garnished with orange and lime zest.

Makes 4 servings.

SPICY SHRIMP PATTIES

12 oz. white fish fillets, such as flounder,
   cod, or whiting
6 oz. peeled, cooked shrimp, chopped
4 scallions, chopped
1-in. piece fresh ginger, grated
2 tablespoons chopped cilantro leaves
1 tablespoon chopped fresh mint
2 cups fresh white breadcrumbs
salt and cayenne pepper
1 egg yolk, beaten
2 tablespoons lemon juice
¾ cup chickpea flour
1 tablespoon ground coriander
¼ cup vegetable oil for frying
mint sprigs and lemon slices, to garnish

Remove any skin and bones from fish, then wash and pat dry with absorbent paper towels. Grind fish, then transfer to a bowl. Stir in shrimp, scallions, ginger, cilantro, mint, 1 cup breadcrumbs, and salt and pepper. Add egg yolk and lemon juice and mix well. Divide mixture into sixteen pieces and form each into a ½-in.-thick round. Roll patties in remaining breadcrumbs to coat completely.

Put flour and ground coriander in a small bowl, season with salt and cayenne pepper, then add ½ cup water and mix to a smooth batter. Heat oil in a skillet. Dip shrimp patties in batter, then fry for 2 or 3 minutes on each side until golden brown. Drain on absorbent paper towels and serve hot, garnished with mint and lemon slices.

Makes 4 servings.

PORK DIM SUM

2 cups ground pork
4 oz. raw, shelled shrimp, ground
1½ tablespoons soy sauce
½ tablespoon Chinese rice wine or dry sherry
½ tablespoon sesame oil
½ tablespoon sugar
pinch pepper
1 egg white
1½ tablespoons cornstarch
30 wonton skins
fresh or frozen peas or chopped hard-boiled egg
  yolks, to garnish

To make filling, mix together ground pork, ground shrimp, soy sauce, rice wine or sherry, sesame oil, sugar, pepper, and egg white until mixture is well blended and smooth. Stir in cornstarch. Divide into thirty portions. Cut off edges of wonton skins to form circles, if necessary. Place one portion of filling in the center of a wonton skin. Gather edges of wonton skin around meat filling. Dip a teaspoon in water and use to smooth the surface of the meat.

Garnish by placing a green pea or piece of chopped egg yolk on top of meat. Gather edge to seal in filling. Repeat with remaining wonton skins and meat filling. Line a steamer with a damp cloth. Steam over high heat for 5 minutes. Remove and serve.

Makes 30 dumplings.

SHRIMP DIM SUM

1 lb. raw, shelled shrimp, ground
4-oz. can bamboo shoots, chopped
¼ cup water
1½ tablespoons soy sauce
½ tablespoon Chinese rice wine or dry sherry
½ teaspoon sugar
½ teaspoon sesame oil
pinch pepper
1½ tablespoons cornstarch
DOUGH:
4 cups all-purpose flour
½ cup boiling water
⅓ cup cold water
1 tablespoon vegetable oil

To make filling, mix together ground shrimp, bamboo shoots, water, soy sauce, rice wine or sherry, sugar, sesame oil, and pepper until well blended and smooth. Stir in cornstarch. Divide into thirty portions. To make dough, put 2½ cups flour in a medium-size bowl. (Reserve remaining flour and use for hands if they become sticky.) Stir in boiling water. Add cold water and oil. Mix to form a dough and knead until smooth. Roll dough into a long rope shape and cut into thirty pieces. Roll each portion into a thin, 2-in. circle.

Place one portion of filling in the center of a dough circle. Bring opposite edges together and pinch them together to hold. Repeat with remaining circles and filling. Line a steamer with a damp cloth. Place dumplings about 1 in. apart. Steam over high heat for 5 minutes. Remove and serve.

Makes 30 dumplings.

FRIED WONTONS

¾ cup lean ground pork
4-oz. can water chestnuts, finely chopped
1 tablespoon cornstarch
½ teaspoon salt
½ teaspoon Chinese rice wine or dry sherry
pinch sesame oil
pinch pepper
30 wonton skins
vegetable oil for frying

Mix together ground pork, water chestnuts, 1 tablespoon water, cornstarch, salt, rice wine or sherry, sesame oil, and pepper until combined. Divide into thirty portions.

Put 1 tablespoon of filling in the center of a wonton skin. Fold skin in half diagonally to form a triangle. Fold the edge containing the filling over about ½ in.

Bring two points together, moisten one inner edge, and pinch edges together to hold. Repeat with remaining wontons and filling. Heat a wok, then add vegetable oil. Deep-fry wontons over medium heat until golden. Drain on absorbent paper towels and serve.

Makes 30 wontons.

CRISPY SEAWEED

7 cups young spring greens
2½ cups vegetable oil
1 tablespoon brown sugar
½ teaspoon sea salt
½ teaspoon ground cinnamon
¾ cup slivered almonds, to garnish (optional)

Remove thick ribs from leaves and discard. Wash leaves and drain and dry thoroughly with absorbent paper towels. Using a very sharp knife or Chinese cleaver, cut leaves into very fine shreds.

Heat the oil in a wok until smoking, then remove from heat and add greens. Return to a medium heat and stir for 2 or 3 minutes or until shreds begin to float. Using a slotted spoon, remove from the oil and drain on absorbent paper towels.

In a small bowl, mix together sugar, salt, and cinnamon. Place "seaweed" on a dish and sprinkle with sugar mixture. Serve cold, garnished with slivered almonds if desired.

Makes 4 servings.

SHRIMP WITH GINGER DIP

CHILI SHRIMP BALLS

16 uncooked large shrimp, peeled, with tails left on
cilantro leaves and fresh ginger strips, to garnish
MARINADE:
1 tablespoon light soy sauce
1 teaspoon rice wine
1 teaspoon sesame oil
1 clove garlic, crushed
DIP:
1 tablespoon white rice vinegar
1 teaspoon sugar
2 tablespoons chopped cilantro leaves
½-in. piece fresh ginger, peeled and finely chopped

1 lb. cooked, peeled large shrimp, thawed and
  dried if frozen
1 fresh red chili, seeded and chopped
3 scallions, finely chopped
grated zest of 1 small lemon
2 tablespoons cornstarch
1 egg white, lightly beaten
salt and freshly ground black pepper
strips of fresh red chili, to garnish

Place shrimp, chili, scallions, lemon zest,
cornstarch, egg white, and black pepper in a
blender or food processor and process to form
a firm, dough-like mixture.

Using a small, sharp knife, cut along back of
each shrimp and remove the thin, black
vein. Rinse and dry shrimp with absorbent
paper towels and place on a plate. Mix
together light soy sauce, rice wine, sesame
oil, and garlic, and brush over the shrimp.
Cover and chill 1 hour.

Divide shrimp mixture into twelve portions
and form each portion into a smooth ball,
flouring hands with extra cornstarch if
necessary to prevent sticking.

To make dip, mix together white rice
vinegar, sugar, chopped cilantro, and fresh
ginger. Cover and chill. Preheat broiler.
Place shrimp on the broiler rack and cook for
1 or 2 minutes on each side, basting with
marinade, until cooked through. Garnish
with cilantro leaves and ginger strips and
serve with dip.

Makes 4 servings.

Bring a wok or large saucepan of water to a
boil, arrange shrimp balls on a layer of waxed
paper in a steamer, and place over water.
Cover and steam for 5 minutes or until
cooked through. Garnish with sliced chili
before serving.

Makes 4 servings.

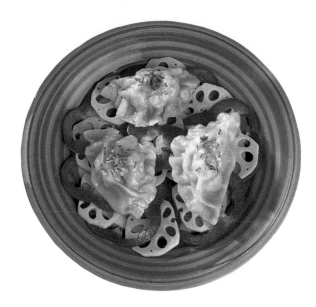

STEAMED FISH DUMPLINGS

6-oz. skinless cod fillet
1 slice lean bacon, trimmed of fat and finely chopped
1 teaspoon light soy sauce
1 teaspoon oyster sauce
1 tablespoon chopped, fresh chives
1 teaspoon cornstarch
12 round wonton skins
1 egg white, lightly beaten
chopped, fresh chives, to garnish

Place cod fillet, bacon, soy sauce, oyster sauce, chives, and cornstarch in a blender or food processor and process to form a firm mixture. Divide into twelve portions.

Place a portion of filling in the center of each wonton skin and lightly brush edges of wonton skin with egg white.

Fold over to form crescent shapes and pinch edges to seal. Bring a wok or large saucepan of water to a boil, arrange dumplings on a layer of waxed paper in a steamer, and place over water. Cover and steam for 10 minutes or until cooked through. Garnish with chives to serve.

Makes 4 servings.

PEARL PATTIES & SHERRY DIP

¾ cup long-grain white rice
1½ cups extra-lean ground beef
2 scallions, finely chopped
1 clove garlic, crushed
1 tablespoon dark soy sauce
1 tablespoon dry sherry
2 teaspoons cornstarch
DIP:
2 tablespoons dry sherry
2 tablespoons dark soy sauce
1 teaspoon sugar
1 clove garlic, crushed

Place rice in a bowl, add enough water to cover, and soak for 1 hour. Drain well and dry on absorbent paper towels. Mix together beef, scallions, garlic, soy sauce, sherry, and cornstarch to form a firm mixture. Divide into sixteen portions and shape into 1½-in.-diameter patties.

Press each patty into rice to coat on both sides. Bring a wok or large saucepan of water to a boil. Arrange patties on a layer of waxed paper in a steamer, making sure they don't overlap—you will probably need two steamers. Place over water, cover, and steam for 20 minutes. To make the dip, mix together dry sherry, soy sauce, sugar, and garlic. Serve dip with patties.

Makes 4 servings.

BROILED FIVE-SPICE CHICKEN

2 boneless, skinless chicken fillets, each weighing
   about 6 oz., trimmed
2 small red bell peppers, halved
2 small yellow bell peppers, halved
chopped, fresh chives, to garnish
MARINADE:
1 clove garlic, crushed
1 fresh red chili, seeded and chopped
3 tablespoons light soy sauce
1 teaspoon five-spice powder
1 teaspoon brown sugar
2 teaspoons sesame oil

Using a small, sharp knife, score chicken fillets on both sides in a crisscross pattern, being careful not to slice all the way through. Place in a shallow dish with bell peppers. To make marinade, mix together garlic, chili, soy sauce, five-spice powder, brown sugar, and sesame oil, and pour over chicken and bell peppers and turn to coat. Cover and chill for 1 hour.

Preheat broiler. Remove chicken and bell peppers from marinade, place on broiler rack, and cook for 4 or 5 minutes on each side or until chicken is cooked through, basting with marinade. Slice chicken fillets and serve with a piece of red and yellow bell pepper, garnished with chives.

Makes 4 servings.

MARINATED MUSHROOMS

1 oz. dried Chinese mushrooms, soaked in hot water
   for 20 minutes
9 oyster mushrooms
9 button mushrooms
1 tablespoon sunflower oil
2 tablespoons light soy sauce
2 stalks celery, chopped
2 cloves garlic, thinly sliced
1 whole cinnamon stick, broken
chopped celery leaves, to garnish
MARINADE:
3 tablespoons light soy sauce
3 tablespoons dry sherry
freshly ground black pepper

Drain Chinese mushrooms and squeeze out excess water. Discard stems and thinly slice caps. Slice oyster and button mushrooms. Heat oil in a wok and stir-fry mushrooms for 2 minutes.

Add soy sauce, celery, garlic, and cinnamon stick, and stir-fry 2 or 3 minutes or until just cooked. Transfer to a shallow dish and let cool. To make marinade, mix together soy sauce, dry sherry, and black pepper, and pour over cooled mushroom mixture. Cover and chill for 1 hour. Discard cinnamon stick, garnish, and serve.

Makes 4 servings.

POT-STICKER DUMPLINGS

1 cup all-purpose flour
1 tablespoon sunflower oil
FILLING:
½ cup lean ground pork
½-in. piece fresh ginger, peeled and finely chopped
1 tablespoon dark soy sauce
1 tablespoon dry sherry
large pinch ground white pepper

Place flour in a bowl and gradually add ½ cup hot water, mixing well to form a dough. Turn out onto a floured surface and knead until smooth.

Return to the bowl, cover, and set aside for 20 minutes. To make filling, mix together ground pork, ginger, soy sauce, sherry, and pepper. Divide dough into sixteen portions and, on a floured surface, flatten each portion into a 2½-in.-diameter round. Take one round at a time, keeping remaining rounds covered with a damp dishcloth, and place a little filling in the center. Brush edge of dough with water and bring together over filling, pinching edges together to seal. Cover with a damp dishcloth while you make the remainder.

Heat oil in a wok and place dumplings, flat side down, in the wok. Cook 2 minutes, until lightly browned on the bottom. Add ⅔ cup water, cover, and cook 10 minutes. Uncover and cook 2 minutes. Drain and serve with a crisp salad and hoisin sauce as a dip.

Makes 4 servings.

GINGERED MELONS

½ honeydew melon
½ cantaloupe melon
4-oz. can water chestnuts, rinsed
1-in. piece fresh ginger, peeled and finely chopped
¼ cup dry sherry
4 pieces preserved ginger in syrup, sliced
2 tablespoons dried melon seeds

Using a spoon, scoop out seeds from both melons. Cut in half, peel away skin, and thinly slice melon flesh. Slice water chestnuts.

Arrange melon slices on serving plates and top with sliced water chestnuts.

Mix together chopped ginger, dry sherry, and preserved ginger with its syrup, and spoon over melon and water chestnuts. Cover and chill for 30 minutes. Sprinkle with melon seeds and serve.

Makes 4 servings.

CURRY PUFFS

2 sticks unsalted butter
5 cups all-purpose flour
3 tablespoons vegetable oil, plus extra for deep-frying
4 shallots, thinly sliced
2 cloves garlic, finely crushed
1 teaspoon grated, fresh ginger
1 fresh green chili, cored, seeded, and finely chopped
4 teaspoons curry powder
2 cups ground beef, lamb, or chicken
1 potato, finely diced
1 tablespoon lime juice, or to taste
⅓ cup chopped celery leaves
celery leaves, to garnish

Melt butter with 2 tablespoons water.

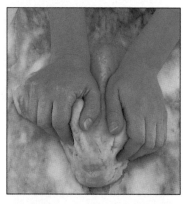

In a bowl, combine butter mixture with flour, a pinch of salt, and about ⅓ cup of water to give a medium-soft dough. Transfer to a work surface and knead for about 10 minutes. Form into a ball. Brush with oil and put in a plastic bag. Let stand at least 30 minutes.

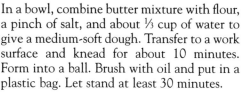

Heat oil in a skillet. Add shallots and fry for 4 or 5 minutes, until browned. Stir in garlic, ginger, chili, and curry powder. Add meat and cook until pale, stirring to break up lumps. Stir in potato, lime juice, salt to taste, and 2 tablespoons water. Simmer gently, covered, 15 to 20 minutes, until meat and potatoes are tender.

Add celery leaves and cook for 2 minutes. If necessary, increase heat and boil to drive off excess moisture, stirring. Knead dough. Break off a 1-in. piece. Form into a smooth ball, then roll into a 4-in. circle.

Put 2 teaspoons meat mixture along the center. Brush edge of dough circle with water and fold dough over filling.

Pinch edges together to seal. Place, pinched end up, on a plate. Repeat with remaining filling and dough. Heat enough oil for deep-frying in a wok or deep-fryer over medium-low heat. Place a few curry puffs in the wok or fryer at one time, so they are not crowded, and fry slowly until golden. Turn them over so they cook evenly. Remove with a slotted spoon and drain on absorbent paper towels. Serve warm, garnished with celery leaves.

Makes about 30.

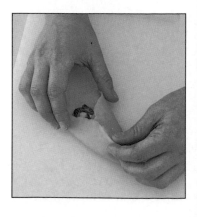

MALAYSIAN SPRING ROLLS

5-oz. boneless, skinless chicken fillet
4 oz. raw shrimp in shells
2 tablespoons peanut oil
½-in. piece fresh ginger, grated
1 clove garlic, finely crushed
3 shallots, very finely chopped
1 small carrot, shredded
1 stalk celery, very finely chopped
1 fresh red chili, cored, seeded, and finely chopped
2 scallions, chopped
1 teaspoon sesame oil
2 teaspoons soy sauce
12 spring roll wrappers
1 egg, beaten
½ cup vegetable oil
Malaysian Dipping Sauce (see page 227), to serve

Skin and finely chop chicken. Peel and finely chop shrimp. In a wok or sauté pan, heat oil. Add chicken and stir-fry until they begin to turn opaque. Stir in shrimp and continue to stir-fry until shrimp begin to turn pink. Add ginger, garlic, shallots, carrot, celery, chili, scallions, sesame oil, and soy sauce, and fry for an additional 1 minute. Transfer to a bowl and leave until cold.

Spread one wrapper on the work surface; keep remaining wrappers between two damp dishcloths. Put 1 or 2 tablespoons filling on lower half of wrapper.

Fold bottom corner up and over filling. Moisten side corners with beaten egg. Fold sides over to cover bottom corner and filling. Press firmly to seal. Moisten top corner with beaten egg.

Roll wrapper over tightly to make a neat cylinder. Press top corner of roll to seal. Place seam side down and cover with a damp dishcloth. Repeat with remaining wrappers and filling.

In a wok or sauté pan, heat vegetable oil. Fry rolls in batches for 3 to 5 minutes, turning occasionally, until golden and crisp. Remove with a slotted spoon and drain on absorbent paper towels. Keep warm while frying remaining rolls. Serve with dipping sauce.

Makes 6 servings.

NONYA PACKAGES

4 dried Chinese black mushrooms
8 oz. boneless, skinless chicken fillets, thinly sliced
  into strips
1 tablespoon oyster sauce
1½ teaspoons rice wine
1½ teaspoons sesame oil
½-in. piece fresh ginger, grated
1½ teaspoons light soy sauce
1 clove garlic, finely crushed
½ fresh red chili, cored, seeded, and finely chopped
2 scallions, including some green, chopped

Soak mushrooms in 3 tablespoons hot water for 30 minutes. Drain. Discard stems and finely slice caps.

In a bowl, mix chicken, oyster sauce, rice wine, sesame oil, ginger, soy sauce, garlic, and chili. Cover and leave in a cool place for up to 1 hour, or in the refrigerator up to 8 hours (return to room temperature 30 minutes before cooking). Cut ten 6-in. squares of waxed paper. Lay one on the work surface with a point toward you. Put several pieces of chicken near the point. Add some mushroom strips and scallions. Fold the point over the filling, making a firm crease. Fold left- and right-hand corners to center.

Continue to fold package over, away from you. Tuck in the last flap to make a package, about 3 x 2 in. Repeat with the remaining chicken and waxed paper. Half-fill a wok or deep-fat fryer with oil and heat to 360° to 375°F. Fry packages in batches for about 8 minutes, pushing them under occasionally and turning over once or twice. Remove with a slotted spoon. Keep warm while cooking the remaining packages. Serve unopened.

Makes 5 or 6 servings.

BROILED CHICKEN SKEWERS

6 large chicken thighs, total weight about 2¼ lbs.
2 cloves garlic, finely chopped
⅔ cup coconut milk
2 teaspoons ground coriander
1 teaspoon each ground cumin and ground turmeric
juice of 1 lime
leaves of 8 cilantro sprigs, chopped
3 tablespoons light soy sauce
2 tablespoons fish sauce
3 tablespoons light brown sugar
½ teaspoon crushed dried chilies

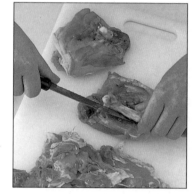

Using a sharp knife, slit along underside of each chicken thigh and remove bone, scraping flesh from bone.

Cut each boned thigh into six pieces. Put in a bowl. In a small bowl, mix together garlic, coconut milk, coriander, cumin, and turmeric. Pour over chicken. Stir to coat, then cover and refrigerate for 2 to 12 hours. To make the sauce, in a small serving bowl, mix together lime juice, cilantro, soy sauce, fish sauce, sugar, and chilies. Set aside.

Soak eight short wooden or bamboo skewers for 30 minutes. Preheat broiler. Thread chicken, skin side up, on skewers. Place on an oiled broiler rack and cook for 4 or 5 minutes. Turn over and cook for an additional 2 or 3 minutes until juices run clear. Serve with sauce.

Makes 4 to 6 servings.

POH PIAH

2 tablespoons vegetable oil
4 shallots, finely chopped
2 cloves garlic, crushed
1 fresh red chili, cored, seeded, and finely chopped
½ cup lean pork, ground
4 oz. crabmeat
8 canned water chestnuts, finely chopped
4 oz. bamboo shoots, shredded
1 tablespoon light soy sauce
1½ tablespoons salted yellow beans
12 spring roll wrappers
Malaysian Spicy Sauce (see page 227), to serve

TO SERVE:
4 oz. small shrimp
4 oz. Chinese sausage, steamed and sliced
1 cup bean sprouts, blanched
1 bunch scallions
2 cups shredded iceberg lettuce leaves
½ medium cucumber, chopped and coarsely shredded

For the filling, in a wok or skillet, heat oil. Add shallots, garlic, and chili. Cook, stirring occasionally, until softened and transparent. Stir pork into wok and stir-fry until it changes color. Add crabmeat, water chestnuts, bamboo shoots, soy sauce, and yellow beans.

Stir together ingredients for about 2 minutes until well mixed. Let cool. Put cooled meat mixture and remaining ingredients in individual bowls. Each person helps themselves to the filling ingredients, then rolls up the wrapper, tucking in the ends, and eats it at once. Serve with spicy sauce and other accompaniments.

Makes 12.

SPICY SPARERIBS

3 lbs. spareribs, trimmed and divided into ribs
¼ cup vegetable oil
2 scallions, thinly sliced
MARINADE:
1-in. piece fresh ginger, grated
4 cloves garlic, finely crushed
1 fresh red chili, cored, seeded, and finely chopped
3 tablespoons rice vinegar
⅓ cup dark soy sauce
2 tablespoons peanut oil
1 tablespoon light brown sugar
1 teaspoon Chinese five-spice powder

Whisk marinade ingredients together. Put ribs in a dish and pour marinade on top.

Turn ribs to coat in marinade, cover, and refrigerate for 2 or 3 hours, turning occasionally. Lift ribs from marinade. Pat dry. Reserve marinade. In a wok or sauté pan, heat oil over high heat. Add three or four ribs and cook, stirring, 2 or 3 minutes, until evenly browned. Transfer to absorbent paper towels. Repeat with remaining ribs.

Pour off all but 2 tablespoons oil from the pan. Return ribs to pan. Add reserved marinade and enough water to completely cover ribs. Bring to a boil. Lower heat, cover, and simmer gently for about 1 hour, stirring occasionally, until meat is tender and comes away slightly from the bone. Boil until cooking liquid is reduced to a thick sauce. Transfer ribs to warmed plates and spoon a little sauce over each serving. Sprinkle with sliced scallions.

Makes 6 servings.

SPLIT PEA FRITTERS

1¼ cups yellow split peas, soaked overnight in
  cold water
3 or 4 fresh red chilies, cored, seeded, and chopped
2 cloves garlic, chopped
2 scallions, sliced
3 tablespoons chopped cilantro leaves
1 teaspoon ground roasted cumin seeds
large pinch ground turmeric
1 egg, beaten
salt
vegetable oil for deep-frying (optional)
banana leaves (optional)
Malaysian Dipping Sauce or Spicy Sauce
  (see page 227), to serve

Drain split peas and put in a saucepan with
1½ cups water. Bring to a boil. Boil, stirring,
for 10 minutes. Drain. Put in a food
processor with chilies, garlic, and scallions.
Mix until coarsely chopped. Add cilantro,
cumin, turmeric, egg, and salt to taste, and
mix together. Form into about fifty small
balls, pressing mixture firmly together with
your hands. Refrigerate for about 1 hour.

Preheat oven to 450°F. Roll patties in a little
oil, put on baking sheets, and bake for
15 to 17 minutes or until golden brown. Turn
over halfway through. Alternatively, heat oil
in a deep-fat fryer to 350°F or until a cube of
bread browns in 30 seconds. Deep-fry fritters
in batches for 2 or 3 minutes or until golden.
Drain on absorbent paper towels. Serve
fritters hot on banana leaves, if desired,
accompanied by the dipping sauce of your
choice.

Makes about 50.

SWEET POTATO RINGS

3 or 4 sweet potatoes, peeled and cubed
2 tablespoons vegetable oil, plus extra for frying
1 onion, finely chopped
2 cloves garlic, finely crushed
1 fresh red chili, cored, seeded, and chopped
1 tablespoon curry powder
1 egg, beaten
salt and freshly ground black pepper
1 cup all-purpose flour
dried breadcrumbs for coating
cilantro sprigs, to garnish

Steam sweet potato cubes 6 to 8 minutes
until tender. Pass through a vegetable mill
into a bowl, or mash thoroughly.

Meanwhile, in a wok or skillet, heat oil and
fry onion, garlic, and chili until onion is
lightly colored. Stir in curry powder and
cook, 1 minute. Add onion mixture to sweet
potato with egg and salt and pepper to taste.
Beat together until evenly mixed, then stir
in flour to bind together; if mixture is too
soft, add a little more flour. Let cool, then
refrigerate for at least 1 hour.

With oiled hands, form mixture into balls
1½ in. in diameter. Press lightly to flatten
into cakes. With floured end of a wooden
spoon, press through center of each cake to
make a ring. Thoroughly coat rings in
breadcrumbs, pressing them in. Chill for at
least 1 hour. Heat ½ in. of oil in a skillet and
fry the rings until crisp and golden. Using a
slotted spoon, transfer to absorbent paper
towels to drain. Serve warm, garnished with
cilantro sprigs.

Makes 4 servings.

GOLD BAGS

4 oz. cooked, peeled shrimp, finely chopped
2 oz. canned water chestnuts, finely chopped
2 scallions, white part only, finely chopped
1 teaspoon fish sauce
freshly ground black pepper
16 wonton skins
vegetable oil for deep-frying
Thai Dipping Sauce 1 (see page 231), to serve
cilantro sprig, to garnish

In a bowl, mix together shrimp, water chestnuts, scallions, fish sauce, and black pepper.

Place a small amount of shrimp mixture in center of each wonton skin. Dampen edges of skins with a little water, then bring up over filling and press edges together to seal.

In a wok, heat oil to 375°F. Add bags in batches and fry for about 2 or 3 minutes until crisp and golden. Using a slotted spoon, transfer to absorbent paper towels to drain. Serve hot with dipping sauce. Garnish with cilantro sprigs.

Makes 16.

CORN CAKES

1½ cups corn kernels
1 tablespoon Green Curry Paste (see page 230)
2 tablespoons all-purpose flour
3 tablespoons rice flour
3 scallions, finely chopped
1 egg, beaten
2 teaspoons fish sauce
vegetable oil for deep-frying
1-in. piece cucumber
Thai Dipping Sauce 2 (see page 232), to serve
1 tablespoon ground roasted peanuts

Place corn in a blender and add curry paste, all-purpose flour, rice flour, scallions, egg, and fish sauce, and mix together until corn is slightly broken up. Form into about sixteen cakes. Heat oil in a wok to 350°F, then deep-fry one batch of corn cakes for about 3 minutes until golden brown.

Using a slotted spoon, transfer to absorbent paper towels to drain. Keep warm while frying the remaining cakes. Peel cucumber, quarter lengthwise, remove seeds, then slice thinly. Place in a small bowl and mix in dipping sauce and ground peanuts. Serve with warm corn cakes.

Makes about 16.

CRAB ROLLS

1½ cups cooked chicken, very finely chopped
4 oz. cooked crabmeat, flaked
4 scallions, finely chopped
¼ cup bean sprouts, finely chopped
1 small carrot, shredded
2 teaspoons fish sauce
freshly ground black pepper
about 9 rice paper wrappers (spring roll wrappers),
    each about 7 in. diameter
vegetable oil for deep-frying
Thai holy basil leaves, Thai mint leaves, and lettuce
    leaves, to serve
Thai Dipping Sauce 1 (see page 231), to serve

In a bowl, mix together chicken, crabmeat, scallions, bean sprouts, carrot, fish sauce, and black pepper. Brush both sides of each wrapper liberally with water and set aside to soften. Cut each wrapper into four wedges. Place a small amount of filling near the wide end of one wedge, fold the end over the filling, tuck in the sides, and roll up. Repeat with the remaining wedges and filling.

In a wok, heat oil to 375°F. Fry rolls in batches for 2 or 3 minutes, until crisp and golden. Drain on absorbent paper towels. Serve hot. To eat, sprinkle each roll with herbs, then wrap in a lettuce leaf and dip into dipping sauce.

Makes about 36.

FISH PACKAGES WITH GALANGAL

2 fresh red chilies, seeded and finely chopped
2 cloves garlic, finely chopped
1 shallot, finely chopped
1½-in. piece galangal, finely chopped
2 stalks lemongrass, finely chopped
1 tablespoon fish sauce
20 Thai holy basil leaves
1 lb. boneless firm white fish, such as halibut, cod,
    hake, or monkfish, cut into ¾-in. pieces
banana leaves (optional)

Using a mortar and pestle or small blender, briefly mix together chilies, garlic, shallot, galangal, lemongrass, and fish sauce. Turn into a bowl, stir in basil leaves and fish. Divide between three or four pieces of banana leaf or aluminum foil. Fold leaves or foil over fish to make neat packages. Secure leaves with a wooden toothpick or fold foil edges tightly together.

Put packages in a steaming basket. Place over boiling water and steam for about 7 minutes, until fish is lightly cooked.

Makes 3 or 4 servings.

STEAMED CRAB

1 clove garlic, chopped
1 small shallot, chopped
6 cilantro sprigs, stalks finely chopped
6 oz. cooked crabmeat
¾ cup cooked, finely shredded lean pork
1 egg, beaten
1 tablespoon coconut cream (see page 8)
2 teaspoons fish sauce
freshly ground black pepper
1 fresh red chili, seeded and cut into fine strips

Grease four individual heatproof dishes and place in a steaming basket.

Using a mortar and pestle, pound garlic, shallot, and cilantro stalks to a paste. In a bowl, stir together crabmeat, pork, garlic paste, egg, coconut cream, fish sauce, and plenty of black pepper until evenly mixed.

Divide between dishes and arrange cilantro leaves and a strip of chili on top of each one. Place the steaming basket over a saucepan of boiling water and steam for about 12 minutes, until mixture is firm.

Makes 4 servings.

Note: Crab shells may be used instead of dishes for cooking.

STUFFED ZUCCHINI

1¼ cups shredded, fresh coconut
⅓ cup chopped cilantro leaves
1 fresh green chili, seeded and finely chopped
4 zucchini, each weighing about 8 oz.
⅓ cup vegetable oil
few drops fish sauce
2 tablespoons lime juice
1 teaspoon crushed palm sugar
freshly ground black pepper

In a small bowl, combine coconut, cilantro, and chili. Set aside.

Cut each zucchini into four lengths about 1½ in. long. Stand each on one cut side and cut two deep slits, like a cross, down 1 in. of the length. Gently open cut sections and fill with coconut mixture. Pour oil and ½ cup water into a wide skillet. Stand zucchini, filled side up, in skillet.

Sprinkle a little fish sauce on top. If any coconut mixture remains, spoon over zucchini. Sprinkle with lime juice, sugar, black pepper, and a few drops of fish sauce. Heat to simmering point, cover tightly, and simmer gently for 5 or 6 minutes. Using two spoons, turn zucchini pieces over, cover again, and continue to cook for an additional 7 to 10 minutes.

Makes 4 to 6 servings.

STEAMED EGGS

4 eggs, beaten
2 scallions, thinly sliced
3 oz. cooked, peeled shrimp, finely chopped
freshly ground black pepper
1 fresh red chili, seeded and thinly sliced
1 tablespoon chopped cilantro leaves
⅓ cup coconut milk (see page 224)
2 teaspoons fish sauce
cilantro sprigs and red chili rings, to garnish

In a small blender or food processor, mix eggs, scallions, shrimp, pepper, chili, cilantro, coconut milk, and fish sauce until evenly combined.

Pour into greased individual heatproof dishes. Place in a steaming basket, then position over a saucepan of boiling water. Cover and steam for 10 to 12 minutes, until just set in center.

Remove from heat, then let stand for a minute or two. Turn out onto a plate, then invert onto a warmed plate. Garnish with cilantro sprigs and red chili rings.

Makes 2 to 4 servings.

STUFFED EGGS

4 large eggs, at room temperature
¼ cup ground cooked pork
¼ cup finely chopped, peeled shrimp
1 teaspoon fish sauce
1 clove garlic, chopped
1½ tablespoons chopped cilantro leaves
finely ground black pepper
lettuce leaves, to serve
cilantro sprigs, to garnish

Form four "nests" from aluminum foil to hold eggs upright. Place in a steaming basket. Cook eggs in pan of gently boiling water for 1½ minutes, then remove.

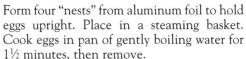

Carefully peel a small part of the pointed end of the eggs. With the point of a slim, sharp knife, cut a small hole down through the exposed white of each egg; reserve pieces of white that are removed. Pour liquid egg yolk and white from egg into a small bowl. Thoroughly mix in pork, shrimp, fish sauce, garlic, cilantro, and pepper. Carefully spoon into eggs and replace removed pieces of white.

Set steaming basket over a saucepan of boiling water and place eggs, cut end up, in the foil nests. Cover the basket and steam the eggs for about 12 minutes. When cool enough to handle, carefully peel off the shells. Serve whole or halved on lettuce leaves, garnished with cilantro sprigs.

Makes 4 servings.

EGG NESTS

1 tablespoon chopped cilantro roots
1 clove garlic, chopped
½ teaspoon black peppercorns, cracked
1 tablespoon peanut oil
½ small onion, finely chopped
¾ cup lean pork, very finely chopped
4 oz. raw, peeled shrimp, chopped
2 teaspoons fish sauce
3 tablespoons vegetable oil
2 eggs
3 fresh red chilies, seeded and cut into fine strips
20 to 30 cilantro leaves
cilantro sprigs, to garnish

Add vegetable oil to wok and place over medium heat. In a small bowl, beat eggs. Spoon egg into a cone of waxed paper with a very small hole in pointed end. Move cone above the surface of the pan so the trail of egg flows onto it and sets in threads. Quickly repeat, moving in another direction directly over threads. Repeat until there are four crisscrossing layers of egg.

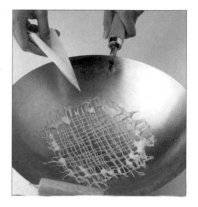

Using a mortar and pestle, pound together cilantro roots, garlic, and peppercorns. In a wok, heat peanut oil, add peppercorn mixture and onion, and stir-fry for 1 minute.

Using a spatula, transfer nest to absorbent paper towels. Repeat with remaining egg to make more nests. Place nests with flat side facing down. Place two strips of chili on each nest to form a cross.

Add pork, stir-fry for 1 minute, then stir in shrimp and cook for 45 seconds. Quickly stir in fish sauce, then transfer mixture to a bowl. Using absorbent paper towels, wipe out wok.

Top with cilantro leaves, then with about 1 tablespoon of pork mixture. Fold nests over filling, turn over, and arrange on a serving plate. Garnish with cilantro sprigs.

Makes 4 servings.

STUFFED CHICKEN WINGS

4 large chicken wings
lean pork, finely ground
2 oz. cooked, peeled shrimp, chopped
3 scallions, finely chopped
2 large cloves garlic, chopped
3 cilantro roots, chopped
2 tablespoons fish sauce
freshly ground black pepper
vegetable oil for deep-frying
rice flour for coating
Thai Dipping Sauce 2 (see page 232), to serve
lettuce leaves, to garnish

Chop chicken flesh from wings. Make up to 6 oz. with pork, if necessary. Place chicken and pork, if used, in a bowl and thoroughly mix together with shrimp and scallions. Divide between chicken wings. Set aside.

Bend chicken wing joints backward against joint. Using a small, sharp knife or kitchen scissors, cut around top of bone that attaches wing to body. Using blade of knife, scrape meat and skin down length of first bone, turning skin back over unboned portion. Break bone free at joint.

Using a mortar and pestle, pound together garlic and cilantro roots. Stir in fish sauce and plenty of black pepper. Pour over chicken wings, stirring them to coat with mixture, then set aside for 30 minutes.

Ease skin over joint and detach from flesh and bone. Working down next adjacent bones, scrape off flesh and skin, being careful not to puncture skin. Break bones free at joint, leaving end section.

Heat oil in a wok to 350°F. Remove chicken wings from bowl, then toss in rice flour to coat completely. Add two at a time to oil and deep-fry for about 3 or 4 minutes until browned. Using a slotted spoon, transfer to absorbent paper towels to drain. Keep warm while frying remaining two chicken wings. Serve with sauce and garnish with lettuce leaves.

Makes 4 servings.

PORK TOASTS

¾ cup lean ground pork
2 oz. cooked, peeled shrimp, finely chopped
2 cloves garlic, finely chopped
1 tablespoon chopped cilantro leaves
1½ scallions, finely chopped
2 eggs, beaten
2 teaspoons fish sauce
freshly ground black pepper
4 day-old slices of bread
1 tablespoon coconut milk
vegetable oil for deep-frying
cilantro leaves, fine rings of fresh red chili, and
    cucumber slices, to garnish

In a bowl, mix together pork and shrimp using a fork, then thoroughly mix in garlic, coriander, scallions, half of egg, fish sauce, and black pepper. Divide between bread, spreading it firmly to edges. In a small bowl, stir together remaining egg and coconut milk and brush over pork mixture. Trim crusts from bread, then cut each slice into squares.

In a wok, heat oil to 375°F. Add several squares at a time, pork-side down, and fry for 3 or 4 minutes or until crisp, turning over halfway through. Using a slotted spoon, transfer to absorbent paper towels to drain, then keep warm in oven. Check temperature of oil in between frying each batch. Serve warm, garnished with coriander and slices of chili and cucumber.

Makes 4 to 6 servings.

PORK & NOODLE PACKAGES

3 cloves garlic, chopped
4 cilantro roots, chopped
¾ cup lean ground pork
1 small egg, beaten
2 teaspoons fish sauce
freshly ground black pepper
1 "nest" of egg thread noodles
vegetable oil for deep-frying
Thai Dipping Sauce 1 (see page 231), to serve

Using a mortar and pestle or small blender, pound or mix together garlic and cilantro roots. In a bowl, mix together pork, egg, fish sauce, and pepper. Stir in garlic mixture.

Place noodles in a heatproof strainer and dip in boiling water for 5 seconds if fresh or about 2 minutes if dried, until separated. Remove and rinse immediately in cold running water. Form pork mixture into approximately twelve balls. Neatly and evenly wind three or four strands of noodles around each ball to cover completely.

In a wok, heat oil to 350°F. Using a slotted spoon, lower four to six balls into oil and cook for about 3 minutes or until golden and pork is cooked through. Using a slotted or draining spoon, transfer to absorbent paper towels to drain. Keep warm while cooking remaining balls. Serve hot with dipping sauce. Garnish with cilantro sprigs.

Makes about 12 packages.

SHRIMP CRYSTAL ROLLS

8 oz. cooked peeled shrimp, cut in half if large
¾ cup coarsely chopped cooked pork
¾ cup coarsely chopped cooked chicken meat
2 tablespoons shredded carrot
2 tablespoons chopped canned water chestnuts
1 tablespoon chopped vegetables chow-chow
1 teaspoon finely chopped garlic
2 scallions, finely chopped
1 teaspoon sugar
2 tablespoons fish sauce
salt and freshly ground black pepper
10 to 12 sheets dried rice paper
flour and water paste
fresh mint and cilantro leaves
crisp lettuce leaves, such as iceberg
Spicy Fish Sauce (see page 233), to serve

In a bowl, mix shrimp, pork, chicken, shredded carrot, water chestnuts, vegetables chow-chow, garlic, scallions, sugar, fish sauce, and salt and pepper. Fill a bowl with warm water, then dip sheets of rice paper in water one at a time. If using large sheets of rice paper, fold in half, then place about 2 tablespoons of filling onto long end of rice paper, fold sides over to enclose filling, and roll up, then seal end with a little flour paste. (The roll will be transparent, hence the name "crystal.")

To serve, place some mint and coriander in a lettuce leaf with a crystal roll and wrap into a neat package, then dip roll into Spicy Fish Sauce before eating.

Makes 4 servings.

SESAME SHRIMP TOASTS

8 to 10 oz. raw, peeled shrimp, chopped
½ teaspoon crushed garlic
½ teaspoon finely chopped fresh ginger
2 shallots or 1 small onion, finely chopped
1 egg, beaten
salt and freshly ground black pepper
1 tablespoon cornstarch
1 loaf French bread
3 or 4 tablespoons white sesame seeds
oil for deep-frying
chopped cilantro leaves, to garnish

In a bowl, mix shrimp, garlic, ginger, shallots, egg, salt, pepper, and cornstarch. Chill in the refrigerator for at least 2 hours.

Cut bread into ½-in. slices and spread thickly with shrimp mixture on one side, then press that side down into sesame seeds so that entire surface is covered by seeds, making sure seeds are firmly pressed into shrimp mixture.

Heat oil in a wok or deep-fat fryer to 350°F and deep-fry toasts, in batches, spread-side down, for 2 or 3 minutes or until they start to turn golden brown around edges. Remove and drain on absorbent paper towels. Serve hot, garnished with chopped cilantro leaves.

Makes 6 to 8 servings.

SHRIMP PASTE ON SUGAR CANE

14 oz. raw, peeled shrimp
2 oz. fresh fatty pork, chopped
½ teaspoon chopped garlic
salt and freshly ground black pepper
1 teaspoon sugar
1 tablespoon cornstarch
1 egg white, beaten
12-in. piece sugar cane
cilantro sprigs, to garnish
Spicy Fish Sauce (see page 233), to serve

Using a mortar and pestle, pound shrimp, pork, and garlic to a smooth paste. Mix with salt, pepper, sugar, cornstarch, and egg white.

Preheat broiler. Peel sugar cane, cut into 4-in. lengths, and split lengthwise into quarters. Mold shrimp paste onto sugar cane, leaving about 1 in. of sugar cane at one end uncovered, to be used as a handle.

Broil sticks under a moderately hot broiler for 5 or 6 minutes, turning to ensure even cooking. Garnish with coriander. To serve, dip each stick in Spicy Fish Sauce before eating. When shrimp paste is eaten, sugar cane can be sucked and chewed.

Makes 4 to 6 servings.

Variation: Instead of broiling, the sugar cane can be deep-fried in hot oil for 4 or 5 minutes or until golden brown.

SQUID WITH SPICY CHILIES

1 lb. fresh squid, cleaned (see page 194)
½ teaspoon crushed garlic
½ teaspoon chopped, fresh ginger
salt and freshly ground black pepper
1 tablespoon fish sauce
2 tablespoons vegetable oil
2 scallions, finely shredded
3 or 4 small red chilies, seeded and sliced
cilantro sprigs, to garnish

Pull head off each squid, discard head and transparent backbone, but reserve tentacles. Cut open body and score inside of flesh in a crisscross pattern.

Cut squid into 1 x 1½-in. pieces. Blanch squid and tentacles in a saucepan of boiling water for 1 minute only—cooking any longer will toughen squid. Remove and drain, then dry well on absorbent paper towels. Mix garlic, ginger, salt, pepper, and fish sauce in a bowl, add blanched squid, and marinate for 25 to 30 minutes.

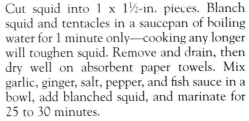

Meanwhile, heat oil in a small saucepan until hot but not smoking. Remove pan from heat, add scallions and chilies, and infuse for 15 to 20 minutes. Arrange squid with marinade on a serving plate, pour oil with scallions and chilies all over squid, and garnish with cilantro sprigs. Serve cold.

Makes 4 to 6 servings.

SEAFOOD SKEWERS

12 scallops
12 large, raw, peeled shrimp
8-oz. firm white fish fillet, such as halibut, cod, or
  monkfish, cut into 12 cubes
1 medium onion, cut into 12 pieces
1 red or green bell pepper, cut into 12 cubes
½ cup dry white wine or sherry
1 tablespoon chopped dill
1 tablespoon chopped Thai holy basil leaves
1 tablespoon lime juice or vinegar
salt and freshly ground black pepper
vegetable oil for brushing
Spicy Fish Sauce (see page 233), to serve

CHICKEN SATAY

1 lb. boneless, skinless chicken fillets, cut into
  1-in. cubes
1 teaspoon crushed garlic
2 shallots or 1 small onion, finely chopped
1 tablespoon ground coriander
1 teaspoon sugar
1 tablespoon mild curry powder
2 tablespoons fish sauce
1 tablespoon lime juice or vinegar
salt and freshly ground black pepper
vegetable oil for brushing
chopped onion and cucumber, to garnish
roasted peanuts, crushed and mixed with Vietnamese
  Hot Sauce (see page 234), to serve

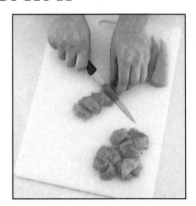

In a bowl, mix scallops, shrimp, fish, onion, and bell peppers with wine, dill, basil, lime juice or vinegar, salt, and pepper. Marinate in a cool place for at least 2 or 3 hours. Meanwhile, soak six bamboo skewers in hot water for 25 to 30 minutes and prepare grill or preheat broiler. Thread seafood and vegetables alternately onto skewers so that each skewer has two pieces of each ingredient.

In a bowl, mix chicken with garlic, shallots or onion, coriander, sugar, curry powder, fish sauce, lime juice or vinegar, and salt and pepper, then marinate for 2 or 3 hours. Meanwhile, soak sixteen bamboo skewers in hot water for 25 to 30 minutes. Prepare grill or preheat broiler.

Brush each skewer with a little oil and cook on a grill or under a hot broiler for 5 or 6 minutes, turning frequently. Serve hot with fish sauce as a dip.

Makes 6 servings.

Thread four meat cubes onto one end of each skewer. Brush each skewer with a little oil and cook on the grill or under the hot broiler for 5 or 6 minutes, turning frequently. Garnish with chopped onion and cucumber and serve hot with sauce as a dip.

Makes 8 servings.

Variation: Pork fillets, beefsteak, or lamb can be prepared and cooked in the same way.

MONGOLIAN-STYLE LAMB

2 cloves garlic, chopped
1 tablespoon chopped fresh ginger
2 shallots or white part of 3 scallions, chopped
1 tablespoon five-spice powder
salt and freshly ground black pepper
1 teaspoon chili sauce
2 tablespoons fish sauce
1½ lbs. leg of lamb fillets, boneless
12 to 16 crisp lettuce leaves
fresh mint and cilantro leaves
Spicy Fish Sauce (see page 233)

With mortar and pestle, pound garlic, ginger, and shallots to a paste. Mix with five-spice powder, salt, pepper, chili, and fish sauces.

Cut lamb fillet into six long strips. Rub spice mixture all over lamb strips and marinate for 3 or 4 hours. Pack meat, with marinade, in a heatproof dish or bowl. Place in a steamer and steam over high heat for 2 or 3 hours.

Prepare grill or preheat broiler. Remove meat strips from steamer and cook them on grill or under the broiler for 3 or 4 minutes, turning frequently so that they are slightly charred but not burned. Pull meat into small shreds and wrap in lettuce leaves with some mint and coriander. Dip rolls in Spicy Fish Sauce before eating.

Makes 6 to 8 servings.

QUAIL WRAPPED IN LETTUCE

1 cup boned and ground quail meat
salt and freshly ground black pepper
½ teaspoon sugar
2 teaspoons fish sauce
3 tablespoons vegetable oil
½ teaspoon crushed garlic
½ teaspoon ground fresh ginger
1 tablespoon chopped scallion
2 tablespoons chopped Chinese mushrooms, soaked
2 tablespoons chopped water chestnuts
1 tablespoon chopped vegetables chow-chow
2 tablespoons oyster sauce
12 iceberg lettuce leaves
fresh mint and cilantro leaves
Spicy Fish Sauce (see page 233)

In a bowl, mix quail meat with salt, pepper, sugar, and fish sauce, and marinate for 15 to 20 minutes. Heat oil in a wok or skillet and lightly brown garlic and ginger. Add quail meat and stir-fry for about 1 minute. Add scallion, mushrooms, water chestnuts, and vegetables chow-chow, and blend well. Stir-fry for 2 minutes, then stir in oyster sauce. Transfer to a serving dish.

To serve, place 2 tablespoons of mixture on a lettuce leaf with some mint and coriander and roll it up tightly, then dip roll into Spicy Fish Sauce before eating.

Makes 4 to 6 servings.

Variation: Pigeon, duck, or other game birds can be cooked and served in the same way.

MIXED SUSHI

3 or 4 dried shiitake mushrooms
1½ tablespoons sugar
3½ tablespoons soy sauce
½ carrot, peeled and shredded
1 to 1½ cups dashi (see page 29)
3 tablespoons sake
3½ oz. crab sticks, shredded
1 oz. green beans, trimmed
vegetable oil for frying
1 egg, beaten, with a pinch of salt
VINEGARED RICE:
3⅔ cups Japanese rice
2 tablespoons mirin
½ cup rice vinegar
2½ tablespoons sugar
¾ teaspoon salt

Soak Japanese rice following method on page 209. Meanwhile, soak mushrooms in warm water for 30 minutes, then drain, reserving ⅓ cup of water. Discard stems and cut caps into thin strips. Put reserved soaking water in a pan with sugar, 1½ tablespoons soy sauce, and mushroom caps, and cook for 20 minutes or until almost all liquid is absorbed. Parboil carrot and cook in dashi, seasoned with 2 tablespoons each soy sauce and sake, for 3 or 4 minutes. Sprinkle remaining sake over crab sticks. Lightly cook beans and slice diagonally.

Heat a skillet, pour in some vegetable oil, then remove from heat and wipe off excess oil. Return to medium heat and pour in egg so that a paper-thin layer covers the entire surface. Break air bubbles and fry both sides for 30 seconds. Turn onto a board, let cool, then cut into shreds. Make sweet vinegared rice (see page 209). While warm, fold in mushrooms, carrots, and crab sticks. Garnish with beans and egg shreds.

Makes 4 to 6 servings.

HAND-ROLLED SUSHI

3⅔ cups Japanese rice
4 or 5 dried shiitake mushrooms
2½ tablespoons sugar
1 tablespoon mirin
2 tablespoons soy sauce, plus extra for dipping
8 oz. fresh tuna
4 oz. smoked salmon
8 raw jumbo shrimp
1 avocado
⅓ cucumber, shredded
1 bunch watercress
8 sheets nori (wafer-thin dried seaweed)

Soak Japanese rice following method on page 209.

Meanwhile, soak shiitake mushrooms in warm water for 30 minutes, then drain, reserving ⅓ cup of soaking water. Trim off stems and discard; cut caps into thin strips. Place in a pan with sugar, mirin, 2 tablespoons soy sauce, and reserved soaking water; cook 10 minutes. Slice tuna into ½ x 2-in. thin pieces. Cut smoked salmon into similar-size slices. Peel, devein, and lightly boil shrimp. Drain and slice horizontally in half. Peel, pit, and thinly slice avocado.

Boil rice (see page 209) and divide between four individual serving bowls with lids to keep rice warm. On a large serving plate, arrange all prepared ingredients and place it in center of table. Lightly broil both sides of nori sheets over low heat and cut each one into four squares so that each diner has eight small sheets. At table, take one sheet in your palm and add a little boiled rice, spreading it with a spatula or fork. Wrap any ingredients in it, dip in soy sauce, and eat.

Makes 4 servings.

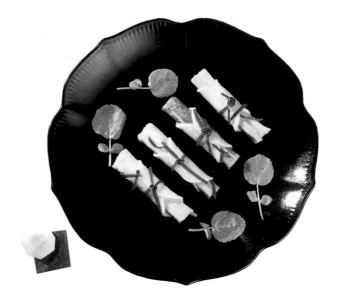

MACKEREL SUSHI

1 lb. 2 oz. mackerel fillets
salt and rice vinegar
VINEGARED RICE:
1 cup Japanese rice
2½ tablespoons rice vinegar
½ tablespoon sugar
½ tablespoon salt
GARNISH:
lemon wedges and watercress
vinegared ginger slices (optional)

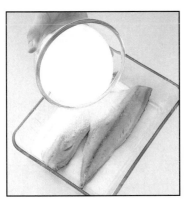

Place mackerel fillets in a dish, cover completely with plenty of salt, and leave overnight in the refrigerator.

Make vinegared rice following the method on page 209. Remove mackerel and rub off salt with absorbent paper towels. Carefully remove all bones with tweezers. Wash off any remaining salt with rice vinegar. Using your fingers, remove transparent skin from each fillet, leaving silver pattern on flesh intact. Place a fillet, skinned side down, in a wet, wooden mold or rectangular container, about 10 x 3 x 2 in., lined with a large piece of plastic wrap. Fill gaps with small pieces taken from the other fillet so the mold is lined.

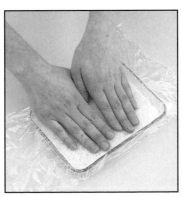

Press rice down firmly on top of fish with fingers. Put the lid on, or fold in plastic wrap, and place a weight on top. Leave in a cool place (but do not refrigerate) for several hours. Remove from container, unwrap, and cut into small pieces with a sharp knife, wiping the knife with a vinegar-soaked cloth after each cut. Garnish with lemon, watercress, and vinegared ginger slices, if desired. Serve with soy sauce.

Makes 4 to 6 servings.

CRAB STICK DAIKON ROLL

4-in. square dried konbu (kelp)
1 large daikon, peeled
7 oz. crab sticks
1½-in. piece fresh ginger, peeled and cut into
  matchsticks
watercress, to garnish
DRESSING:
2 dried or fresh red chilies
1 cup dashi (see page 29)
¼ cup rice vinegar
3 tablespoons sugar
salt and 2 or 3 teaspoons vegetable oil

Slice daikon into very thin rounds and spread out on a wire rack. Dry 24 hours.

The next day, soak konbu in warm water for 10 minutes, then cut lengthwise into thin strings. Divide each crab stick lengthwise into two or three pieces. Place a piece of crab stick and one or two shreds of ginger on a dried and softened piece of daikon and roll up. Tie with a string of konbu so that it won't open up. Repeat with remaining ingredients. Put all rolls in a mesh bowl or colander and pour over boiling water. Drain and set aside.

If using dried chilies, soak in warm water for 10 minutes. Whether using dried or fresh, cut in half lengthwise and remove seeds, then slice diagonally into thin strips. Put dashi, rice vinegar, sugar, a little salt, and oil in a saucepan and bring to a boil. Stir to dissolve sugar and add chili strips. Boil a few seconds and remove from heat. Let cool. Place daikon rolls in a bowl, pour over dressing, and marinate overnight. Transfer to a serving dish and garnish with watercress.

Makes 4 to 8 servings.

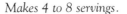

VEGETABLE TEMPURA

1 carrot
1 turnip or parsnip
7 oz. green beans, trimmed
vegetable oil for deep-frying
½ daikon, peeled and shredded
1½ to 2-in. piece fresh ginger, peeled and grated
lemon wedges, to garnish
BATTER:
1 egg yolk
1 cup ice-cold water
1¾ cups all-purpose flour, sifted
SAUCE:
1 cup dashi (see page 29)
⅓ cup soy sauce
⅓ cup mirin

Cut carrot and turnip into 2-in.-long shreds. Cut beans diagonally into fine strips. Heat plenty of oil in a wok or deep skillet to 340°F. Meanwhile, make batter. In a large mixing bowl, lightly beat egg and pour in ice-cold water. Stir just two or three times, then add flour. Using three or four chopsticks or a fork, very lightly mix batter with just a few strokes. Do not whisk or overmix—the batter should be very lumpy. Put all the vegetable shreds into the bowl and gently fold in.

Carefully drop the battered vegetables into the oil, a tablespoon at a time. Fry a few at a time and remove from oil when both sides are light golden and drain on absorbent paper towels. Repeat until all battered vegetables are cooked. Arrange them on a large serving plate or individual plates with heaps of shredded daikon and ginger. Garnish with lemon wedges. Quickly heat dashi, soy sauce, and mirin in a pan and pour it into small individual bowls. Serve hot.

Makes 4 servings.

BROILED TOFU WITH MISO SAUCE

1 lb. 2 oz. firm tofu
toasted sesame seeds for sprinkling
bamboo leaves, to garnish
MISO SAUCE:
3½ oz. miso
1 egg yolk
1 tablespoon each sake, mirin, and sugar
¼ cup dashi (see page 29)
juice of ½ lime

Wrap each tofu cake in a dishcloth and place a light weight, such as a plate, on top to squeeze out water. Let stand for at least 1 hour.

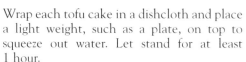

To make sauce, put miso in a bowl and blend in egg yolk, sake, mirin, and sugar. Place bowl over a saucepan of simmering water. Gradually add dashi and stir until sauce becomes thick but not too hard, then add lime juice. Remove from heat immediately and cool to room temperature (it will keep well in the refrigerator, if desired).

Preheat broiler. Unwrap tofu cakes and cut into 2 x ¾ x ½-in. slices. Skewer each slice lengthwise with two bamboo skewers. Broil them under high heat, a few minutes on each side, until lightly browned and heated through. Remove from heat and, using a butter knife, thickly spread one side with miso sauce. Sprinkle with toasted sesame seeds. Broil miso-covered side for 1 or 2 minutes. Serve hot on skewers on a bed of bamboo leaves.

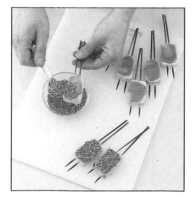

Makes 4 servings as a starter.

SEAFOOD

INDIAN	60
CHINESE	65
MALAYSIAN	74
THAI	80
VIETNAMESE	86
JAPANESE	92

SHRIMP & FISH BALL CURRY

1 lb. white fish fillets, such as sole, flounder, cod,
  whiting, or monkfish, skinned
4 oz. peeled, cooked shrimp
1½ cups fresh white breadcrumbs
2 eggs, beaten separately
2 tablespoons chopped cilantro leaves
2 teaspoons lemon juice
salt and pepper
2 tablespoons vegetable oil, plus extra for frying
1 large onion, finely chopped
2 fresh green chilies, seeded and chopped
4 cloves garlic, crushed
½ teaspoon turmeric
⅔ cup coconut milk (see page 224)
14½-oz. can diced tomatoes

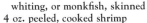

Wash fish and remove any bones. Mince fish
and shrimp, then transfer to a large bowl.
Stir in 1 cup breadcrumbs, 1 egg, coriander,
and lemon juice, and season with salt and
pepper. Mix well and form into twenty-four
balls. Roll balls in remaining egg, then in
remaining breadcrumbs to coat completely.
Chill for 30 minutes. Meanwhile, heat
2 tablespoons oil in a heavy-bottomed pan,
add onion, and cook, stirring, for 5 minutes
or until soft.

Add chilies, garlic, and turmeric, and fry for
an additional 2 minutes. Stir in coconut
milk and tomatoes and cook, uncovered, for
20 minutes, stirring occasionally, until
thickened. Half-fill a deep-fat pan or fryer
with oil and heat to 375°F or until a cube of
day-old bread browns in 40 seconds. Fry fish
balls for 3 to 5 minutes or until golden. Drain
well and serve with sauce.

Makes 4 servings.

HOT MUSSELS WITH CUMIN

3½ lbs. mussels
2 tablespoons vegetable oil
1 large onion, finely chopped
1-in. piece fresh ginger, grated
6 cloves garlic, crushed
2 fresh green chilies, seeded and finely chopped
½ teaspoon turmeric
2 teaspoons ground cumin
1¾ cups shredded, fresh coconut
2 tablespoons chopped cilantro leaves
cilantro sprigs, to garnish

Scrub mussels clean in several changes of
fresh, cold water and pull off beards.

Discard any mussels that are cracked or do
not close tightly when tapped. Set aside.
Heat oil in a large saucepan and add onion.
Fry, stirring, 5 minutes or until soft, then add
ginger, garlic, chilies, turmeric, and cumin.
Fry 2 minutes, stirring constantly.

Add mussels, coconut, and 1 cup water and
bring to a boil. Cover and cook over a high
heat, shaking pan frequently, for about
5 minutes or until almost all the shells have
opened. Discard any that do not open.
Spoon mussels into a serving dish, pour over
cooking liquid, and sprinkle with chopped
coriander. Garnish with cilantro sprigs and
serve at once.

Makes 4 servings.

CILANTRO & CHILI FISH

1¾ lbs. white fish fillets, such as monkfish, sole,
   or flounder
4 teaspoons lemon juice
salt and pepper
2½ cups cilantro leaves
4 fresh green chilies, seeded and chopped
3 cloves garlic, crushed
1 cup plain yogurt
vegetable oil for deep-frying
lemon wedges and cilantro leaves, to garnish

Trim any skin and bones from fish, then cut
flesh into 1 x 3-in. strips.

Spread the fish strips in a shallow,
nonmetallic dish and sprinkle with lemon
juice, salt, and pepper. Set aside in a cool
place. Put the coriander, chilies, garlic, and
1 or 2 tablespoons water in a blender or food
processor fitted with a metal blade and
process until smooth, frequently scraping
mixture down from sides. Squeeze out excess
liquid from paste, place in a shallow dish,
and stir in yogurt.

Heat oil in a deep skillet to 350°F or until a
cube of day-old bread browns in 35 seconds.
Drain fish and pat dry with absorbent paper
towels. Dip strips in yogurt mixture, coating
them all over, and fry a few at a time for
2 or 3 minutes or until golden brown. Drain
on absorbent paper towels, then serve at
once, garnished with lemon wedges and
cilantro leaves.

Makes 4 servings.

SOLE WITH DILL STUFFING

4 sole fillets, each weighing about 6 oz., skinned
3 tablespoons lemon juice
salt and pepper
2 tablespoons vegetable oil
1 clove garlic, crushed
1-in. piece fresh ginger, grated
¼ teaspoon cayenne pepper
¼ teaspoon turmeric
4 scallions, finely chopped
1 cup finely chopped fresh dill
dill sprigs, to garnish

Wash fish fillets and pat dry with absorbent
paper towels.

Lay fillets, skin-side up, on a work surface
and sprinkle with lemon juice and salt and
pepper, then set aside. Preheat oven to 350°F.
Heat 1½ tablespoons oil in a skillet. Add
garlic, ginger, cayenne, turmeric, and
scallions, and cook over a low heat for
3 minutes or until onions are soft and
golden, stirring occasionally. Remove from
heat and set aside to cool, then stir in dill.

Divide stuffing between fillets and spread
evenly over skinned side of fish. Roll fillets
up from thickest end. Grease a shallow
ovenproof dish with remaining oil and
arrange sole rolls, seam-side down, in the
dish with ¼ cup water. Cover with
aluminum foil and cook for 15 to 20 minutes
or until fish flakes easily. Serve hot, with
cooking juices spooned over and garnished
with sprigs of dill.

Makes 4 servings.

FISH IN HOT SAUCE

4 whole fish, such as mackerel, trout or gray mullet, each weighing about 8 oz., cleaned
4 dill sprigs
4 lime slices
¼ cup vegetable oil
4 scallions, sliced
½-in. piece fresh ginger, grated
1 clove garlic, crushed
1 teaspoon mustard seeds
¼ teaspoon cayenne pepper
1 tablespoon tamarind paste (see page 11)
2 tablespoons tomato paste
dill sprigs and lime slices, to garnish

Wash fish and pat dry with absorbent paper towels. Slash two or three times on each side, tuck a sprig of dill and a lime slice inside each fish, then set aside. Heat 2 tablespoons of oil in a small pan. Add onions and cook, stirring, 2 or 3 minutes or until softened. Add ginger, garlic, and mustard seeds, and fry for an additional 1 minute or until mustard seeds start to pop.

Stir in cayenne pepper, tamarind paste, tomato paste, and ⅓ cup water. Bring to a boil and simmer, uncovered, for about 5 minutes or until thickened slightly. Meanwhile, heat broiler. Place fish on broiler rack, brush with remaining oil, and broil for about 5 minutes on each side, basting occasionally with oil, until flesh flakes easily. Serve hot with sauce, garnished with dill and lime slices.

Makes 4 servings.

STEAMED FISH & VEGETABLES

4 whole red mullet, red snapper, or sea bream, each weighing about 8 oz., cleaned
4 teaspoons Garam Masala (see page 224)
½ teaspoon turmeric
2 tablespoons chopped cilantro leaves
1 tablespoon chopped fresh parsley
1-in. piece fresh ginger, grated
4 lemon slices
2 tablespoons vegetable oil
8 new potatoes, sliced
3 carrots, sliced
4 zucchini, sliced
salt and pepper
cilantro leaves, to garnish

Wash fish and pat dry with absorbent paper towels, then slash three times on each side. Mix Garam Masala, turmeric, cilantro, parsley, and ginger together and rub into flesh and skin of fish. Tuck a slice of lemon inside each fish and set aside. Heat oil in a skillet, add potatoes and carrots, and fry, stirring frequently, for 5 or 6 minutes or until slightly softened and beginning to brown.

Add zucchini to skillet and fry for 1 minute. Season with salt and pepper. Using a slotted spoon, transfer vegetables to a steamer. Lay the fish on top, cover, and steam for 20 to 25 minutes or until fish flakes easily and vegetables are tender. Serve at once, garnished with cilantro.

Makes 4 servings.

COCONUT SPICED COD

4 cod steaks, each weighing 6 to 8 oz.
salt and pepper
2 tablespoons vegetable oil
1 onion, chopped
1⅓ cups dried coconut
2-in. piece fresh ginger, grated
2 cloves garlic, crushed
2 green chilies, seeded and chopped
½ teaspoon chili powder
grated zest and juice of 1 lemon
2 tablespoons chopped cilantro leaves
2 tomatoes, skinned, seeded, and diced
oregano leaves, to garnish

Wash cod steaks and pat dry with absorbent paper towels. Place in a greased ovenproof dish and sprinkle with salt and pepper. Heat oil in a skillet, add onion, and fry, stirring, for about 5 minutes or until soft. Stir in coconut, ginger, garlic, chilies, and chili powder, and fry, stirring, for 3 to 5 minutes or until golden brown.

Stir in lemon zest and juice and simmer, covered, for 10 minutes to soften coconut. Preheat oven to 325°F. Stir cilantro and tomatoes into coconut mixture and spoon over cod steaks. Cook for 20 to 25 minutes or until fish flakes easily. Serve hot, garnished with oregano leaves.

Makes 4 servings.

Note: Cover with foil during cooking if coconut begins to brown too much.

BROILED SPICED FISH

4 whole flounder, each weighing about 8 oz., skinned
salt and pepper
⅔ cup plain yogurt
2 cloves garlic, crushed
2 teaspoons Garam Masala (see page 224)
1 teaspoon ground coriander
½ teaspoon chili powder
1 tablespoon lemon juice
lemon wedges and parsley sprigs, to garnish

Wash fish, pat dry with absorbent paper towels, and place in a shallow, nonmetallic dish. Sprinkle with salt and pepper.

Mix together yogurt, garlic, Garam Masala, coriander, chili powder, and lemon juice. Pour over fish and cover. Leave in a cool place for 2 or 3 hours to allow fish to absorb the flavors.

Heat broiler. Transfer fish to a broiler rack and cook for about 8 minutes, basting with cooking juices and turning over halfway through cooking, until fish flakes easily. Serve hot, garnished with lemon wedges and parsley sprigs.

Makes 4 servings.

Note: Use fillets instead of whole fish, if preferred, and broil for about 2 minutes less.

FISH IN A PACKET

4 fish steaks, such as sea bass, cod, or salmon, each
  weighing 6 to 8 oz.
1 or 2 fresh or frozen banana leaves (optional)
salt and pepper
1¼ cups finely shredded fresh coconut
1½ cups chopped fresh mint
4 cloves garlic, crushed
1 teaspoon ground cumin
4 fresh green chilies, seeded and chopped
2 tablespoons lemon juice
¼ cup cider vinegar
1 tablespoon vegetable oil
8 dried curry leaves (optional)
mint leaves and lemon slices, to garnish

Wipe fish steaks and place each in the center
of a 12-in. square of banana leaf or piece of
aluminum foil. Sprinkle fish with salt and
pepper. Mix together coconut, mint, garlic,
cumin, chilies, and lemon juice. Spoon a
quarter of the mixture over each fish steak.
Fold sides of banana leaf or foil over to seal
completely. Tie banana leaf packages with
fine string, if necessary.

Pour vinegar, oil, and ¾ cup water into
bottom of a large steamer, add curry leaves (if
using), and bring to a boil. Steam packages
for 12 to 15 minutes or until fish flakes easily.
Open packages and serve, garnished with
mint and lemon slices.

Makes 4 servings.

CREAMY SAFFRON FISH CURRY

1½ lbs. white fish fillets, such as sole, flounder,
  whiting, or cod
pinch saffron threads
3 tablespoons vegetable oil
2 onions, chopped
3 cloves garlic, crushed
1-in. piece fresh ginger, grated
1 teaspoon turmeric
1 tablespoon ground coriander
2 teaspoons Garam Masala (see page 224)
salt and cayenne pepper
2 teaspoons chickpea flour
1 cup plain yogurt
¼ cup thick cream
lemon zest and red bell pepper strips, to garnish

Wash fish, remove any skin and bones, and
pat dry with absorbent paper towels. Cut
into large chunks and set aside. Put saffron in
a small bowl with 2 tablespoons boiling
water and let soak for about 5 minutes. Heat
oil in a large, shallow pan, add onions, and
cook, stirring, for about 5 minutes or until
soft but not colored.

Add garlic, ginger, turmeric, coriander,
Garam Masala, and salt and pepper, and fry
for an additional 1 minute. Stir in flour and
cook for 1 minute, then remove from heat.
Stir in yogurt and cream, then return to heat
and slowly bring to a boil. Add fish, saffron,
and soaking water, and simmer gently,
covered, for 10 to 15 minutes or until fish is
tender and flakes easily. Serve fish hot,
garnished with shreds of lemon zest and
strips of red bell pepper.

Makes 4 servings.

KUNG PO SHRIMP

1 lb. prepared raw shrimp
¼ cup cornstarch mixed with ⅓ cup water
2½ cups peanut oil
2 scallions, finely chopped
½-in. piece fresh ginger, peeled and finely chopped
1 tablespoon rice wine or dry sherry
1 tablespoon light soy sauce
1 teaspoon brown sugar
2 teaspoons sherry vinegar
sea salt and black pepper

Dip shrimp in cornstarch mixture to coat evenly; allow excess batter to drain off.

In a wok, heat oil until smoking, add shrimp, and deep-fry for about 3 minutes or until golden brown. Remove using a slotted spoon and then drain on absorbent paper towels. Pour the oil from the wok, leaving just 2 tablespoonsful.

Add scallion and ginger to wok and stir-fry for 1 minute. Stir in rice wine, soy sauce, brown sugar, sherry vinegar, salt, and pepper, and bring to a boil. Add shrimp to sauce and heat gently until sauce has thickened.

Makes 4 servings.

PHOENIX SHRIMP

8 large prepared shrimp
1-in. piece fresh ginger, peeled and grated
3 scallions, chopped
2 tablespoons rice wine or dry sherry
1 teaspoon sesame oil
1 tablespoon light soy sauce
½ teaspoon sea salt
2½ cups vegetable oil
BATTER:
4 egg whites
2 tablespoons cornstarch
2 tablespoons all-purpose flour
1½ cups dry breadcrumbs, for coating

Using a cleaver or large knife, slightly flatten shrimp along their length; place in a dish. In a bowl, mix together ginger, scallions, rice wine or dry sherry, sesame oil, soy sauce, and salt. Pour over the shrimp and leave for 30 minutes. Make batter in a bowl by beating together egg whites until thick, then beat in cornstarch and flour. Dip shrimp in batter to coat thickly and evenly, then coat well with dry breadcrumbs.

In a wok, heat vegetable oil until very hot, add shrimp, and deep-fry for 5 minutes or until golden. Drain on absorbent paper towels.

Makes 4 servings.

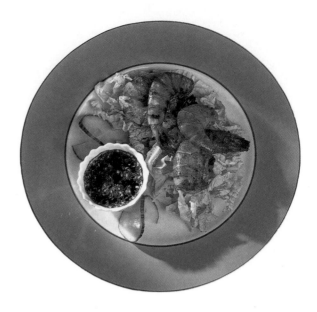

MUSSELS WITH BEANS & CHILI

8 lbs. mussels, scrubbed and rinsed
½ cup vegetable oil
4 cloves garlic, finely chopped
2 red chilies, seeded if desired, finely chopped
½ green bell pepper, seeded and chopped
3 scallions, sliced
1 teaspoon cornstarch mixed with 2 teaspoons
  cold water
¼ cup rice wine or dry sherry
3 tablespoons black bean paste
2 teaspoons ground ginger
1 tablespoon brown sugar
2 tablespoons hot chili paste
3 tablespoons oyster sauce
3 cups Chinese Chicken Stock (see page 16)

Place mussels in a large saucepan, add 2 cups water, cover, and place over a high flame for about 5 minutes, shaking pan occasionally, or until mussels have opened; this may have to be done in batches. Remove from heat, drain, and discard any mussels that have not opened.

In a wok, heat oil, add garlic, chilies, green bell pepper, and scallions, and stir-fry for 1 minute. In a bowl, mix together cornstarch mixture, rice wine or dry sherry, black bean paste, ground ginger, brown sugar, hot chili paste, oyster sauce, and stock. Stir into wok and bring to a boil, stirring. Simmer until lightly thickened. Add mussels to wok and heat through for 5 minutes, occasionally shaking wok.

Makes 4 to 6 servings.

SALT & PEPPER SHRIMP

16 uncooked large shrimp
1 teaspoon chili powder
1 teaspoon coarse sea salt
1 teaspoon Szechuan peppercorns, crushed
2 cloves garlic, finely chopped
1 tablespoon peanut oil
DIP:
½ teaspoon Szechuan peppercorns, toasted
  and ground
2 tablespoons light soy sauce
2 tablespoons dry sherry
1 teaspoon brown sugar

Cut heads off shrimp. Use scissors to remove legs, leaving shells intact.

Rinse shrimp and pat dry with absorbent paper towels. In a bowl, mix together shrimp, chili powder, salt, peppercorns, and garlic. Heat oil in a wok until very hot and stir-fry shrimp for 2 to 3 minutes or until shrimp are pink and cooked through. Drain on absorbent paper towels.

Mix together ingredients for dip. Serve shrimp immediately with dip and a salad.

Makes 4 servings.

Note: Serve with finger bowls of water and lemon slices, to freshen hands.

STIR-FRIED SCALLOPS

SCALLOPS WITH BLACK BEANS

1 lb. fresh bay scallops, cleaned and trimmed
8 oz. baby corn
8 oz. snow peas
1 tablespoon sunflower oil
2 shallots, chopped
1 clove garlic, finely chopped
½-in. piece fresh ginger, peeled and finely chopped
2 tablespoons yellow bean sauce
1 tablespoon light soy sauce
1 teaspoon sugar
1 tablespoon dry sherry

Rinse scallops and dry with absorbent paper towels.

Slice baby corn in half lengthwise and trim ends from snow peas. Heat oil in a wok and stir-fry the shallots, garlic, and ginger for 1 minute.

Add scallops, baby corn, and snow peas, and stir-fry for 1 minute. Stir in yellow bean sauce, soy sauce, sugar, and sherry, and simmer for 4 minutes or until scallops and vegetables are cooked through. Serve on a bed of rice.

Makes 4 servings.

Note: Scallops are sometimes sold with edible orange roe still attached.

12 scallops on their half-shells
2 tablespoons peanut oil
2 cloves garlic, finely chopped
3 scallions, finely chopped
1 fresh hot green chili, seeded and chopped
3 tablespoons fermented salted black beans, soaked for 20 minutes, then drained
2 tablespoons dark soy sauce
2 teaspoons brown sugar
3 tablespoons Chinese Chicken Stock (see page 16)
2 teaspoons cornstarch

Place scallops on their shells in a steaming basket, place over a wok or saucepan of boiling water, cover, and cook for 6 minutes.

Meanwhile, in a wok, heat oil, add garlic, scallions, chili, and black beans, and stir-fry for 2 minutes, mashing the beans. Stir in soy sauce and sugar for 1-2 minutes.

Blend stock with cornstarch until smooth. Stir into wok, bring to a boil, stirring, and simmer until thickened. Keep warm. Transfer scallops to a warmed serving plate and spoon a little sauce over each.

Makes 4 servings.

CURRIED CRAB

1½ lbs. cooked large crab claws, thawed and
  dried if frozen
1 tablespoon sunflower oil
2 cloves garlic, thinly sliced
⅓ cup Chinese Vegetable Stock (see page 17)
1 tablespoon Madras curry paste
1 tablespoon light soy sauce
1 teaspoon brown sugar
1 large green bell pepper, thinly sliced
1 cup small broccoli florets

Wrap the end of a rolling pin in plastic wrap
and tap the main part of the crab claws until
shell cracks, leaving pincers intact. Peel
away hard shell to expose crab flesh, leaving
shell on pincers. Heat oil in a wok and stir-
fry crab and garlic for 1 or 2 minutes or until
crab is lightly browned. Drain on absorbent
paper towels and set aside.

Mix together stock, curry paste, soy sauce,
and brown sugar, and add to wok with green
bell pepper and broccoli. Simmer 5 minutes,
stirring occasionally. Return crab and garlic
to wok and simmer 2 or 3 minutes, stirring to
coat crab with sauce. Serve immediately
with rice, vegetables, and lemon wedges.

Makes 4 servings.

SQUID FLOWERS & BELL PEPPERS

2½ cups peanut oil
1 lb. squid, cleaned (see page 194)
2 slices fresh ginger, peeled and finely chopped
1 large green bell pepper, seeded and cut into
  1-in. squares
1 teaspoon sea salt
1 tablespoon dark soy sauce
1 teaspoon rice vinegar
½ teaspoon brown sugar
ground black pepper
1 teaspoon sesame oil

In a wok, heat oil until smoking, add squid,
and fry for 1 minute. Remove and drain on
absorbent paper towels.

Pour oil from wok, leaving just 1 tablespoon.
Add ginger and green bell pepper and stir-fry
for 5 minutes or until pepper begins to
soften. Stir in sea salt, soy sauce, rice vinegar,
brown sugar, and black pepper.

Bring to a boil, stirring, then reduce heat so
sauce is simmering, add squid, and gently
heat through. Transfer to a warmed serving
plate and sprinkle with sesame oil.

Makes 4 servings.

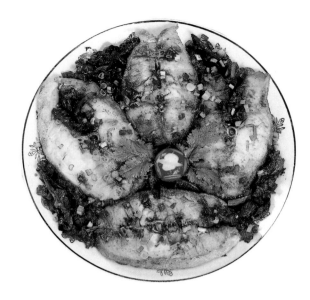

HUNAN FISH STEAKS

2½ cups vegetable oil
4 cod steaks, each weighing about 6 oz.
SAUCE:
4 dried black winter mushrooms
2 medium onions, finely chopped
3 slices fresh ginger, peeled and finely chopped
2 cloves garlic, finely chopped
2 tablespoons Chinese radish pickle, chopped
3 dried red chilies
¾ cup Chinese Chicken Stock (see page 16)
3 tablespoons dark soy sauce
2 tablespoons brown sugar
2 teaspoons sea salt
¼ cup rice wine or dry sherry
4 scallions, chopped, to garnish
2 teaspoons sesame oil, to serve

Soak the mushrooms in hot water for 25 minutes, then drain. In a wok, heat oil until just smoking. Add fish steaks two at a time and deep-fry for 1½ minutes each side. Remove, drain on absorbent paper towels, and keep warm. Reheat oil before adding remaining steaks. Pour oil from wok, leaving just 3 tablespoons. Stir in all sauce ingredients and boil, stirring, until reduced by half.

Reduce heat so sauce is just simmering, add fish steaks, and heat through gently, turning occasionally, for 5 minutes. Transfer fish to a warmed serving plate, pour over sauce, and sprinkle with finely chopped scallions and sesame oil.

Makes 4 servings.

CANTONESE LOBSTER

3 lbs. lobster
2 tablespoons peanut oil
½-in. piece fresh ginger, peeled and grated
4 scallions, coarsely chopped
1 teaspoon sea salt
¾ cup Chinese Chicken Stock (see page 16)
2 tablespoons dark soy sauce
2 tablespoons rice wine or dry sherry

Insert the point of a large, heavy knife in the back of the lobster's head, then move the knife toward the tail in a series of cutting movements to split the lobster in half.

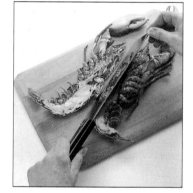

Remove and discard head sac and black intestinal thread. Crack the claws. In a wok, over a moderate heat, heat oil, add lobster pieces, cover, and cook for 4 minutes. Remove and drain on absorbent paper towels. Pour oil from wok, leaving just 1 tablespoon. Stir ginger, scallions, salt, stock, soy sauce, and rice wine into the wok and bring to a boil.

Return lobster pieces to wok, cover, and simmer for 5 minutes. Transfer lobster to a warmed serving plate and pour sauce on top.

Makes 4 servings.

COD WITH OYSTER SAUCE

1½-lb. cod fillet, skinned
2 shallots, shredded
8 oyster mushrooms, sliced
2 cloves garlic, finely sliced
4 oz. cooked, peeled large shrimp, thawed and
   dried if frozen
¼ cup oyster sauce
2 tablespoons dry sherry
salt and freshly ground black pepper
grated zest of 1 lime and 1 lemon
2 tablespoons chopped cilantro leaves

COD WITH VINEGAR SAUCE

1 tablespoon sunflower oil
6 shallots, sliced
2 tablespoons white rice vinegar
2 teaspoons sugar
1 tablespoon light soy sauce
1¼ cups Chinese Vegetable Stock (see page 17)
1 teaspoon cornstarch mixed with 2 teaspoons
   cold water
4 cod steaks, each weighing about 6 oz.
salt and freshly ground black pepper
2 tablespoons chopped fresh chives

Heat half of the oil in a wok and stir-fry
shallots for 2 to 3 minutes.

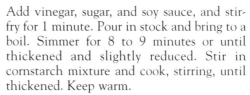

Preheat oven to 350°F. Rinse cod fillet and
pat dry with absorbent paper towels. Place
on a large piece of waxed paper and put in a
baking pan. Top cod with shallots,
mushrooms, garlic, and shrimp, then
sprinkle with oyster sauce and sherry. Season
with salt and freshly ground pepper.

Add vinegar, sugar, and soy sauce, and stir-
fry for 1 minute. Pour in stock and bring to a
boil. Simmer for 8 to 9 minutes or until
thickened and slightly reduced. Stir in
cornstarch mixture and cook, stirring, until
thickened. Keep warm.

Bring ends of waxed paper over fish and pleat
together to seal. Bake 25 minutes or until
cod is cooked through. Carefully lift from
paper, sprinkle with lime and lemon zest and
cilantro, and serve with rice and salad.

Makes 4 servings.

Preheat broiler. Season cod steaks on both
sides and place on broiler rack. Brush with
remaining oil and cook for 4 minutes on
each side or until cooked through. Drain on
absorbent paper towels. Remove skin. Stir
chives into vinegar sauce, spoon over cod
steaks, and serve with noodles and broiled
tomatoes.

Makes 4 servings.

SMOKY GARLIC FISH STEW

1½ lbs. firm white fish fillets, such as cod or
   monkfish, skinned and cut into 1-in. cubes
4 large cloves garlic, roughly chopped
2 teaspoons light soy sauce
3 tablespoons sweet sherry
1 tablespoon cornstarch
1 tablespoon sunflower oil
14 shallots, sliced
2 tablespoons fermented black beans
4 scallions, cut into 1-in. pieces
2 tablespoons dark soy sauce

In a bowl, mix together cubed fish, garlic,
light soy sauce, sherry, and cornstarch. Cover
and chill for 30 minutes. Heat oil in a wok
and stir-fry fish mixture and shallots for
3 minutes or until fish is lightly colored.
Remove with a slotted spoon, drain on
absorbent paper towels, and set aside.

Add black beans, scallions, and dark soy
sauce to wok and stir-fry for 2 or 3 minutes
over high heat or until thick and syrupy.
Replace fish mixture and cook for 2 minutes,
stirring gently. Serve immediately with
noodles and salad.

Makes 4 servings.

LIME-BROILED FISH KABOBS

12 oz. monkfish tails, skinned and cut into
   ¾-in. cubes
12 oz. trout fillets, skinned and cut into ¾-in. pieces
2 limes
1 teaspoon sesame oil
large pinch five-spice powder
freshly ground pepper
strips of lime zest, to garnish

Place monkfish and trout in a shallow dish.
Juice one lime and grate the zest. Mix juice
and zest with sesame oil and five-spice
powder, pour over fish, cover, and chill for
30 minutes.

Soak four bamboo skewers in cold water.
Halve and quarter remaining lime
lengthwise, then halve each quarter to make
eight wedges. Slice each piece of lime in half
crosswise to make sixteen small pieces.

Preheat broiler. Thread monkfish, trout, and
lime pieces onto skewers and place on broiler
rack. Brush with marinade and season with
pepper. Broil for 2 minutes on each side,
brushing occasionally with marinade to keep
them from drying out. Drain on absorbent
paper towels, garnish with lime zest, and
serve with rice, vegetables, and lime wedges.

Makes 4 servings.

STUFFED RED MULLET

4 oyster mushrooms
2 oz. cooked, peeled large shrimp, thawed and
    dried if frozen
grated zest of 1 small lemon
2 tablespoons oyster sauce
4 red mullet or red snapper fillets, each weighing
    about 8 oz., cleaned and scaled
¼ cup dry sherry
1 large carrot, cut into thin strips
1 daikon, peeled and cut into thin strips
1 cup small broccoli florets
lemon zest and chopped scallions, to garnish

Finely chop mushrooms and shrimp. Place in
a small bowl and mix in lemon zest. Stir in
oyster sauce and set aside. Rinse fish and pat
dry with absorbent paper towels. Divide
mushroom mixture into four portions and
press into cavity of each fish. Place stuffed
fish in a shallow dish and spoon over sherry.
Cover and chill for 30 minutes.

Bring a wok or large saucepan of water to a
boil. Arrange carrot and daikon strips and
broccoli florets on waxed paper in two
steamers, lay fish on top, and spoon sherry
marinade on top. Place over boiling water,
cover, and steam for 10 minutes. Carefully
turn fish over and steam for an additional
8 to 10 minutes or until cooked through.
Garnish with lemon zest and chopped
scallions to serve.

Makes 4 servings.

STEAMED FISH CAKES

1-in. piece fresh ginger, peeled
1½ lbs. cod fillets, skinned and chopped
1 egg white, lightly beaten
2 teaspoons cornstarch
2 tablespoons chopped, fresh chives
salt and ground white pepper
8 oyster mushrooms
2 shallots
2 zucchini
1 red bell pepper, halved
1 yellow bell pepper, halved
1 clove garlic
fresh chives, to garnish
oyster sauce, to serve (optional)

Chop half the ginger and place in a food
processor or blender with cod, egg white,
cornstarch, chives, salt, and pepper. Process
until finely chopped. Divide into twelve
portions and shape into 3-in.-diameter
patties. Line a large plate with waxed paper,
arrange fish cakes on plate, cover, and chill
for 30 minutes. Using a sharp knife, thinly
slice mushrooms, shallots, zucchini, bell
peppers, remaining ginger, and garlic.

Bring a wok or large saucepan of water to a
boil. Arrange vegetables on waxed paper in a
steamer, place fish cakes on top, and place
over boiling water. Cover and steam for
10 minutes or until cooked, turning fish
cakes halfway through cooking time.
Garnish with chives and serve with a salad
and oyster sauce.

Makes 4 servings.

SALMON WITH GINGER DIP

FIVE-SPICE SALMON STEAKS

4 salmon fillets, each weighing about 6 oz., skinned
2 tablespoons light soy sauce
1 tablespoon dry sherry
1-in. piece fresh ginger, peeled and cut into
  thin strips
1 teaspoon sunflower oil
freshly ground pepper
4 scallions, shredded, to garnish
DIP:
2 tablespoons sweet sherry
1 tablespoon light soy sauce

Using a sharp knife, lightly score top of
salmon fillets in diagonal lines, being careful
not to slice all the way through.

Place salmon in a shallow dish. Mix together
soy sauce, sherry, and ginger strips, and
spoon over salmon. Cover and chill for
1 hour.

Preheat broiler and brush broiler rack lightly
with oil. Remove salmon from marinade and
place on rack. Season with pepper and broil
for 2 or 3 minutes on each side. Meanwhile,
mix together sweet sherry and light soy sauce
for dip and set aside. Drain salmon on
absorbent paper towels. Garnish with
scallions and serve with dip.

Makes 4 servings.

4 salmon steaks, each weighing about 6 oz.
2 teaspoons five-spice powder
freshly ground black pepper
1 tablespoon peanut oil
1 clove garlic, finely chopped
2 tablespoons rice wine
1 tablespoon light soy sauce
1 teaspoon sesame oil
zest of 1 lemon, cut into fine strips

Rinse salmon steaks and pat dry with
absorbent paper towels. Rub both sides with
five-spice powder and freshly ground black
pepper.

Heat oil in a wok, add garlic and salmon, and
cook for 1 to 2 minutes on each side or until
salmon is lightly browned.

Add rice wine, soy sauce, and sesame oil, and
simmer for 3 or 4 minutes or until salmon is
just cooked through. Stir in lemon zest.
Remove salmon with a slotted spoon and
remove skin.

Makes 4 servings.

FRAGRANT SHRIMP

2 dried shrimp
2 tablespoons vegetable oil
5 whole, small, fresh red chilies
1 small onion, finely chopped
3 cloves garlic, finely chopped
1-in. piece fresh ginger, grated
1 teaspoon curry powder
leaves from 2 stalks of fresh curry leaves
1 lb. raw, unpeeled medium shrimp, peeled
  and deveined
1 tablespoon yellow bean sauce
1 teaspoon oyster sauce
1 teaspoon dark soy sauce
2 teaspoons rice wine
pinch sugar

Soak the dried shrimp in hot water for 10 minutes. Drain and pound in a mortar or mix in a small blender. In a wok or sauté pan, heat oil over medium heat. Add chilies, onion, garlic, and ginger. Fry for 1 minute. Add curry powder and curry leaves. Stir for 30 seconds.

Stir in shrimp and dried shrimp, then add yellow bean sauce, oyster sauce, and soy sauce. Bring to a simmer, cover pan, then cook gently for 2 or 3 minutes or until shrimp are beginning to turn pink. Add rice wine, and sugar to taste. Increase heat and stir for a few seconds. Serve immediately.

Makes 4 servings.

SHRIMP ROBED IN SPICES

8 candlenuts or cashews
2 teaspoons lime juice
2 large shallots, chopped
4 cloves garlic, crushed
1-in. piece galangal, chopped
1-in. piece fresh ginger, chopped
1 stalk lemongrass, chopped
½ teaspoon ground turmeric
¼ cup vegetable oil
1¼ lbs. raw, unpeeled medium shrimp, peeled
  and deveined

Put nuts in a blender and grind to a powder. Transfer to a small bowl. Stir in lime juice and 1 tablespoon water. Set aside.

Put shallots, garlic, galangal, ginger, lemongrass, and turmeric in blender. Add 2 or 3 tablespoons water and mix to a paste. Heat oil in a wok or large, nonstick skillet over medium heat. Add spice paste and cook, stirring, for about 5 minutes or until reduced and reddish-brown in color.

Add shrimp and nut mixture. Increase heat to high and fry, stirring, for 2 or 3 minutes or until shrimp are cooked and spice mixture clings to them. Using a slotted spoon, transfer to a warm plate, leaving all oil behind.

Makes 3 or 4 servings.

SHRIMP KABOBS

½ cup vegetable oil
⅓ cup lime juice
½-in. piece fresh ginger, grated
2 large cloves garlic, finely crushed
1 fresh red chili, cored, seeded, and finely chopped
leaves from a small bunch of cilantro, chopped
1 tablespoon light soy sauce
½ teaspoon light brown sugar
1½ lbs. raw, unpeeled large shrimp
Malaysian Dipping Sauce (see page 227), to serve

In a bowl, whisk together oil, lime juice, ginger, garlic, and chili. Stir in cilantro, soy sauce, and sugar.

Soak eight long wooden or bamboo skewers in water for 20 to 30 minutes, drain, then thread with shrimp. Place skewers in a shallow, nonreactive dish. Pour ginger mixture evenly over shrimp. Turn skewers, cover, and refrigerate for 1 to 2 hours, turning occasionally. Return to room temperature for 30 minutes.

Preheat broiler. Transfer kabobs to oiled broiler rack; reserve marinade. Cook shrimp 2 or 3 in. from heat, for 4 to 6 minutes, turning halfway through cooking time, until they turn pink. Brush with reserved marinade occasionally. Serve accompanied by Malaysian Dipping Sauce (see page 227).

Makes 4 servings.

MUSSELS IN HOT SPICY SAUCE

4 dried red chilies, seeded
2 teaspoons shrimp paste, roasted (see page 11)
1 small onion, chopped
1-in. piece fresh galangal
4 cloves garlic, 3 coarsely chopped and 1 finely chopped
1 stalk lemongrass, sliced
6 to 8 candlenuts or cashews
1 teaspoon paprika
¼ cup vegetable oil
2 to 3 lbs. live mussels, cleaned

Put chilies in a small bowl. Add ¼ cup hot water and soak until slightly softened. Pour into a blender.

Add shrimp paste, onion, galangal, coarsely chopped garlic, lemongrass, nuts, and paprika. Mix to a paste, adding a little extra water if necessary. In a wok or large sauté pan, heat oil over medium-high heat. Add finely chopped garlic and stir until just beginning to brown. Add spice paste and stir for 3 minutes.

Pour in 1½ cups water and bring to a boil. Add mussels. Return quickly to boil, then cover pan and cook over medium-high heat for 3 to 5 minutes, shaking the pan halfway through, until all mussels have opened; discard any mussels that remain closed. Serve mussels in deep bowls with cooking juices spooned on top.

Makes 4 servings.

MILD FISH CURRY

1¼ cups dried coconut
3 small onions, chopped
2 cloves garlic, crushed
1 fresh red chili, cored, seeded, and chopped
1-in. piece fresh ginger, chopped
2 stalks lemongrass, chopped
2 teaspoons ground turmeric
3 tablespoons peanut oil
2¼ cups coconut milk
1 lb. firm white fish fillet, such as cod, haddock, or
    monkfish, skinned and cubed
3 tablespoons thick coconut milk
fresh red chili, shredded, to garnish

Heat dried coconut in a small skillet over medium-high heat until lightly darkened with a roasted aroma. Cool slightly, then pound in a mortar and pestle, or in small bowl using the end of a rolling pin. Set aside until required. Put onions, garlic, chili, ginger, lemongrass, and turmeric in a blender and mix to a paste. Heat oil in a wok or skillet over medium-high heat. Add spice paste and fry for 3 to 4 minutes or until fragrant but not colored.

Stir coconut milk into spice paste. Bring to a boil, stirring, then lower heat and simmer for 3 minutes. Add fish to pan and cook gently for 3 or 4 minutes or until just cooked through. Stir in thick coconut milk and pounded coconut. Serve garnished with shredded chili.

Makes 3 or 4 servings.

COCONUT CURRIED FISH

6 cloves garlic, chopped
1-in. piece fresh ginger, chopped
1 large, fresh red chili, cored, seeded, and chopped
¼ cup vegetable oil
1 large onion, quartered and sliced
2 teaspoons ground cumin
½ teaspoon ground turmeric
1¾ cups coconut milk
salt
1 lb. firm white fish fillet, such as cod or halibut,
    cut into 2-in. pieces
cilantro sprigs and lime wedges, to garnish

Put garlic, ginger, and chili in a blender. Add ⅔ cup water. Mix until smooth.

Heat oil in a wok or sauté pan over medium heat. Add onion and fry for 5 to 7 minutes or until beginning to color. Add cumin and turmeric and stir for 30 seconds. Stir in garlic mixture. Cook, stirring, for about 2 minutes or until liquid has evaporated.

Stir coconut milk into pan. Bring to a boil and bubble until sauce is reduced by half. Add salt to taste. Add fish and spoon sauce over it so it is covered. Heat to a simmer and cook gently for 4 to 6 minutes or until fish just flakes when tested with the point of a sharp knife. Garnish with cilantro sprigs and lime wedges. Serve with rice.

Makes 3 or 4 servings.

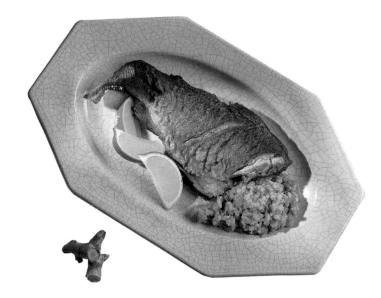

CRISP FISH WITH TURMERIC

2 whole fish, such as trout or bream, each weighing
   about 12 oz.
1 teaspoon ground turmeric
1½ teaspoons salt
½ cup vegetable oil
SAUCE:
1 tablespoon tamarind
4 dried red chilies
1 stalk lemongrass, chopped
1 clove garlic, chopped
4 shallots, chopped
¼-in. piece galangal, chopped
3 tablespoons vegetable oil
1 cup peanuts, toasted, skinned, and ground
about 2 teaspoons light brown sugar
salt

To make sauce, soak the tamarind in
2 tablespoons hot water for 4 hours. Press
firmly through a sieve. In blender, soak
chilies in 2 tablespoons hot water for
10 minutes. Add lemongrass, garlic, shallots,
and galangal. Grind to a paste. Heat oil in a
wok or small skillet over medium-high heat.
Add chili mixture and fry, stirring, for
3 minutes. Add tamarind liquid, peanuts,
and sugar and salt to taste. Simmer for
2 or 3 minutes. Set aside.

With point of a sharp knife, score three
diagonal lines on both sides of each fish.
Score each lengthwise down backbone. Mix
together turmeric and salt. Rub into fish,
working mixture into cuts. Leave for 1 hour.
In a wok or sauté pan over medium heat,
heat the oil to 350°F. Cook the fish for
5 or 6 minutes each side or until golden and
crisp. Remove and drain on absorbent paper
towels. Serve hot, accompanied by lime
wedges and sauce.

Makes 4 servings.

SPICED FISH IN BANANA LEAVES

1¼ lbs. white fish fillets
banana leaves (optional)
oil for brushing
SPICE PASTE:
6 shallots, chopped
2 cloves garlic, crushed
2 fresh red chilies, seeded and chopped
1-in. piece fresh ginger, chopped
4 candlenuts or cashews
½ teaspoon tamarind paste (see page 11)
2 teaspoons each ground coriander and ground cumin
¼ teaspoon ground turmeric

To make spice paste, put all ingredients in a
blender with a pinch salt and mix to a paste.

Cut fish into fourteen 2-in. pieces, ½ in.
thick. Coat top of each piece thickly with
spice paste. If using banana leaves, hold
them over a flame to soften. Oil leaves
thoroughly and cut into pieces to wrap
around pieces of fish (or do this with
aluminum foil). Secure with wooden
toothpicks.

Preheat grill or broiler. Cook fish packages
for 8 to 10 minutes, turning halfway through.
Serve with banana leaf or foil partially torn
away to reveal fish, and with lime wedges.

Makes 4 servings.

MARINATED BROILED FISH

SPICED SWEET & SOUR FISH

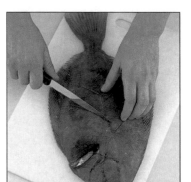

4 flat fish, such as flounder, each weighing
about 12 oz.
4 large cloves garlic, cut into fine slivers
1-in. piece fresh ginger, cut into fine slivers
¼ cup peanut oil
¼ cup light soy sauce
1 tablespoon sesame oil
1 tablespoon rice wine
4 scallions, thinly sliced

With the point of a sharp knife, cut five
diagonal slashes, herringbone style, in both
sides of each fish. Place in a shallow dish.

Put garlic, ginger, oil, soy sauce, sesame oil,
and rice wine in a small saucepan. Heat to
simmering point and pour over fish,
spooning marinade into slashes. Refrigerate
at least 1 hour, turning fish every 30 minutes.

Preheat broiler. Lift fish from marinade and
broil, pale skin side down, for 3 minutes.
Turn carefully and broil for an additional
1 or 2 minutes, depending on thickness of
fish. Broil in batches if necessary, keeping
broiled fish warm. Reheat any remaining
marinade and pour over fish. Sprinkle with
scallions and serve.

Makes 4 servings.

1 tablespoon cumin seeds
1 teaspoon coriander seeds
3 tablespoons vegetable oil
½ fresh red chili, cored, seeded, and chopped
3 cloves garlic, crushed
2 onions, chopped
1 in. shrimp paste, roasted (see page 11)
3½ tablespoons lime juice
3 tablespoons dark soy sauce
brown sugar, to taste
2 whole fish, each weighing about 1½ lbs.

Heat cumin and coriander seeds in skillet
over medium-high heat until toasted, with a
fragrant roasted aroma.

Cool slightly, then grind in a small blender,
a mortar and pestle, or a small bowl using the
end of a rolling pin. Heat oil in a small skillet
over medium-high heat. Add chili, garlic,
and onions, and fry until lightly browned.
Tip into the blender with cumin and
coriander and add shrimp paste, lime juice,
and soy sauce. Mix to a thin paste. Add
1 cup hot water, and sugar to taste. Set aside.

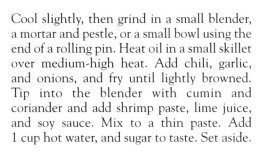

Preheat broiler. Cut three deep slashes on
both sides of each fish and score along
backbone. Cook fish for 5 or 6 minutes on
each side, depending on thickness. The flesh
should just flake when tested with point of a
sharp knife, and the skin should be brown.
Reheat sauce and pour some over each fish.
Serve remaining sauce separately.

Makes 4 or 5 servings.

SARAWAK MARINATED FISH

FISH STEAKS WITH CHILI

1 lb. very fresh white fish fillets, skinned and
   thinly sliced
⅓ cup lime juice
2 fresh red chilies, cored, seeded, and chopped
pinch salt
2-in. piece fresh ginger, grated
6 shallots, finely chopped
2 cilantro sprigs, chopped
2 sprigs Chinese celery, or inner stalks celery, chopped

5 dried red chilies, cored and seeded
½ small red bell pepper, chopped
5 shallots, chopped
4 cloves garlic, chopped
¼ cup vegetable oil
1 lb. fish steaks, such as cod, monkfish, salmon,
   or snapper
cilantro sprigs, to garnish
rice and lime juice, to serve

Put fish in a nonreactive dish. Pour
3 tablespoons lime juice on top and leave for
at least 30 minutes, occasionally stirring
gently, until fish turns opaque.

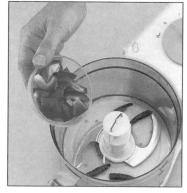

Put chilies in a blender. Add ¼ cup hot water
and leave until softened. Add red bell
pepper, shallots, and garlic. Mix to a coarse
paste.

Meanwhile, in a mortar and pestle, pound
chilies with a pinch of salt. Mix with
remaining lime juice.

Heat 2 tablespoons oil in a skillet over
medium heat. Add fish and fry until lightly
browned on both sides and almost, but not
quite, cooked through. Remove, then
transfer to absorbent paper towels to drain.

Drain lime juice from fish. Sprinkle ginger,
shallots, cilantro, and celery over fish.
Trickle chili mixture evenly over fish and stir
gently to mix ingredients together. Serve
immediately.

Makes 4 servings.

Add remaining oil to pan. Add chili paste
and cook over medium-high heat for about
3 minutes or until paste looks dry. Stir in
2 tablespoons water. Lower heat, return fish
to pan, and baste with chili paste. Cook
gently for 1 or 2 minutes, basting with paste.
Garnish with cilantro and serve with rice,
with plenty of lime juice squeezed on top.

Makes 3 or 4 servings.

STIR-FRIED SHRIMP & GINGER

3 cloves garlic, crushed
1½-in. piece fresh ginger, thinly sliced
2 tablespoons vegetable oil
12 to 16 raw jumbo shrimp, peeled and deveined
2 red shallots, finely chopped
grated zest of ½ kaffir lime
2 teaspoons fish sauce
3 scallions, thinly sliced
lime juice, to serve
scallion brushes (see page 14), to garnish

Using a mortar and pestle or small blender, pound or mix together garlic and ginger. In a wok, heat oil, add garlic paste, and stir-fry for 2 or 3 minutes. Stir in shrimp and shallots and stir-fry for 2 minutes.

Stir in the lime zest, fish sauce, and 3 tablespoons water. Allow to bubble for 1 minute or until shrimp become opaque and are cooked through. Stir in scallions, then remove from heat. Serve in a warmed dish, sprinkled with lime juice and garnished with scallion brushes.

Makes 3 or 4 servings.

SHRIMP IN COCONUT SAUCE

2 fresh red chilies, seeded and chopped
1 red onion, chopped
1 thick stalk lemongrass, chopped
1-in. piece galangal, chopped
1 teaspoon ground turmeric
1 cup coconut milk
14 to 16 raw jumbo shrimp, peeled and deveined
8 Thai holy basil leaves
2 teaspoons lime juice
1 teaspoon fish sauce
1 scallion, including some green, cut into fine strips

Using a small blender, mix the chilies, onion, lemongrass, and galangal to a paste. Transfer to a wok and heat, stirring, for 2 or 3 minutes. Stir in turmeric and ½ cup water, bring to a boil, and simmer for 3 or 4 minutes or until most of the water has evaporated.

Stir in the coconut milk and shrimp and cook gently, stirring occasionally, for about 4 minutes or until shrimp are just firm and pink. Stir in basil leaves, lime juice, and fish sauce. Sprinkle with strips of scallion, and serve.

Makes 4 servings.

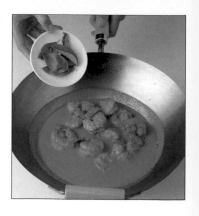

SHRIMP WITH GARLIC

2 tablespoons vegetable oil
5 cloves garlic, chopped
¼-in. slice fresh ginger, very finely chopped
14 to 16 jumbo shrimp, peeled, tails left on
2 teaspoons fish sauce
2 tablespoons chopped cilantro leaves
freshly ground black pepper
lettuce leaves, lime juice, and diced cucumber,
    to serve

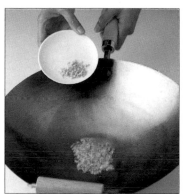

In a wok, heat oil, add garlic, and fry until browned.

Stir in ginger, heat for 30 seconds, then add shrimp and stir-fry for 2 or 3 minutes or until beginning to turn opaque. Stir in fish sauce, cilantro, 1 or 2 tablespoons water, and plenty of black pepper. Simmer for 1 or 2 minutes.

Serve shrimp on a bed of lettuce leaves with lime juice squeezed on top and sprinkled with cucumber.

Makes 4 servings.

JACKETED SHRIMP

1½-in. piece cucumber
Thai Dipping Sauce 1 (see page 231)
8 raw jumbo shrimp
vegetable oil for deep-frying
leaves from 1 cilantro sprig, chopped
BATTER:
⅔ cup rice flour
3 tablespoons dried coconut
1 egg, separated
¾ cup coconut milk
1 teaspoon fish sauce

Cut cucumber into quarters lengthwise, remove and discard seeds, then slice thickly. Place in a small bowl and add dipping sauce. Set aside. Peel shrimp, leaving tails on. Cut along back of each shrimp and devein. Set shrimp aside.

To make batter, stir together flour and coconut in a bowl. Gradually stir in egg yolk, coconut milk, and fish sauce. In a clean bowl, whisk egg white until stiff; fold into batter. In a wok, heat oil to 350°F. Dip shrimp in batter to coat evenly. Deep-fry in batches for 2 or 3 minutes or until golden. Using a slotted spoon, transfer to absorbent paper towels. Keep warm while frying the rest. Add cilantro to sauce and serve with the shrimp.

Makes 3 or 4 servings.

SHRIMP & CUCUMBER CURRY

¼ cup coconut cream (see page 8)
3 or 4 tablespoons Red Curry Paste (see page 230)
8 oz. raw, large, peeled shrimp
8-in. length cucumber, halved lengthwise, seeded and cut into ¼-in. pieces
1¼ cups coconut milk
2 tablespoons tamarind water (see page 11)
1 teaspoon crushed palm sugar
cilantro leaves, to garnish

MUSSELS WITH BASIL

1½ lbs. fresh mussels in shells, cleaned, bearded, and rinsed
1 large clove garlic, chopped
3-in. piece galangal, thickly sliced
2 stalks lemongrass, chopped
10 Thai holy basil sprigs
1 tablespoon fish sauce
Thai holy basil leaves, to garnish
Thai Dipping Sauce 2 (see page 232), to serve

In a wok, heat coconut cream, stirring, until it boils, thickens, and oil begins to form. Add curry paste. Stir in shrimp to coat, then stir in cucumber. Add coconut milk, tamarind water, and sugar.

Place mussels, garlic, galangal, lemongrass, basil sprigs, and fish sauce in a large saucepan. Add water to a depth of ½ in., cover pan, and bring to a boil. Cook for about 5 minutes, shaking pan frequently, until mussels have opened; discard any that remain closed.

Cook gently for about 3 or 4 minutes or until shrimp are just cooked through. Transfer to a warmed serving dish and garnish with cilantro.

Makes 3 servings.

Transfer mussels to a large, warmed bowl, or individual bowls, and strain over cooking liquid. Sprinkle with basil leaves. Serve with sauce for dipping.

Makes 2 or 3 servings.

FISH IN BANANA LEAF CUPS

FISH WITH CHILI SAUCE

3 oz. firm white fish, such as cod, hake, or monkfish,
  very finely chopped
3 oz. cooked, peeled shrimp, very finely chopped
2 or 3 teaspoons Red Curry Paste (see page 230)
2 tablespoons ground peanuts
1 kaffir lime leaf, finely chopped
2 tablespoons coconut milk
1 egg
2 teaspoons fish sauce
leaf part of ½ head of Chinese cabbage, finely
  shredded
2 banana leaf cups (see Note), if desired
2 teaspoons coconut cream (see page 8)
strips of fresh red chili, to garnish

1 flatfish, such as flounder or pomfret, gutted
  and cleaned
vegetable oil for brushing
2 teaspoons vegetable oil
3 small dried red chilies, halved lengthwise
2 cloves garlic, finely chopped
1 teaspoon fish sauce
⅓ cup tamarind water (see page 11)
1 teaspoon crushed palm sugar

In a bowl, mix fish and shrimp together using
a fork. Mix in curry paste, peanuts, and lime
leaf. In a small bowl, mix together coconut
milk, egg, and fish sauce. Stir into fish
mixture to evenly combine. Set aside for
30 minutes. Divide Chinese cabbage
between banana leaf cups or heatproof
individual dishes to make a fine layer. Stir
fish mixture and divide between cups or
dishes.

Preheat broiler. Brush fish lightly with oil,
then broil for about 4 minutes on each side
or until lightly colored and flesh flakes when
tested with the point of a knife. Transfer to a
warmed plate and keep warm.

Place in a steaming basket over a saucepan of
boiling water. Cover and steam for about
15 minutes or until just set in center. Place
on a warmed serving plate, trickle coconut
cream on top, and garnish with red chili.

Makes 2 servings.

Note: To make a banana leaf cup, cut two
4-in. circles from a banana leaf and place dull
sides together. Form a ½-in. pleat about 1½ in.
deep in the edge of circle and staple together.
Repeat to make four corners.

In a small saucepan, heat vegetable oil, add
chilies and garlic, and cook for 1 minute. Stir
in fish sauce, tamarind water, and palm sugar,
and simmer for 2 or 3 minutes or until lightly
thickened. Spoon over fish.

Makes 2 servings.

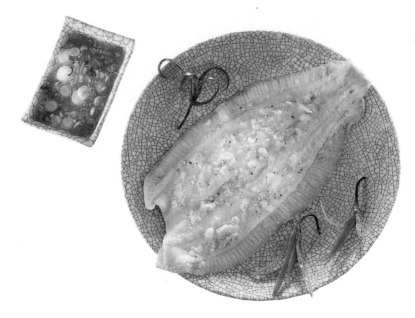

FISH WITH LEMONGRASS

2 tablespoons vegetable oil
1 flatfish, such as flounder, gutted and cleaned
4 cloves garlic, finely chopped
2 fresh red chilies, seeded and finely chopped
1 red shallot, chopped
1 cup lime juice
½ teaspoon crushed palm sugar
1½ tablespoons finely chopped lemongrass
2 teaspoons fish sauce
chili flowers (see page 14), to garnish

In a wok, heat oil and add fish, skin-side down first, and cook for 3 to 5 minutes on each side until lightly browned and cooked. Transfer to a warmed serving plate, cover, and keep warm. Add garlic to wok and fry, stirring occasionally, until browned.

Stir in chilies, shallot, lime juice, palm sugar, lemongrass, and fish sauce. Allow to simmer gently for 1 or 2 minutes. Pour over fish and garnish with chili flowers.

Makes 2 servings.

CILANTRO FISH & GARLIC

6 cilantro roots, chopped
3 large cloves garlic, chopped
5 black peppercorns, crushed
2 fish fillets, such as trout or flounder
2 pieces banana leaf (optional)
3 tablespoons lime juice
½ teaspoon crushed palm sugar
1 scallion, finely chopped
½ small, fresh green chili, seeded and thinly sliced
½ small, fresh red chili, seeded and thinly sliced
chili flowers (see page 14), to garnish

Using a mortar and pestle or small blender, briefly mix together cilantro roots, garlic, and peppercorns. Spread evenly over inside of fish fillets; set aside for 30 minutes.

Wrap fish in banana leaves or pieces of aluminum foil, securing leaf with a wooden toothpick or folding edges of foil tightly together. Broil for about 8 minutes. Meanwhile, in a bowl, stir together lime juice and sugar, then stir in scallion and chilies. Serve with fish. Garnish with chili flowers.

Makes 2 servings.

FISH WITH MUSHROOM SAUCE

all-purpose flour for coating
salt and freshly ground black pepper
1 whole flatfish, such as flounder, weighing about
  1½ lbs., gutted and cleaned
2 tablespoons vegetable oil, plus extra for deep-frying
3 cloves garlic, thinly sliced
1 small onion, halved and thinly sliced
1¾-in. piece fresh ginger, finely chopped
6 to 8 shiitake mushrooms, sliced
2 teaspoons fish sauce
3 scallions, sliced
scallion brushes (see page 14), to garnish

Season flour with salt and pepper, then use to lightly dust fish. Heat oil in a large deep-fat fryer to 350°F, add fish, and cook for 4 or 5 minutes, turning halfway through, until crisp and browned.

Meanwhile, heat 2 tablespoons oil in a wok, add garlic, onion, and ginger, and cook, stirring occasionally, for 2 minutes. Add mushrooms and stir-fry for 2 minutes. Stir in fish sauce, 3 or 4 tablespoons water, and scallions. Simmer briefly. Transfer fish to absorbent paper towels to drain. Place fish on a warmed serving plate and spoon sauce on top. Garnish with scallion brushes.

Makes 2 servings.

COCONUT FISH WITH GALANGAL

¼ cup vegetable oil
1 shallot, chopped
1½-in. piece galangal, finely chopped
2 stalks lemongrass, finely chopped
1 small fresh red chili, seeded and chopped
½ cup coconut milk
2 teaspoons fish sauce
5 cilantro sprigs
12 oz. white fish fillets, such as halibut or
  red snapper
1 small onion, sliced
freshly ground black pepper

In a wok, heat 1 tablespoon oil, add shallot, galangal, lemongrass, and chili. Stir for 3 minutes or until lightly colored. Transfer to a small blender, add coconut milk, fish sauce, and stalks from cilantro sprigs, and process until well mixed. Place fish in a heatproof, shallow, round dish that fits over a saucepan and pour spice sauce on top. Cover dish, place over pan of boiling water, and steam for 8 to 10 minutes or until flesh flakes.

Meanwhile, heat remaining oil in a wok over moderate heat, add onion, and cook, stirring occasionally, until browned. Using a slotted spoon, transfer to absorbent paper towels. Add cilantro leaves to oil and fry for a few seconds. Using a slotted spoon, transfer to absorbent paper towels to drain. Sprinkle with fried onions and cilantro and plenty of freshly ground black pepper.

Makes 3 or 4 servings.

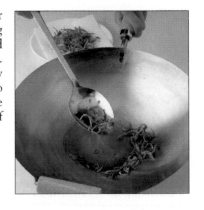

CURRIED SHRIMP

STIR-FRIED SHRIMP

2 tablespoons vegetable oil
1 teaspoon chopped garlic
2 shallots, or 1 small onion, chopped
2 or 3 tablespoons mild curry powder
1 cup Vietnamese Hot Sauce (see page 234)
1 cup chicken stock or water
1 cup coconut milk
2 medium red potatoes, cut into chunks
2 or 3 carrots, sliced
3 or 4 lime or bay leaves
2 tablespoons fish sauce
10 oz. raw, peeled shrimp
½ teaspoon salt
1 teaspoon sugar
cilantro sprigs, to garnish

3 tablespoons vegetable oil
1 teaspoon chopped garlic
½ teaspoon chopped fresh ginger
1 tablespoon chopped scallion
10 oz. raw, peeled shrimp, halved lengthwise
4 oz. straw mushrooms, halved lengthwise
2 oz. water chestnuts, sliced
3 tablespoons fish sauce
1 tablespoon sugar
about 2 or 3 tablespoons chicken stock or water
1 teaspoon chili sauce (optional)
salt and freshly ground black pepper
cilantro sprigs, to garnish

Heat oil in a pan or pot and stir-fry garlic and shallots or onion for about 30 seconds. Blend in curry powder and cook for 30 seconds or until fragrant. Add Vietnamese Hot Sauce, stock or water, and coconut milk, then bring to a boil, stirring constantly. Add potatoes, carrots, lime or bay leaves, and fish sauce, cover, and simmer gently for 25 to 30 minutes.

Heat oil in a wok or pan and stir-fry garlic, ginger, and scallion for about 20 seconds. Add shrimp, mushrooms, and water chestnuts, and stir-fry for about 2 minutes.

Add shrimp, salt, and sugar, then increase the heat and cook for 5 or 6 minutes, stirring continuously. Serve at once, garnished with cilantro sprigs.

Makes 4 servings.

Add fish sauce and sugar, stir a few times, then add stock or water. Bring to a boil and stir for another minute or so. Finally, add chili sauce, if using, and season with salt and pepper. Garnish with cilantro sprigs and serve at once.

Makes 4 servings.

SCALLOPS WITH VEGETABLES

SHRIMP WITH LEMONGRASS

3 tablespoons vegetable oil
1 teaspoon chopped garlic
1 or 2 small red chilies, seeded and chopped
2 shallots or 1 small onion, chopped
2 oz. snow peas
1 small carrot, thinly sliced
8 oz. fresh scallops, sliced
2 oz. sliced bamboo shoots
2 tablespoons black fungus, soaked and sliced
2 or 3 scallions, cut into short sections
2 tablespoons fish sauce
1 teaspoon sugar
2 or 3 tablespoons chicken stock or water
1 tablespoon oyster sauce
salt and freshly ground black pepper
cilantro sprigs, to garnish

2 cloves garlic, chopped
1 tablespoon chopped cilantro
2 tablespoons chopped lemongrass
½ teaspoon black or white peppercorns
3 tablespoons vegetable oil
12 to 14 oz. raw, peeled shrimp, cut in half
  lengthwise if large
2 shallots, or 1 small onion, sliced
2 or 3 small fresh chilies, seeded and chopped
2 or 3 tomatoes, cut into wedges
1 tablespoon fish sauce
1 tablespoon oyster sauce
2 or 3 tablespoons chicken stock or water
cilantro sprigs, to garnish

Heat oil in a wok or pan and stir-fry garlic, chilies, and shallots or onion for about 20 seconds. Add snow peas and carrot and stir-fry for about 20 minutes. Add scallops, bamboo shoots, black fungus, and scallions, and stir-fry for 1 minute.

Using a mortar and pestle, pound garlic, cilantro, lemongrass, and peppercorns to a paste. Heat oil in a wok or skillet and stir-fry spicy paste for 15 to 20 seconds or until fragrant. Add shrimp, shallots or onion, chilies, and tomatoes, and stir-fry for 2 or 3 minutes.

Add fish sauce and sugar, blend well, and stir for another minute, then add stock or water. Bring to a boil and stir for a few more seconds. Add oyster sauce and season with salt and pepper. Garnish with cilantro sprigs and serve at once.

Makes 4 servings.

Add fish sauce, oyster sauce, and stock or water, bring to a boil, and simmer for 2 or 3 minutes. Serve garnished with cilantro sprigs.

Makes 4 servings.

SPICY CRAB

STUFFED SQUID

1 clove garlic, chopped
2 shallots or white parts of 3 or 4 scallions, chopped
1 teaspoon chopped, fresh ginger
1 tablespoon chopped lemongrass
2 or 3 tablespoons vegetable oil
1 teaspoon chili sauce
1 tablespoon sugar
3 or 4 tablespoons coconut milk
2 cups chicken stock
3 tablespoons fish sauce
2 tablespoons lime juice or vinegar
meat from 1 large or 2 medium cooked crabs, cut
   into small pieces
salt and freshly ground black pepper
cilantro sprigs, to garnish

1 oz. bean thread vermicelli, soaked then cut into
   short strands
½ oz. black fungus, soaked then shredded
1 cup lean ground pork
salt and ground black pepper
2 scallions, chopped
1 tablespoon fish sauce
1 egg, beaten
8 to 12 small squid, headless, cleaned (see page 194)
1 or 2 tablespoons vegetable oil
lettuce leaves
Spicy Fish Sauce (see page 233), for dipping

In a bowl, mix vermicelli, fungus, pork, salt, pepper, scallions, fish sauce, and egg.

Using a mortar and pestle, pound garlic, shallots or scallions, ginger, and lemongrass to a fine paste. Heat oil in clay pot or flameproof casserole, add garlic mixture, chili sauce, and sugar, and stir-fry for about 1 minute. Add coconut milk, stock, fish sauce, and lime juice or vinegar, and bring to a boil.

Fill squid with stuffing mixture, then steam for 25 to 30 minutes.

Add the crab pieces and season with salt and pepper. Blend well and cook for 3 or 4 minutes, stirring constantly, then serve hot, garnished with cilantro sprigs.

Makes 4 servings.

Note: Uncooked crabs can be used in this dish, but you will need to increase the cooking time by about 8 to 10 minutes.

Remove squid from the steamer. Heat the oil in a skillet and fry the stuffed squid for 3 or 4 minutes, turning once. Serve hot on a bed of lettuce with Spicy Fish Sauce as a dip.

Makes 4 to 6 servings.

Note: Squid are sometimes available ready-cleaned, with tentacles still attached. If desired, the squid can be steamed in advance and then fried just before serving.

FISH IN CURRY SAUCE

1-lb. fish fillet or steak, such as halibut, cod, or
  monkfish, cut into bite-size pieces
freshly ground black pepper
2 tablespoons fish sauce
1 tablespoon sugar
1 tablespoon vegetable oil
1 clove garlic, finely chopped
2 or 3 shallots, finely chopped
2 or 3 tablespoons mild curry powder
1 cup Vietnamese Hot Sauce (see page 234)
1½ cups chicken stock or water
9 oz. tofu, cut into small cubes
½ teaspoon salt
2 or 3 scallions, cut into short lengths, to garnish
1 or 2 small red chilies, seeded and chopped
  (optional)

In a dish, marinate fish with pepper, fish
sauce, and sugar for 15 to 20 minutes. Heat
oil in a saucepan and stir-fry garlic and
shallots for about 1 minute. Add curry
powder and hot sauce and cook for another
minute, stirring constantly. Add stock or
water, blend well, and bring to a boil.

Add fish, tofu pieces, and salt, stir very
gently, then reduce heat, cover, and simmer
for 10 minutes. Serve hot, garnished with
scallions and chilies, if using.

Makes 4 servings.

VIETNAMESE MIXED SEAFOOD

3 tablespoons vegetable oil
1 teaspoon crushed garlic
2 shallots, chopped
4-oz. fish fillet, cut into bite-size pieces
4 oz. prepared squid
4 oz. raw, peeled shrimp
4 oz. fresh scallops
4 oz. crabmeat
¼ cup Sweet & Sour Sauce or Vietnamese Hot
  Sauce (see page 234)
3 tablespoons fish sauce
3 or 4 tablespoons chicken stock or water
2 scallions, thinly sliced
freshly ground black pepper

Heat oil in a clay pot or flameproof casserole
and stir-fry garlic and shallots for about
1 minute or until fragrant. Add seafood and
stir-fry very gently so that fish fillet does not
break up. Cook for 2 or 3 minutes, then add
Sweet and Sour Sauce or Vietnamese Hot
Sauce and fish sauce with stock or water.
Blend well and bring to a boil.

Cover and simmer gently for 3 or 4 minutes,
then remove the lid and turn off the heat.
Garnish with scallions and pepper and serve
hot straight from the pot.

Makes 4 servings.

Variation: It is not essential to use as many
as five different types of fish this dish; if
preferred, use any combination of two or
three types.

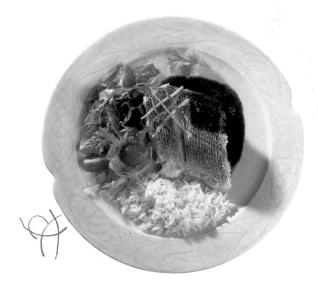

VIETNAMESE STEAMED FISH

BROILED FLATFISH

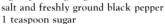

1 whole fish, such as sea bass, gray mullet, or
   grouper, weighing about 2 lbs., cleaned
salt and freshly ground black pepper
1 teaspoon sugar
1 teaspoon chopped, fresh ginger
1 tablespoon each chopped white and green
   parts of a scallion
1 tablespoon fish sauce
2 teaspoons sesame oil
1 tablespoon shredded, fresh ginger
1 tablespoon vegetable oil
1 tablespoon black bean sauce
1 tablespoon soy sauce
2 small fresh red chilies, seeded and shredded
cilantro sprigs, to garnish

1¼ lbs. flatfish, such as flounder, cleaned
salt and freshly ground black pepper
1 tablespoon vegetable oil, plus extra for brushing
½ teaspoon crushed garlic
½ teaspoon chopped, fresh ginger
2 shallots, finely chopped
2 or 3 small fresh red chilies, seeded and chopped
1 tablespoon chopped scallion
2 tablespoons fish sauce
1 teaspoon sugar
1 tablespoon tamarind water or lime juice
2 or 3 tablespoons chicken stock or water
2 teaspoons cornstarch

Score fish on both sides at 1-in. intervals.
Rub inside and out with salt and pepper,
then marinate in a shallow dish with sugar,
ginger, white parts of scallion, fish sauce, and
sesame oil for 30 minutes. Place the
fish with marinade in a hot steamer, or on a
rack inside a wok, cover, and steam for
15 to 20 minutes.

Score both sides of fish at 1-in. intervals and
rub with salt and pepper. Let stand for
25 minutes. Meanwhile, preheat broiler.
Brush both sides of fish with oil and cook
under a hot broiler for about 4 minutes each
side until lightly brown but not burned.
Place on a warmed serving dish.

Remove dish from the steamer or wok, place
ginger and green part of scallion on top of
fish. Heat vegetable oil in a small saucepan,
add black bean sauce, soy sauce, and chilies,
and stir-fry for 30 seconds, then drizzle over
the fish. Garnish with cilantro and serve
with rice and a salad.

Makes 4 servings.

Note: If fish is too big to fit into your steamer
or wok, cut it in half crosswise and
reassemble on a warmed plate to serve.

Heat the oil in a small pan and stir-fry the
garlic, ginger, shallots, chilies, and scallion
for 1 minute, then add fish sauce, sugar,
tamarind water or lime juice, and stock
or water. Bring to a boil and simmer for
30 seconds. Mix the cornstarch with
1 tablespoon water and stir into sauce to
thicken. Pour sauce over fish.

Makes 2 servings.

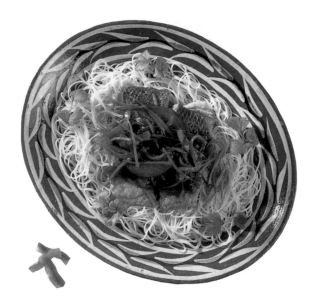

SWEET & SOUR FISH

1 (2-lb.) whole fish, such as sea bass, gray mullet,
  or carp, cleaned
salt and freshly ground black pepper
vegetable oil for deep-frying
2 tablespoons all-purpose flour
1 small onion, shredded
1 small carrot, thinly shredded
1 small green bell pepper, seeded and thinly shredded
2 tomatoes, cut into small wedges
2 tablespoons fish sauce
1 cup Sweet & Sour Sauce (see page 234)
½ cup stock or water
1 teaspoon sesame oil (optional)
cilantro sprigs, to garnish

Score both sides of fish at 1-in. intervals.
Rub fish inside and out with salt and pepper,
then let stand for 15 to 20 minutes. Heat oil
in a wok or deep-fat fryer to 350°F. Coat fish
with flour and deep-fry for 3 or 4 minutes on
each side until golden. Remove and drain on
absorbent paper towels, then place fish on a
warmed serving platter.

Pour off all but about 1 tablespoon oil from
the wok, add onion, carrot, green bell
pepper, and tomatoes. Stir-fry for about
1 minute, then add fish sauce, Sweet and
Sour Sauce, and stock or water. Bring to a
boil, then add sesame oil, if using. Pour sauce
over fish, garnish with cilantro, and serve
with rice vermicelli.

Makes 4 servings.

Variation: Fish fillets or steak can be cooked
in the same way.

FRIED FISH FILLET

1-lb. firm white fish fillet, such as halibut, cod,
  haddock, or monkfish, cut into ¾-in. pieces
salt and freshly ground black pepper
1 egg, beaten
3 tablespoons all-purpose flour mixed with
  2 tablespoons water
vegetable oil for deep-frying
fresh Thai holy basil and cilantro sprigs, to garnish
Spicy Fish Sauce (see page 233), to serve

In a dish, season fish with salt and pepper
and leave for 25 to 30 minutes. Make a
batter by blending egg with flour and water
paste.

Heat oil in a wok or deep-fat fryer to 350°F.
Coat fish pieces with batter and deep-fry, in
batches, for 3 or 4 minutes or until golden.
Remove and drain on absorbent paper
towels.

Place fish pieces on a warmed serving dish
with garnishes. Serve at once with Spicy
Fish Sauce as a dip.

Makes 4 servings.

Variation: A whole fish, boned, skinned,
and coated in batter, can be deep-fried and
then cut into bite-size pieces for serving.

TEMPURA

4 raw jumbo shrimp or 8 medium shrimp
12 to 14 oz. whiting fillets
all-purpose flour for coating
4 to 8 fresh shiitake or button mushrooms
8 asparagus tips or okra
vegetable oil for deep-frying
shredded daikon, to garnish
fresh ginger, to garnish
BATTER:
1 egg yolk, beaten
scant 1 cup ice-cold water
scant 1 cup all-purpose flour, sifted
DIPPING SAUCE:
scant 1 cup dashi (see page 29)
¼ cup mirin
⅓ cup soy sauce

Peel shrimp, retaining tail shell, and devein. Make a few slits along the belly to keep it from curling during cooking. Cut whiting fillets into pieces about 2 in. long and roll in all-purpose flour. If mushrooms are large, cut them in half. Heat oil for deep-frying to 340°F. Meanwhile, prepare the batter. Lightly mix egg yolk with ice-cold water and add all-purpose flour immediately. Using chopsticks or a fork, very lightly fold in flour with just four or five strokes. The batter should be loosely mixed but still very lumpy.

Deep-fry asparagus tips or okra without any batter for 2 or 3 minutes, then drain on a wire rack. Dip mushrooms, shrimp (one at a time, holding by tail), and whiting fillets in batter. Deep-fry one at a time in this order for 1 to 3 minutes or until light golden. Drain, then arrange a fourth of each on absorbent paper towels on individual plates. Boil dashi, mirin, and soy sauce in a pan and pour into small individual bowls. Serve garnished with daikon and ginger.

Makes 4 servings.

MACKEREL TATSUTA FRY

1½ lbs. mackerel, filleted
1 cup cornstarch
vegetable oil for deep-frying
lemon wedges, to garnish
MARINADE:
¼ cup sake
2 tablespoons soy sauce
1-in. piece fresh ginger, peeled and grated

Remove large bones from mackerel fillets. Slice fillets crosswise into bite-size pieces, inserting the blade diagonally.

To make marinade, combine sake, soy sauce, and ginger in a mixing bowl. Add mackerel pieces, turning to coat with marinade, then marinate for 30 minutes. Drain and toss mackerel in cornstarch to dust thoroughly.

Heat oil in a wok or deep skillet to 325°F. Slide mackerel pieces into hot oil, a few pieces at a time, and fry for 2 or 3 minutes or until golden brown, turning a few times. Remove from oil and drain on a wire rack. Arrange a quarter of the fried mackerel pieces on each of four individual plates, on folded absorbent paper towels if desired. Alternatively, heap all the fish in the center of a bamboo basket tray. Garnish with lemon wedges and serve at once.

Makes 4 servings.

SALMON & NANBAN SAUCE

1-lb. salmon fillet, descaled
pinch salt
all-purpose flour for coating
vegetable oil for deep-frying
3 scallions, shredded, to garnish
NANBAN SAUCE:
¼ cup soy sauce
3 tablespoons rice vinegar
1½ tablespoons sake
2 teaspoons sugar
4½ tablespoons dashi (see page 29)
1 or 2 dried or fresh red chilies, seeded and chopped

Cut salmon fillet, with skin on, into twelve pieces and sprinkle with salt.

To make sauce, combine soy sauce, rice vinegar, sake, sugar, dashi, and chilies in a saucepan and bring to a boil. Let cool. Pat dry salmon pieces with absorbent paper towels and dredge in all-purpose flour. Heat oil in a wok or deep skillet to 340°F. Shake off any excess flour from salmon pieces and deep-fry for 3 or 4 minutes or until golden brown. Drain on a wire rack.

Transfer fried salmon pieces to a large serving plate and spread shredded scallion on top. Drizzle with the sauce and serve immediately.

Makes 4 servings.

SWORDFISH TERIYAKI

2 or 3 swordfish steaks, each weighing 7 to 9 oz.
⅓ cup soy sauce
2 tablespoons sake
3 tablespoons mirin
4 or 5 fresh mint leaves, chopped
vegetable oil for frying
watercress sprigs, to garnish

Slice swordfish steaks in half horizontally to make a thickness of ½ in., then cut into 2½ x 1½-in. pieces. In a bowl, mix soy sauce, sake, mirin, and mint. Add fish, mix well, and marinate for 30 to 40 minutes, turning over occasionally.

Heat a skillet and spread a little oil evenly over the bottom. Drain fish pieces, reserving marinade, and fry a few pieces at a time over high heat until both sides become dark brown.

When all swordfish pieces are cooked, return them to the skillet. Add the marinade, gently mix in, and remove from heat. Divide fish between four individual plates or heap it in the center of a serving plate. Garnish with sprigs of watercress and serve at once.

Makes 4 servings.

TOFU & FISH HOT POT

1 lb. 2 oz. tofu
9 oz. white fish or fillets, such as cod
4 Chinese cabbage leaves
1½ cups cilantro leaves and/or 1¾ cups
    spinach leaves
2 or 3 scallions, finely chopped, to serve
SOUP:
6-in. piece dried konbu (kelp) (optional)
2¼ cups dashi (see page 29)
3 tablespoons soy sauce
½ tablespoon sugar

Cut the tofu into bite-size cubes and the fish
steaks or fillets into chunks with bone and
skin left on.

Cut Chinese cabbage leaves in half
lengthwise, and then crosswise into 1-in.-
long pieces. Chop cilantro leaves and/or
spinach roughly into 2-in. lengths.

To make soup, put konbu in a pot (ideally a
clay pot or enamelled casserole) and add
dashi, soy sauce, and sugar. Bring to a boil
and then add some of each of the prepared
ingredients. When it begins to boil again,
transfer pot to a portable gas ring or electric
hotplate on the dining table. Diners may
then serve themselves to some soup and
ingredients in individual bowls, sprinkled
with chopped scallion.

Makes 4 servings.

ISHIKARI HOT POT

4 salmon steaks, scaled, skin left on
1 onion
2 potatoes
1 or 2 carrots
4 to 8 fresh shiitake or button mushrooms
1½ cups cilantro leaves or watercress
9 oz. firm tofu
10 oz. (1 cake) konnyaku (optional)
2 tablespoons butter
4-in. piece dried konbu (kelp) (optional)
3 to 5 tablespoons miso
2 scallions, finely chopped, to serve

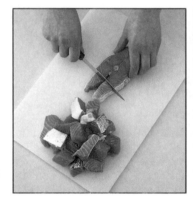

Cut salmon steaks into chunks. Halve onion
and cut into ¼-in.-thick slices.

Slice potatoes and carrots into ½-in.-thick
rounds (if large, cut into half-moons) and
parboil separately. Drain and set aside. Slice
shiitake mushrooms diagonally into four
slices. Chop cilantro leaves or watercress
into 2¼-in. lengths. Cut tofu and konnyaku,
if using, in half lengthwise, then cut tofu
into ½-in. squares and konnyaku into ¼-in.
slices. Melt butter in a large cast-iron pot
and stir-fry onion slices for 1 or 2 minutes.
Add konbu and enough water to half-fill pot.

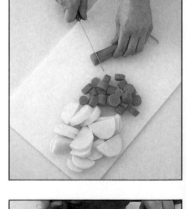

Bring to a boil over medium heat, discard
konbu, and lower heat. Dissolve miso in a
bowl with some of the soup, then stir back
into pan. Add potatoes, carrots, salmon,
mushrooms, and konnyaku, cover, and cook
over low heat for 5 minutes. Add cilantro or
watercress and tofu; simmer 3 or 4 minutes.
Serve sprinkled with chopped scallion.

Makes 4 to 6 servings.

Note: Ishikari is a river on the northern
island of Japan, and is famous for its salmon.

POULTRY

LEMON & CILANTRO CHICKEN

4 chicken thighs, skinned
4 chicken drumsticks, skinned
¼ cup vegetable oil
2-in. piece fresh ginger, grated
4 cloves garlic, crushed
1 fresh green chili, seeded and finely chopped
½ teaspoon turmeric
1 teaspoon ground cumin
1 teaspoon ground coriander
salt and cayenne pepper
grated zest and juice of 1 lemon
3 cups chopped cilantro leaves
cilantro leaves and lemon slices, to garnish

Wash chicken joints and pat dry with absorbent paper towels. Heat oil in a large skillet, add chicken, and fry, stirring frequently, until browned all over. Remove from skillet with a slotted spoon and set aside. Add ginger and garlic to pan and fry 1 minute. Stir in chili, turmeric, cumin, and ground coriander, and season with salt and cayenne pepper, then cook an additional 1 minute.

Return chicken to skillet, add ½ cup water and lemon zest and juice. Bring to a boil, then cover and cook over a medium heat 25 to 30 minutes or until chicken is tender. Stir in chopped cilantro, then serve hot, garnished with cilantro leaves and lemon slices.

Makes 4 servings.

Variation: Use fresh parsley, or parsley and mint, instead of cilantro, if preferred.

APRICOT & CHICKEN CURRY

2½ lbs. chicken joints, skinned
½ teaspoon chili powder
1 tablespoon Garam Masala (see page 224)
1-in. piece fresh ginger, grated
2 cloves garlic, crushed
1 cup ready-to-eat dried apricots
2 tablespoons vegetable oil
2 onions, finely sliced
14½-oz. can diced tomatoes
1 tablespoon sugar
2 tablespoons white wine vinegar
salt

Wash chicken and pat dry with absorbent paper towels. Cut each joint into 4 pieces and put in a large bowl. Add chili powder, Garam Masala, ginger, and garlic, and toss well to coat chicken pieces. Cover and let stand in a cool place 2 to 3 hours to allow chicken to absorb flavors. In a separate bowl, put apricots and ⅔ cup water and let soak 2 or 3 hours.

Heat oil in a large, heavy-bottomed pan and add chicken. Fry over a high heat 5 minutes or until browned all over. Remove from pan and set aside. Add onions to pan and cook, stirring, about 5 minutes, until soft. Return chicken to pan with tomatoes and cook, covered, over low heat 20 minutes. Drain apricots, add to pan with sugar and vinegar. Season with salt. Simmer, covered, 10 to 15 minutes. Serve hot.

Makes 4 servings.

TANDOORI CHICKEN

2½ lbs. chicken joints, skinned
1 tablespoon lime juice
salt
1 small onion
1 tablespoon Tandoori Masala (see Note)
2 teaspoons Garam Masala (see page 224)
1-in. piece fresh ginger, grated
1¼ cups plain yogurt
lime wedges and cilantro leaves, to garnish

CHICKEN BIRYANI

1¼ lbs. boneless chicken fillets, skinned
2½ cups basmati rice, washed
⅓ cup vegetable oil
6 green cardamom pods, bruised
½ teaspoon cumin seeds
2 onions, finely sliced
4 cloves garlic, crushed
2-in. piece fresh ginger, grated
⅔ cup plain yogurt
salt and pepper
large pinch saffron threads
2 tablespoons boiling water
few drops red food coloring
3 tablespoons slivered almonds, toasted, to garnish
2 tablespoons golden raisins, to garnish

Wash chicken joints and pat dry with absorbent paper towels, then make 2 or 3 cuts in meaty parts.

Cut chicken into ¾-in. cubes. Set aside. Soak rice in cold water 30 minutes, then drain. Heat ¼ cup oil in a large, heavy-bottomed pan, add cardamom pods and cumin seeds, and fry 1 minute. Stir in onions, garlic, ginger, and chicken and cook about 5 minutes, stirring, over a high heat until chicken is browned all over. Stir in yogurt 1 tablespoon at a time, then add ½ cup water. Cover and simmer 15 minutes.

Place chicken in a shallow, nonmetallic dish. Sprinkle with lime juice and salt and set aside. Put onion, Tandoori Masala, Garam Masala, ginger, salt, and yogurt into a blender or food processor fitted with a metal blade and process until smooth and frothy. Pour over chicken and cover loosely. Marinate in a cool place 6 hours or overnight.

Preheat oven to 400°F. Drain excess marinade from chicken joints and place them in a baking pan. Cook 25 to 30 minutes, until tender and well browned. Serve hot, garnished with lime wedges and cilantro leaves.

Makes 4 servings.

Note: To make Tandoori Masala, grind 1 tablespoon each cumin and coriander seeds, stir in 1 tablespoon cayenne pepper and a few drops red food coloring, and mix well.

Heat remaining oil in separate pan, stir in rice, and fry 2 or 3 minutes, until golden, stirring all the time. Stir into chicken mixture and season with salt and pepper. Cover and simmer 12 to 15 minutes, until rice and chicken are tender. Soak saffron in boiling water 5 minutes. Stir food coloring into 2 tablespoons water. Pour liquids into separate parts of rice and fork in to color it yellow, red, and white. Serve hot, garnished with almonds and golden raisins.

Makes 4 servings.

GOLDEN STEAMED CHICKEN

CHICKEN WITH LENTILS

⅔ cup basmati rice
1 (3½-lb.) chicken
3 tablespoons vegetable oil
½ teaspoon chili powder
⅓ cup raisins
⅓ cup slivered almonds
1 tablespoon chopped fresh thyme
salt
½ teaspoon ground cumin
½ teaspoon turmeric
1 teaspoon ground coriander
2 teaspoons Garam Masala (see page 224)
cayenne pepper
½ cup hot water
thyme sprigs, to garnish

8 oz. boneless, skinless chicken fillets
1¼ cups red split lentils
½ teaspoon turmeric
¼ cup vegetable oil
6 green cardamom pods, bruised
1 onion, finely sliced
½-in. piece fresh ginger, grated
salt and cayenne pepper
2 tablespoons lemon juice
1 teaspoon cumin seeds
2 cloves garlic, finely sliced

Wash chicken, pat dry, and cut into cubes. Set aside.

Wash rice thoroughly and soak in cold water 30 minutes, then drain. Wash chicken, pat dry with absorbent paper towels, and set aside. Heat 1 tablespoon oil in a saucepan, add rice, and fry, stirring, 2 or 3 minutes, until golden brown. Stir in chili powder, raisins, almonds, thyme, ¾ cup water, and salt. Bring to a boil, then cover and simmer 10 to 12 minutes, until rice has absorbed all the liquid. Let cool, then use to stuff chicken.

Wash lentils, put in a large saucepan, and add 3¾ cups water and turmeric. Bring to a boil, then cover and simmer 20 to 30 minutes or until tender. Drain thoroughly. Meanwhile, heat half the oil in a large saucepan, add cardamom pods, and fry 1 minute. Add onion and fry, stirring frequently, about 8 minutes, until golden brown. Add chicken and fry 5 minutes, until browned all over. Add ginger and fry an additional 1 minute. Season with salt and cayenne pepper.

Truss chicken, then place in a steamer and steam 1 hour. Heat remaining oil in a large pan, add cumin, turmeric, coriander, and Garam Masala. Season with salt and cayenne pepper and fry 1 minute. Transfer chicken to this pan and fry 5 minutes, turning chicken until well coated. Pour hot water down side of pan, cover, and cook over a low heat 15 to 20 minutes, until tender. Serve hot, garnished with thyme sprigs.

Makes 4 servings.

Stir in lemon juice and ⅔ cup water and cover. Simmer 25 to 30 minutes or until chicken is tender. Stir in lentil mixture and cook, stirring, 5 minutes. Meanwhile, heat remaining oil, add cumin and garlic, and fry, stirring, until garlic is golden. Transfer chicken and lentils to serving dish and pour over garlic mixture. Serve hot.

Makes 4 servings.

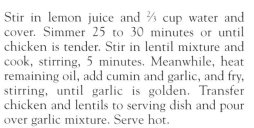

CHICKEN IN SPICY SAUCE

8 chicken thighs, skinned
10-oz. can tomatoes, drained
2 tablespoons tomato paste
2 tablespoons chili sauce
2 teaspoons sugar
1 tablespoon Garam Masala (see page 224)
2 tablespoons light soy sauce
2-in. piece fresh ginger, grated
2 cloves garlic, crushed
juice of 1 lime and 1 lemon
twists of lime and lemon, to garnish

Wash chicken and dry with absorbent paper towels. Make 2 or 3 cuts in meaty parts and place in a shallow, nonmetallic dish.

Put tomatoes, tomato paste, chili sauce, sugar, Garam Masala, soy sauce, ginger, garlic, and lime and lemon juice in a blender or food processor fitted with a metal blade and process until smooth. Pour over chicken, cover, and leave in a cool place 2 or 3 hours to allow chicken to absorb flavors.

Preheat oven to 375°F. Put chicken and sauce in a baking pan and cook, uncovered, 45 to 50 minutes, basting with sauce 2 or 3 times, until tender and cooked. Serve hot, garnished with lime and lemon twists.

Makes 4 servings.

CURRIED CHICKEN LIVERS

8 oz. chicken livers
2 tablespoons vegetable oil
2 onions, finely sliced
3 cloves garlic, crushed
2 teaspoons Garam Masala (see page 224)
½ teaspoon turmeric
salt and pepper
2 tablespoons lemon juice
2 tablespoons chopped fresh parsley
parsley sprigs, to garnish

Wash chicken livers and remove any green-tinged parts. Set aside.

Heat oil in a skillet, add onions, and cook over a medium heat, stirring, about 8 minutes, until soft and golden brown. Stir in garlic, Garam Masala, and turmeric, and season with salt and pepper.

Fry 1 minute, then stir in chicken livers and fry about 5 minutes, stirring frequently, until livers are browned on outsides but still slightly pink in the center. Sprinkle with lemon juice and parsley. Serve hot, garnished with sprigs of parsley.

Makes 4 servings as a starter.

Note: Frozen chicken livers can be used: thaw at room temperature 3 to 4 hours before using.

DUCK & COCONUT CURRY

4 duck portions, skinned
2 tablespoons vegetable oil
1 teaspoon mustard seeds
1 onion, finely chopped
3 cloves garlic, crushed
2-in. piece fresh ginger, grated
2 fresh green chilies, seeded and chopped
1 teaspoon ground cumin
1 tablespoon ground coriander
1 teaspoon turmeric
1 tablespoon white wine vinegar
salt and cayenne pepper
1¼ cups coconut milk (see page 224)
2 tablespoons shredded coconut, toasted, and lemon
  wedges, to garnish

Wash duck and pat dry with absorbent paper towels. Heat oil in a large skillet, add duck, and fry, stirring, over a high heat 8 to 10 minutes, until browned all over, then remove from skillet. Pour off all but 2 tablespoons of fat, add mustard seeds, and fry 1 minute or until they begin to pop.

Add onion to skillet and cook, stirring, over a medium heat 8 minutes or until soft and golden. Stir in garlic, ginger, chilies, cumin, coriander, and turmeric, and fry 2 minutes. Stir in vinegar and season with salt and cayenne pepper. Return duck to skillet and turn pieces to coat them in spice mixture. Stir in coconut milk and bring to a boil. Cover and cook over a low heat about 40 minutes or until duck is tender. Garnish and serve hot.

Makes 4 servings.

ROAST DUCK IN FRUIT SAUCE

1 (4½-lb.) duck
3 onions, chopped
1 cup chopped mixed nuts
1 cup fresh breadcrumbs
¼ cup chopped cilantro leaves
1 egg yolk
salt and cayenne pepper
1 tablespoon Garam Masala (see page 224)
2 tablespoons vegetable oil
2 cloves garlic, crushed
1-in. piece fresh ginger, grated
1 teaspoon turmeric
2 tablespoons ground coriander
1 teaspoon chickpea flour
1¼ cups plain yogurt
juice of 2 lemons and 2 oranges

Preheat oven to 375°F. Wash duck and pat dry with absorbent paper towels, then prick skin with a fork. In a bowl, mix together 1 onion, nuts, breadcrumbs, 3 tablespoons cilantro leaves, egg yolk, and a pinch each of salt and cayenne pepper. Use to stuff duck, then truss neatly. Rub Garam Masala into skin, place duck in a baking pan, and cook 1¼ hours or until tender. Remove duck and keep warm. Heat oil in a saucepan, add remaining onions, and cook, stirring, 5 minutes, until soft.

Stir in garlic, ginger, turmeric, ground coriander, chickpea flour, and salt and cayenne pepper to taste. Cook 1 minute, then stir in yogurt. Simmer 10 minutes, then stir in lemon and orange juice and heat gently without boiling. Carve duck, pour over sauce, and sprinkle with remaining cilantro. Serve hot.

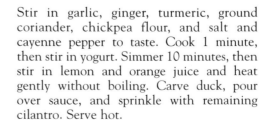

Makes 4 servings.

Note: This looks very attractive garnished with twists of lemon and orange zest.

MURGHAL SHREDDED DUCK

1 lb. boneless duck fillets, skinned
¼ cup vegetable oil
1 onion, finely chopped
1 quantity Cashew Masala made with ¾ cup cashews
  (see page 224)
1 teaspoon turmeric
⅔ cup dried coconut
½ cup golden raisins
⅔ cup plain yogurt
⅓ cup thick cream
⅓ cup unsalted cashews
1 green chili, seeded and chopped

Wash duck fillets and pat dry with absorbent paper towels.

Slice duck into ¼-in.-thick strips. Heat 3 tablespoons oil in a large skillet, add duck, and cook over a high heat about 5 minutes, until browned all over. Remove duck from pan with a slotted spoon and set aside. Add onion to pan and cook, stirring, 5 minutes or until soft. Stir in Cashew Masala and turmeric and fry 2 minutes. Stir in coconut, golden raisins, yogurt, cream, and duck.

Cover and cook over a low heat 15 to 20 minutes, stirring occasionally, until duck is tender. Just before serving, heat remaining oil in a small pan, add cashews, and fry 2 or 3 minutes, until golden. Add chili and fry an additional 1 minute. Transfer duck to a warm serving dish and spoon cashew and chili mixture on top. Serve hot.

Makes 4 to 6 servings.

DUCK WITH HONEY & LIME

4 duck portions, each weighing about 8 oz., skinned
2 tablespoons vegetable oil
1 onion, finely chopped
2 cloves garlic, crushed
1-in. piece fresh ginger, finely sliced
8 green cardamom pods, bruised
3-in. cinnamon stick
3 tablespoons clear honey
juice of 2 limes
twists of lime, to garnish

Wash duck and pat dry with absorbent paper towels. Make 2 or 3 cuts in meaty parts of duck.

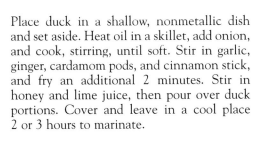

Place duck in a shallow, nonmetallic dish and set aside. Heat oil in a skillet, add onion, and cook, stirring, until soft. Stir in garlic, ginger, cardamom pods, and cinnamon stick, and fry an additional 2 minutes. Stir in honey and lime juice, then pour over duck portions. Cover and leave in a cool place 2 or 3 hours to marinate.

Preheat oven to 400°F. Transfer duck to a baking pan if shallow dish is not ovenproof, then cook 45 to 60 minutes, basting occasionally with marinade, until browned and tender. Serve hot, garnished with lime twists.

Makes 4 servings.

CHICKEN WITH MUSHROOMS

1 lb. skinless, boneless chicken thighs
1 tablespoon sunflower oil
16 button mushrooms, sliced
2 bunches scallions, chopped
1 clove garlic, finely chopped
1-in. piece fresh ginger, peeled and finely chopped
⅔ cup Chinese Chicken Stock (see page 16)
2 tablespoons rice wine
2 tablespoons dark soy sauce
2 tablespoons oyster sauce
15-oz. can straw mushrooms, drained
1 teaspoon cornstarch mixed with 2 teaspoons
  cold water

Trim fat from chicken thighs. Cut meat into 1-in. strips. Heat oil in a wok and stir-fry chicken strips 3 or 4 minutes or until chicken is lightly browned all over.

Add sliced mushrooms, scallions, garlic, and ginger, and stir-fry 2 minutes. Stir in stock, rice wine, soy sauce, oyster sauce, straw mushrooms, and cornstarch mixture, and simmer, stirring, 5 minutes. Serve with noodles.

Makes 4 servings.

GINGER CHICKEN PATTIES

2 cups lean ground chicken
1 clove garlic, finely chopped
1-in. piece fresh ginger, peeled and finely chopped
3 tablespoons chopped cilantro
1 tablespoon cornstarch
2 cups cooked long-grain white rice
salt and freshly ground pepper
1 egg white, lightly beaten
2 teaspoons sunflower oil
cilantro leaves, to garnish
DIP:
2 tablespoons light soy sauce
2 tablespoons dry sherry
½-in. piece fresh ginger, peeled and grated

In a bowl, mix together chicken, garlic, ginger, and cilantro. Stir in cornstarch, rice, salt, and pepper. Stir in egg white. Divide mixture into 8 portions and shape into 3-in.-diameter patties, dusting hands with extra cornstarch if needed. Place on a plate, cover, and chill 30 minutes.

Preheat broiler. Brush broiler rack lightly with oil and place patties on rack. Brush tops lightly with oil and cook 4 minutes. Turn patties over, brush again with oil, and cook an additional 3 or 4 minutes or until cooked through. Drain on absorbent paper towels. To make dip, mix together soy sauce, sherry, and ginger in a small bowl. Garnish patties with cilantro and serve with dip.

Makes 4 servings.

CHICKEN & BASIL STIR-FRY

1 lb. boneless chicken thighs
1 tablespoon dark soy sauce
1 tablespoon cornstarch
1 tablespoon peanut oil
2 cloves garlic, thinly sliced
1 fresh red chili, seeded and thinly sliced
1 teaspoon chili powder
1 tablespoon hoisin sauce
small bunch basil leaves, shredded
basil leaves and blanched red chili strips, to garnish

Remove skin and fat from chicken. Cut meat into 1-in. strips and place in a bowl. Stir in soy sauce and cornstarch.

Heat oil in a wok and stir-fry chicken with garlic and chili 7 or 8 minutes.

Add chili powder and hoisin sauce and cook another 2 minutes. Remove from heat and stir in shredded basil. Garnish with basil leaves and chili strips and serve on a bed of rice.

Makes 4 servings.

LEMON & HONEY CHICKEN

4 boneless chicken fillets, each weighing about 4 oz.
3 tablespoons honey
4 teaspoons light soy sauce
grated zest and juice of 2 lemons
1 clove garlic, finely chopped
freshly ground pepper
1 tablespoon sunflower oil
2 tablespoons chopped fresh chives
thin strips of lemon zest, to garnish

Remove skin and fat from chicken fillets. Using a sharp knife, score chicken fillets in a cross on both sides, taking care not to slice all the way through. Place in a shallow dish.

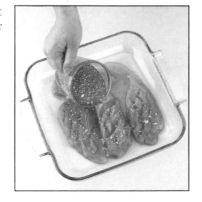

Mix together honey, soy sauce, lemon zest and juice, garlic, and pepper. Pour over chicken, cover, and chill 1 hour.

Heat oil in a wok. Drain chicken, reserving marinade, and cook 2 or 3 minutes on each side, until lightly golden. Add marinade and simmer 5 minutes, turning frequently, until chicken is cooked through and sauce is syrupy. Stir in chives, garnish with lemon zest, and serve on a bed of noodles.

Makes 4 servings.

CHICKEN CHOW MEIN

4 nests dried egg noodles
8 oz. boneless, skinless chicken fillets
1 tablespoon light soy sauce
1 tablespoon dry sherry
1 tablespoon sunflower oil
4 shallots, finely chopped
4 oz. snow peas, sliced diagonally
1 oz. prosciutto, trimmed and finely diced
1 teaspoon sesame oil
1 teaspoon sugar
2 scallions, finely shredded, to garnish

CHICKEN & PLUM CASSEROLE

1 oz. dried Chinese mushrooms, soaked in hot water
  20 minutes
1 lb. skinless, boneless chicken thighs
1 tablespoon sunflower oil
2 cloves garlic, thinly sliced
1 oz. prosciutto, trimmed and diced
3 plums, halved and pitted
1 tablespoon brown sugar
3 tablespoons light soy sauce
2 tablespoons rice wine
3 tablespoons plum sauce
1 tablespoon chili sauce
2½ cups Chinese Chicken Stock (see page 16)
2 teaspoons cornstarch mixed with 4 teaspoons
  cold water

Bring a large saucepan of water to a boil and cook noodles 3 or 4 minutes. Drain well, rinse, put in cold water, and set aside. Trim chicken fillets. Using a sharp knife, shred into ¼-in. strips. In a bowl, mix chicken strips with soy sauce and sherry.

Drain mushrooms and squeeze out excess water. Discard mushroom stems and thinly slice caps. Trim fat from chicken thighs and cut meat into 1-in. strips. Heat oil in a wok and stir-fry chicken, garlic, and prosciutto 3 or 4 minutes. Add mushrooms and stir-fry 1 minute.

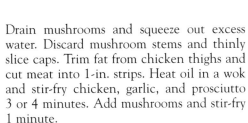

Heat sunflower oil in a wok and stir-fry chicken and shallots 2 minutes. Add snow peas and prosciutto and stir-fry 1 minute. Drain noodles well and add to pan along with sesame oil and sugar. Cook, stirring, 2 minutes to warm through. Garnish with scallions and serve.

Makes 4 servings.

Add plums, brown sugar, soy sauce, rice wine, plum sauce, chili sauce, and stock, and simmer 20 minutes or until plums have softened. Add cornstarch mixture and cook, stirring, until thickened. Serve on a bed of rice.

Makes 4 servings.

CHICKEN WITH PEANUTS

1 lb. boneless chicken fillets
1 tablespoon chili oil
1-in. piece fresh ginger, peeled and finely chopped
⅓ cup peanuts, skins removed
1 tablespoon Chinese Chicken Stock (see page 16)
1 tablespoon dry sherry
1 tablespoon dark soy sauce
1 teaspoon brown sugar
1 teaspoon five-spice powder
1 teaspoon white rice vinegar
4 scallions, finely chopped

Remove skin and fat from chicken fillets. Cut into 1-in. pieces.

Heat oil in a wok and gently stir-fry chicken, ginger, and peanuts 2 minutes or until chicken is just colored.

Add stock, sherry, soy sauce, sugar, five-spice powder, and rice vinegar, and simmer 5 minutes, stirring occasionally. Remove from heat and stir in scallions.

Makes 4 servings.

CHICKEN WITH CUCUMBER

1 medium cucumber
2 teaspoons salt
1 lb. boneless chicken fillets
1 tablespoon peanut oil
2 cloves garlic, finely chopped
1 tablespoon light soy sauce
1 tablespoon dry sherry
2 tablespoons chopped fresh chives
cucumber twists, to garnish

Peel cucumber, halve lengthwise, and scoop out seeds with a teaspoon. Cut into 1-in. cubes, place in a bowl, and sprinkle with salt. Set aside 20 minutes.

Remove skin and fat from chicken. Cut into ½-in. strips. Drain cucumber and rinse well. Pat dry with absorbent paper towels.

Heat oil in a wok and stir-fry chicken and garlic 5 minutes. Add soy sauce, sherry, chives, and cucumber and cook 3 minutes. Garnish with cucumber twists and serve with noodles.

Makes 4 servings.

PEPPERED CHICKEN KABOBS

1 lb. boneless, skinless chicken fillets, cubed
1 tablespoon rice wine
1 tablespoon dark soy sauce
grated zest and juice of 1 lime
2 teaspoons brown sugar
1 teaspoon ground cinnamon
1 teaspoon sunflower oil
1 teaspoon Szechuan peppercorns, toasted and
    crushed
strips of lime zest and lime wedges, to serve

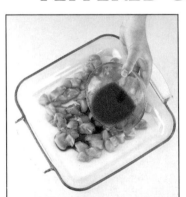

Place chicken in a shallow dish. Mix together
rice wine, soy sauce, lime zest and juice,
sugar, and cinnamon. Pour over chicken.

Cover chicken and chill 1 hour. Meanwhile,
soak 8 bamboo skewers in cold water
30 minutes. Remove chicken pieces from
marinade, reserving marinade, and thread
chicken onto skewers.

Preheat broiler. Brush broiler rack lightly
with oil and place skewers on rack. Brush
with   marinade   and   sprinkle   with
peppercorns. Broil 3 minutes, turn, brush
again, and broil another 2 or 3 minutes or
until cooked through. Drain on absorbent
paper towels. Garnish with lime zest and
serve with lime wedges.

Makes 4 servings.

CHINESE GRILLED CHICKEN

4 chicken quarters, each weighing about 8 oz., skin
    and fat removed
2 cloves garlic, finely chopped
1-in. piece fresh ginger, peeled and finely chopped
¼ cup hoisin sauce
2 tablespoons dry sherry
1 teaspoon chili sauce
1 tablespoon dark soy sauce
1 tablespoon brown sugar
1 tablespoon chopped fresh chives, to garnish

Rinse chicken quarters and pat dry with
absorbent paper towels. Using a sharp knife,
score top of quarters in diagonal lines.

Place chicken in a shallow dish. Mix
together garlic, ginger, hoisin sauce, sherry,
chili sauce, soy sauce, and brown sugar, and
spoon over prepared chicken quarters. Cover
and chill overnight.

Preheat broiler. Place chicken on broiler
rack and cook 20 minutes, turning once,
until cooked through. Garnish with chives
and serve with rice and salad.

Makes 4 servings.

CRISPY SKIN CHICKEN

1 (3½-lb.) chicken
salt
1 tablespoon light corn syrup
¼ cup plus 1 teaspoon sea salt
1 tablespoon Chinese five-spice powder
2 tablespoons rice vinegar
3¾ cups vegetable oil

Bring a large saucepan of salted water to a boil. Lower in chicken, return to a boil, then remove pan from heat, cover tightly, and leave chicken in the water 30 minutes.

Drain chicken, dry with absorbent paper towels, and leave in a cold, dry place at least 12 hours. In a small bowl, mix together light corn syrup, 1 teaspoon salt, ½ teaspoon five-spice powder, and rice vinegar. Brush over chicken and chill in refrigerator 20 minutes. Repeat until all coating is used. Refrigerate chicken at least 4 hours to allow coating to dry thoroughly on the skin.

Split chicken in half through the breast. In a wok, heat oil, add chicken halves, and deep-fry 5 minutes or until golden brown. Lift chicken from oil and drain on absorbent paper towels. Cut into bite-size pieces. In a small saucepan over a low heat, stir together remaining sea salt and remaining five-spice powder 2 minutes. Sprinkle over chicken.

Makes 4 servings.

CHICKEN IN BLACK BEAN SAUCE

1 cup peanut oil
1-lb. boneless, skinless chicken fillet, cubed
10 button mushrooms, halved
½ red bell pepper, seeded and diced
½ green bell pepper, seeded and diced
4 scallions, finely chopped
2 carrots, thinly sliced
2 tablespoons dried black beans, washed
½-in. piece fresh ginger, peeled and grated
1 clove garlic, finely chopped
2 tablespoons rice wine or dry sherry
1 cup Chinese Vegetable Stock (see page 17)
1 tablespoon light soy sauce
2 teaspoons cornstarch mixed with 4 teaspoons cold water

In a wok, heat oil until smoking, add chicken cubes, and deep-fry 2 minutes. Using a slotted spoon, lift chicken from oil and drain on absorbent paper towels. Pour oil from wok, leaving just 2 tablespoons.

Add mushrooms to wok and stir-fry 1 minute. Add red and green bell peppers, scallions, and carrots, and stir-fry 3 minutes. In a bowl, mash black beans with ginger, garlic, and rice wine or dry sherry. Stir into wok, then stir in stock and soy sauce. Cook another 2 minutes. Stir in cornstarch mixture and bring to a boil, stirring. Stir in chicken and heat through gently.

Makes 4 servings.

DUCK WITH KIWI FRUIT

SOY-ROAST DUCKLING

2 boneless duck fillets, each weighing about 8 oz.
½-in. piece fresh ginger, peeled and finely chopped
1 clove garlic, finely chopped
2 tablespoons dry sherry
2 kiwi fruit
1 teaspoon sesame oil
SAUCE:
¼ cup dry sherry
2 tablespoons light soy sauce
4 teaspoons honey

Remove skin and fat from duck. With a sharp knife, score flesh in diagonal lines. Beat with a meat tenderizer until ½ in. thick.

Place duck fillets in a shallow dish and add ginger, garlic, and sherry. Cover and chill 1 hour. Peel and thinly slice kiwi fruit and halve crosswise. Cover and chill until required. Preheat broiler. Drain duck fillets and place on broiler rack. Brush with sesame oil and cook 8 minutes. Turn and brush again with oil. Cook 8 to 10 minutes or until tender and cooked through.

Meanwhile, make sauce. Put sherry, soy sauce, and honey in a saucepan, bring to a boil, and simmer 5 minutes or until syrupy. Drain duck fillets on absorbent paper towels and slice thinly. Arrange duck slices and kiwi fruit on serving plates. Pour sauce over duck and serve with rice and vegetables.

Makes 4 servings.

1 (5-lb.) duckling, giblets removed
¼ cup dark soy sauce
2 tablespoons brown sugar
2 cloves garlic, finely chopped
soft pancakes, scallions, and cucumber, to serve
DIP:
1 tablespoon sunflower oil
4 scallions, finely chopped
1 clove garlic, finely chopped
3 tablespoons dark soy sauce
2 teaspoons brown sugar
2 tablespoons dry sherry

Rinse duckling and pat dry. Place on a wire rack in a baking pan. Prick all over with a fork.

Sprinkle duckling with soy sauce, brown sugar, and garlic. Bake 2 hours 15 minutes or until juices run clear and skin is well browned. To make dip, heat oil in a wok and stir-fry scallions and garlic 1 minute. Combine with soy sauce, sugar, and sherry in a bowl.

To serve, remove all skin and fat from duckling and shred flesh away from bone. Serve with dip, soft pancakes, and shredded scallions and cucumber.

Makes 4 servings.

Note: Soft pancakes can be bought ready-made from Asian markets.

DUCK WITH GREEN BELL PEPPERS

1 egg white
3 tablespoons cornstarch
sea salt
1 lb. boned duck fillets, cubed
2½ cups peanut oil
2 green bell peppers, seeded and cut into
    1-in. squares
2 tablespoons light soy sauce
1 tablespoon rice wine or dry sherry
1 teaspoon brown sugar
½ cup Chinese Chicken Stock (see page 16)
1 teaspoon sesame oil
white pepper

In a bowl, whisk together egg white, cornstarch, and 1 teaspoon salt. Stir in duck cubes to mix thoroughly. Leave 20 minutes. In a wok, heat peanut oil until very hot. Add duck and deep-fry about 4 minutes, until crisp. Remove and drain on absorbent paper towels.

Add bell peppers to wok and deep-fry 2 minutes, then drain on absorbent paper towels. Pour oil from wok, leaving about 2 tablespoonsful. Add soy sauce, rice wine or dry sherry, sugar, stock, sesame oil, and salt and pepper to taste. Boil to a boil, then add cooked duck and bell peppers, reduce heat, and gently heat through.

Makes 4 servings.

STIR-FRIED DUCK WITH LEEKS

4 tablespoons vegetable oil
2 leeks, thinly shredded
1 red bell pepper, seeded and sliced
½-in. piece fresh ginger, peeled and thinly sliced
3 cloves garlic, finely chopped
2 tablespoons black bean paste
1 lb. cooked boned duck, cut into strips
¼ cup Chinese Chicken Stock (see page 16)
2 tablespoons light soy sauce
2 tablespoons rice vinegar
2 teaspoons brown sugar
2 teaspoons chili sauce

In a wok, heat oil until just smoking. Add leeks, pepper, ginger, and garlic. Stir-fry briefly to coat with oil, then stir in black bean paste and stir-fry 5 minutes or until vegetables begin to soften.

Add duck, stock, soy sauce, rice vinegar, brown sugar, and chili sauce, and stir-fry 2 or 3 minutes or until duck is heated through.

Makes 4 servings.

SZECHUAN TURKEY

1 lb. lean boneless turkey
1 egg white, lightly beaten
large pinch salt
1 teaspoon cornstarch
1 tablespoon sunflower oil
½ teaspoon Szechuan peppercorns, toasted
  and crushed
8 oz. vegetables chow-chow, shredded
8 oz. snow peas
4-oz. can water chestnuts, rinsed and sliced

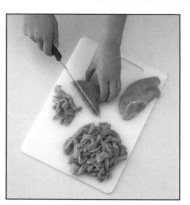

Remove skin and fat from turkey. Cut into
thin strips about ¼ in. thick.

Place turkey strips in a bowl and mix with
egg white, salt, and cornstarch. Cover and
chill 30 minutes.

Heat oil in a wok and stir-fry turkey with
crushed peppercorns 2 minutes or until
turkey is just colored. Add vegetables chow-
chow, snow peas, and water chestnuts, and
stir-fry 3 minutes or until just cooked
through. Serve immediately.

Makes 4 servings.

SWEET & SOUR TURKEY

1 lb. lean skinless boneless turkey
1 tablespoon sunflower oil
2 shallots, chopped
2 stalks celery, sliced
2 tablespoons light soy sauce
1 red bell pepper, sliced
1 yellow bell pepper, sliced
1 green bell pepper, sliced
4-oz. can bamboo shoots, drained
3 tablespoons plum sauce
2 tablespoons white rice vinegar
1 teaspoon sesame oil
2 tablespoons sesame seeds

Trim away any excess fat from turkey. Cut
into 1-in. cubes. Heat oil in a wok and stir-
fry turkey, shallots, and celery 2 or 3 minutes
or until lightly colored.

Add soy sauce and bell peppers and stir-fry
2 minutes. Stir in bamboo shoots, plum
sauce, and vinegar, and simmer 2 minutes.
Stir in sesame oil, sprinkle with sesame
seeds, and serve.

Makes 4 servings.

BRAISED CHICKEN WITH SPICES

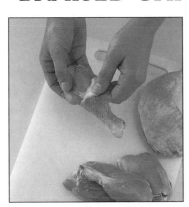

4 chicken thighs and 4 chicken drumsticks, total
  weight about 2¼ lbs.
4 cloves garlic, chopped
2 shallots, chopped
2-in. piece fresh ginger, chopped
1¾ cups coconut milk
2 teaspoons ground coriander
2 teaspoons ground cumin
¼ teaspoon ground turmeric
2 tablespoons vegetable oil
6 green cardamom pods
6 star anise
6 dried red chilies
1 cinnamon stick
4 cloves
20 fresh curry leaves

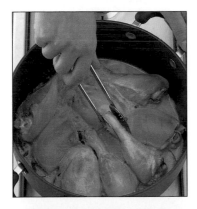

Skin chicken pieces and set aside. Place
garlic, shallots, ginger, coconut milk,
cilantro, cumin, and turmeric into a small
blender. Mix to a fine paste. In a heavy-
bottomed saucepan large enough to hold
chicken in a single layer, heat oil over
medium heat. Add cardamom pods, star
anise, chilies, cinnamon, cloves, and curry
leaves. Fry, stirring, 2 or 3 minutes. Add ⅓ of
the coconut milk mixture. Bring to a boil,
then add chicken. Turn to coat, then cook
5 minutes.

Add remaining coconut milk mixture. Bring
to a simmer, then lower heat and cook
gently, uncovered, 50 minutes, stirring
frequently. Cook an additional 10 minutes,
stirring every minute. The chicken should be
golden brown and most of the milk
evaporated. Pour away oily residue. Increase
heat to high. Add 3 or 4 tablespoons water
and stir to deglaze pan. Serve chicken with
Thai rice and sauce.

Makes 4 servings.

CHICKEN & PINEAPPLE CURRY

5 shallots, chopped
3 large fresh red chilies, cored, seeded, and chopped
3 cloves garlic, crushed
2-in. piece galangal, chopped
1 stalk lemongrass, chopped
2 tablespoons vegetable oil
1½ lbs. boneless, skinless chicken fillets, cut
  into strips
2 tablespoons light brown sugar
3½ cups coconut milk
2 teaspoons tamarind paste (see page 11)
2 tablespoons fish sauce
4 kaffir lime leaves
1 small pineapple, weighing about 1 lb., thinly sliced
grated zest and juice of 1 lime, or to taste
small handful cilantro leaves, chopped

Put shallots, chilies, garlic, galangal, and
lemongrass in a small blender. Mix to a
paste; add 1 tablespoon of the oil, if
necessary. In a wok or sauté pan, heat
remaining oil. Add chicken and stir-fry until
just turning pale golden brown. Remove and
set aside.

Stir chili paste into pan and stir-fry 3 or 4
minutes or until fragrant. Stir in sugar,
coconut milk, tamarind, fish sauce, and kaffir
lime leaves. Bring to a boil, and boil 4 or 5
minutes or until reduced by half and lightly
thickened. Return chicken to pan. Add
pineapple and simmer 3 or 4 minutes or until
chicken juices run clear. Add lime zest and
lime juice to taste. Stir in cilantro.

Makes 6 servings.

DEVIL'S CURRY

10 fresh red chilies, cored, seeded, and chopped
2-in. piece fresh ginger, chopped
6 shallots, chopped
3 cloves garlic, chopped
1 tablespoon ground coriander
½ teaspoon ground turmeric
8 candlenuts or cashews
⅓ cup vegetable oil
6 shallots, thinly sliced
3 cloves garlic, thinly sliced
1 teaspoon black mustard seeds, lightly crushed
1 (3½-lb.) chicken, jointed, or small chicken portions
5 to 7 small potatoes, halved
2 teaspoons mustard powder
2 tablespoons rice vinegar
1 tablespoon dark soy sauce

Place chilies, ginger, chopped shallots and garlic, cilantro, turmeric, and candlenuts or cashews in a blender and mix to a paste. In a large wok or sauté pan, heat oil over medium-high heat. Add sliced shallots and garlic and fry until lightly browned. Stir in spice paste and cook about 5 minutes, stirring. Add mustard seeds, stir once or twice, then add chicken. Cook, stirring frequently, until chicken pieces turn white.

Add potatoes and 2½ cups water. Bring to a boil, cover, then simmer 15 minutes. Stir together mustard, vinegar, and soy sauce. Stir into pan, re-cover, and cook another 15 to 20 minutes, stirring occasionally, until chicken is tender.

Makes 4 to 6 servings.

AROMATIC CHICKEN

2 teaspoons tamarind paste (see page 11)
salt
1 (3½-lb.) chicken, cut into pieces, or chicken portions, chopped
12 fresh green chilies, cored, seeded, and chopped
2 small onions, chopped
5 cloves garlic, crushed
1 ripe tomato, chopped
⅓ cup vegetable oil
4 kaffir lime leaves
1 stalk lemongrass, crushed

Blend tamarind paste with 1 teaspoon salt and 2 tablespoons hot water. Pour mixture over chicken and rub in. Leave 1 hour.

Put chilies, onions, garlic, and tomato in a blender and mix to a paste. In a wok or large heavy sauté pan, heat oil. Add chicken and marinade. Turn to brown on both sides, then remove with a slotted spoon.

Add spice paste, lime leaves, and lemongrass to pan. Cook, stirring, 6 or 7 minutes or until paste is browned. Return chicken to pan, add 1¼ cups water, and bring to a simmer. Cover and simmer gently 30 minutes or until chicken juices run clear, turning chicken occasionally.

Makes 4 servings.

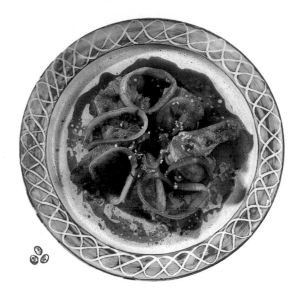

MALAY CHICKEN

2 teaspoons cumin seeds
2 teaspoons coriander seeds
8 boneless chicken thighs, total weight about 1½ lbs.
1 bunch scallions, white part only, finely chopped
2 tablespoons chopped cilantro leaves
2 oz. creamed coconut, chopped
1 clove garlic, crushed and finely chopped
½ fresh red chili, cored, seeded, and chopped
2 teaspoons sunflower oil
1 teaspoon sesame oil
2 tablespoons lime juice
salt
lime slices
cilantro sprigs, to garnish

Place cumin and coriander seeds in a small pan and heat until aroma is released. Grind in a blender or using a mortar and pestle and set aside. Open out chicken thighs. Mix together scallions and cilantro and spoon an equal quantity on each opened chicken thigh. Re-form thighs. Place in a single layer in a nonreactive dish. Put coconut in a bowl and stir in scant 1 cup boiling water until dissolved. Stir in garlic, chili, sunflower and sesame oil, lime juice, spices, and salt. Pour over chicken, turn to coat in marinade, then cover and refrigerate overnight.

Preheat broiler or grill. Transfer chicken to room temperature. Soak bamboo skewers in water 20 to 30 minutes. Remove chicken from marinade (reserve marinade) and thread 1 or 2 chicken thighs onto each skewer with a lime slice. Broil or grill about 20 minutes, basting with remaining marinade, until chicken juices run clear when tested with the point of a sharp knife. Garnish with cilantro sprigs.

Makes 4 servings.

NONYA CHICKEN

2 tablespoons vegetable oil
1¾ lbs. chicken portions, cut into large, bite-size pieces
2 fresh red chilies, sliced into rings
1 tablespoon dark soy sauce
1 tablespoon light soy sauce
1½ teaspoons light brown sugar
1 onion, sliced into ¼-in. rings
sesame oil for sprinkling
toasted sesame seeds, to garnish

In a wok or large skillet over medium-high heat, heat oil. Add chicken and fry until evenly browned.

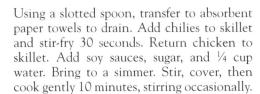

Using a slotted spoon, transfer to absorbent paper towels to drain. Add chilies to skillet and stir-fry 30 seconds. Return chicken to skillet. Add soy sauces, sugar, and ¼ cup water. Bring to a simmer. Stir, cover, then cook gently 10 minutes, stirring occasionally.

Stir in onion, re-cover skillet, and continue to cook gently, stirring occasionally, 5 minutes or until onion is soft and chicken juices run clear when chicken is pierced with a sharp knife. Sprinkle in a few drops of sesame oil. Serve sprinkled with toasted sesame seeds to garnish.

Makes 3 or 4 servings.

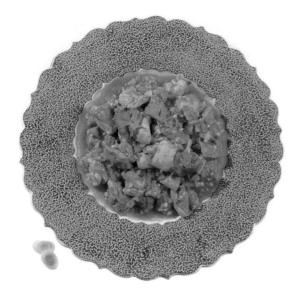

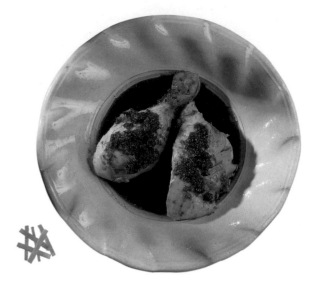

MALAYSIAN SPICED CHICKEN

8 chicken thighs, boned (see page 42) and chopped
3 tablespoons vegetable oil
1 clove garlic, finely chopped
2 tablespoons fish sauce
6 shallots, finely chopped
cilantro leaves, to garnish
MARINADE:
2 small fresh red chilies, cored, seeded, and chopped
1 stalk lemongrass, chopped
1 clove garlic, crushed
1½-in. piece fresh ginger, chopped
1 tablespoon ground turmeric
10-oz. can tomatoes
1 tablespoon light brown sugar
salt

To make marinade, put chilies, lemongrass, garlic, ginger, turmeric, tomatoes, brown sugar, and salt in a blender and mix together well. Put chicken in a nonreactive bowl. Pour marinade over chicken. Stir together, cover, and refrigerate overnight. Return bowl of chicken to room temperature 1 hour. In a wok or heavy sauté pan over high heat, heat oil. Add garlic and fry 30 seconds. Add chicken and marinade. Stir and toss together, then stir in fish sauce and ¼ cup hot water. Cover, lower heat, and simmer 5 minutes.

Add shallots and continue to cook, uncovered, stirring occasionally, about 10 minutes, until chicken juices run clear. Serve garnished with cilantro.

Makes 4 servings.

GINGER & SOY ROAST CHICKEN

1½-in. piece fresh ginger, coarsely chopped
1 onion, coarsely chopped
3 cloves garlic, coarsely chopped
1 (3½-lb.) chicken
⅓ cup vegetable oil
3 tablespoons dark soy sauce
3 tablespoons rice vinegar
2½ tablespoons light brown sugar

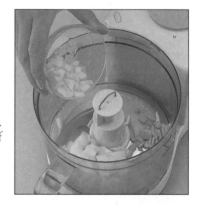

Put ginger, onion, and garlic in a blender. Mix to a paste, adding a little water if necessary.

Put chicken in a baking pan. Rub inside and outside of chicken with half of ginger mixture. Cover and leave 1 hour. Put remaining ginger paste in a bowl and stir in oil, soy sauce, rice vinegar, sugar, and ⅓ cup water.

Preheat oven to 350°F. Prop up tail end of chicken. Pour as much soy sauce mixture as possible into cavity of chicken. Roast chicken 25 minutes, basting occasionally with remaining soy mixture. Pour remaining soy mixture around chicken and cook an additional 50 minutes, basting occasionally, until chicken juices run clear. Stir a little water into the pan if sauce begins to dry out too much.

Makes 4 servings.

CHICKEN WITH RICE

1-in. piece fresh ginger, grated
4 scallions, including some green, finely chopped
2 teaspoons rice wine
1 (2½-lb.) chicken
4 cloves garlic, lightly crushed
1¼ cups long-grain white rice
TO SERVE:
2-in. piece fresh ginger, grated
¾ teaspoon salt
2 teaspoons soy sauce
2 teaspoons rice vinegar
1 teaspoon sesame oil
2 scallions, including some green, sliced

CHICKEN IN SPICED SAUCE

2 tablespoons vegetable oil
6 chicken thighs and 6 chicken drumsticks
2 stalks lemongrass, chopped
4 shallots, chopped
4 cloves garlic, chopped
2½-in. piece fresh ginger, chopped
3 tablespoons ground coriander
2 teaspoons ground turmeric
4 fresh bay leaves
1½ cups coconut milk
¼ cup Chinese chili sauce
about 2 tablespoons brown sugar, or to taste
½ cup chopped roasted candlenuts or cashews
salt

In a small bowl, mix together ginger, scallions, and rice wine. Rub over chicken and put some in cavity. Set aside to cool 1 hour. Put chicken in a large saucepan and cover with water. Add garlic and bring to a boil over medium heat. Skim off any impurities. Cover pan and poach 25 minutes. Remove from heat and let cool 1½ hours. Remove chicken and plunge into a bowl of water and ice cubes 10 minutes. Strain stock and measure 2 cups. Remove chicken skin and cut meat into chunks. Keep warm.

In a large skillet over medium heat, heat oil. Add chicken and brown evenly. Transfer to absorbent paper towels to drain. Pour all but 1½ tablespoons fat from skillet. Put lemongrass, shallots, garlic, and ginger in a blender. Mix to a paste. Gently heat fat, add spice paste, and stir 2 minutes. Stir in cilantro, turmeric, and bay leaves and stir-fry 1 minute. Stir in coconut milk, chili sauce, sugar, nuts, and salt, and stir-fry an additional minute.

In another serving bowl, mix ginger and salt. In another bowl, mix soy sauce, rice vinegar, and sesame oil. Put scallions in a third bowl. Bring measured stock to a boil; add rice. Return to a boil, stir, cover, and simmer 12 minutes. Remove from heat and leave 5 minutes or until tender. Divide rice between 4 warm serving bowls and put chicken on top. Bring remaining stock to a boil. Spoon over chicken or serve separately. Serve with accompaniments.

Return chicken to skillet and turn in sauce. Cover and cook gently 20 minutes, stirring and turning chicken frequently, until chicken juices run clear. Discard bay leaves before serving.

Makes 6 servings.

Makes 4 servings.

CHICKEN IN COCONUT MILK

CHICKEN WITH CILANTRO

8 black peppercorns, cracked
6 cilantro roots, finely chopped
1¾-in. piece galangal, thinly sliced
2 fresh green chilies, seeded and thinly sliced
2½ cups coconut milk
grated zest of 1 kaffir lime
4 kaffir lime leaves, shredded
1 (3-lb.) chicken, cut into 8 pieces
1 tablespoon fish sauce
3 tablespoons lime juice
3 tablespoons chopped cilantro leaves

Using a mortar and pestle or small blender, pound or mix together peppercorns, cilantro roots, and galangal.

6 cilantro sprigs
1 tablespoon black peppercorns, crushed
2 cloves garlic, chopped
juice of 1 lime
2 teaspoons fish sauce
4 large or 6 medium chicken drumsticks or thighs
lime wedges, to serve
scallion brushes (see page 14), to garnish

Using a mortar and pestle or small blender, pound or mix together cilantro, peppercorns, garlic, lime juice, and fish sauce; set aside.

In a wok, briefly heat peppercorn mixture, stirring, then stir in chilies, coconut milk, lime zest, and leaves. Heat to just simmering point and add chicken portions. Adjust heat so liquid is barely moving, then cook gently about 40 to 45 minutes or until chicken is very tender and liquid reduced.

Using the point of a sharp knife, cut slashes in chicken. Spread spice mixture over chicken. Cover and set aside in a cool place 2 to 3 hours, turning occasionally.

Stir in fish sauce and lime juice. Scatter cilantro leaves over chicken and serve.

Makes 6 to 8 servings.

Preheat broiler. Broil chicken, basting and turning occasionally, about 10 minutes or until cooked through and golden. Serve with wedges of lime and garnish with scallion brushes.

Makes 2 to 4 servings.

LEMONGRASS CHICKEN CURRY

12 oz. boneless chicken, chopped into small pieces
1 tablespoon Red Curry Paste (see page 230)
3 tablespoons vegetable oil
2 cloves garlic, finely chopped
1 tablespoon fish sauce
2 stalks lemongrass, finely chopped
5 kaffir lime leaves, shredded
½ teaspoon crushed palm sugar

Place chicken in a bowl, add curry paste, and stir to coat chicken; set aside 30 minutes.

In a wok, heat oil, add garlic, and fry until golden. Stir in chicken, then fish sauce, lemongrass, lime leaves, sugar, and ½ cup water.

Adjust heat so liquid is barely moving and cook 15 to 20 minutes or until chicken is cooked through. If chicken becomes too dry, add a little more water, but the final dish should be quite dry.

Makes 3 or 4 servings.

GRILLED THAI CHICKEN

4 fresh red chilies, seeded and sliced
2 cloves garlic, chopped
5 shallots, finely sliced
2 teaspoons crushed palm sugar
½ cup coconut cream (see page 8)
2 teaspoons fish sauce
1 tablespoon tamarind water (see page 11)
4 boneless chicken fillets
Thai holy basil leaves or cilantro leaves, to garnish

Using a mortar and pestle or small blender, pound or blend chilies, garlic, and shallots to a paste. Work in sugar, then stir in coconut cream, fish sauce, and tamarind water.

Using the point of a sharp knife, cut 4 slashes in chicken fillets. Place chicken in a shallow dish and pour spice mixture on top. Turn to coat, cover dish, and set aside 1 hour.

Preheat broiler. Place chicken on a piece of aluminum foil and broil about 4 minutes each side, basting occasionally, until cooked through. Garnish with basil or cilantro leaves.

Makes 4 servings.

THAI SPICED CHICKEN

5 shallots, chopped
3 cloves garlic, chopped
5 cilantro roots, chopped
2 stalks lemongrass, chopped
2 fresh red chilies, seeded and chopped
1½-in. piece fresh ginger, finely chopped
1 teaspoon shrimp paste
1½ tablespoons vegetable oil
2 chicken legs, divided into thighs and drumsticks
1½ tablespoons tamarind water (see page 11)

Using a mortar and pestle or blender, pound or mix shallots, garlic, cilantro, lemongrass, chilies, ginger, and shrimp paste until smooth.

In a wok, heat oil, stir in spicy paste, and cook, stirring, 3 or 4 minutes. Stir in chicken pieces to coat evenly.

Add tamarind water and ⅓ cup water. Cover and cook gently about 25 minutes or until chicken is tender.

Makes 3 or 4 servings.

CHICKEN WITH BASIL LEAVES

2 tablespoons vegetable oil
2 cloves garlic, chopped
12 oz. boneless, skinless chicken fillets, chopped
1 small onion, finely chopped
3 fresh chilies, seeded and thinly sliced
20 Thai holy basil leaves
1 tablespoon fish sauce
¼ cup coconut milk
squeeze of lime juice
Thai holy basil leaves and chili flower, to garnish

In a wok, heat 1 tablespoon oil, add garlic, chicken, onion, and chilies, and cook, stirring occasionally, 3 to 5 minutes or until cooked through.

Stir in basil leaves, fish sauce, and coconut milk. Stir briefly over heat. Squeeze over lime juice. Serve garnished with basil leaves and chili flower.

Makes 2 or 3 servings.

CHICKEN WITH GALANGAL

CHICKEN WITH PEANUT SAUCE

1 lb. boneless, skinless chicken fillets
3 tablespoons vegetable oil
2 cloves garlic, finely chopped
1 onion, quartered and sliced
1-in. piece galangal, finely chopped
8 pieces dried Chinese black mushrooms, soaked
   30 minutes, drained and chopped
1 fresh red chili, seeded and cut into fine strips
1 tablespoon fish sauce
1½ teaspoons crushed palm sugar
1 tablespoon lime juice
12 Thai mint leaves
4 scallions, including some green, chopped
Thai mint leaves, to garnish

1-in. piece galangal, chopped
2 cloves garlic, chopped
1½ tablespoons Fragrant Curry Paste (see page 231)
¼ cup coconut cream (see page 8)
1 lb. boneless, skinless chicken fillets, cut into
   large pieces
3 shallots, chopped
¼ cup dry-roasted peanuts, chopped
1 cup coconut milk
½ teaspoon finely chopped dried red chili
2 teaspoons fish sauce
freshly cooked broccoli, to serve

Using a sharp knife, cut chicken into 2 x 1-in. pieces; set aside. In a wok, heat oil, add garlic and onion, and cook, stirring occasionally, until golden. Stir in chicken and stir-fry about 2 minutes.

Using a mortar and pestle or small blender, pound or mix together galangal, garlic, and curry paste. Mix in coconut cream. Place chicken in a bowl and stir in spice mixture; set aside 1 hour.

Add galangal, mushrooms, and chili, and stir-fry 1 minute. Stir in fish sauce, sugar, lime juice, mint leaves, scallions, and 3 or 4 tablespoons water. Cook, stirring, about 1 minute. Transfer to a warmed serving dish and sprinkle with mint leaves.

Makes 4 servings.

Heat a wok, add shallots and coated chicken, and stir-fry 3 or 4 minutes. In a blender, mix peanuts with coconut milk, then stir into chicken with chili and fish sauce. Cook gently about 30 minutes or until chicken is tender and thick sauce formed. Transfer to center of a warmed serving plate and arrange cooked broccoli around the chicken.

Makes 4 servings.

CHICKEN WITH SNOW PEAS

STEAMED CHICKEN CURRY

3 tablespoons vegetable oil
3 cloves garlic, chopped
1 dried red chili, seeded and chopped
3 red shallots, chopped
2 tablespoons lime juice
2 teaspoons fish sauce
12 oz. chicken, finely chopped
1½ stalks lemongrass, chopped
1 kaffir lime leaf, sliced
6 oz. snow peas
1½ tablespoons coarsely ground brown rice
 (see page 10)
3 scallions, chopped
chopped cilantro leaves, to garnish

1 quantity Fragrant Curry Paste (see page 231)
1⅔ cups coconut milk
1 lb. boneless, skinless chicken fillets, sliced
4 kaffir lime leaves, shredded
8 Thai holy basil leaves
Thai holy basil sprig, to garnish

Using a small blender, mix together curry
paste, ⅓ cup coconut milk, and ⅓ cup water;
set aside. Place chicken in a heatproof bowl
or dish, stir in remaining coconut milk, and
set aside 30 minutes.

In a wok, heat 2 tablespoons oil, add garlic,
and cook, stirring occasionally, until lightly
browned. Stir in chili, shallots, lime juice,
fish sauce, and ¼ cup water. Simmer 1 or 2
minutes, then stir in chicken, lemongrass,
and lime leaf. Cook, stirring, 2 or 3 minutes
or until chicken is just cooked through.
Transfer to a warmed plate and keep warm.

Stir curry-flavored coconut milk, lime leaves,
and basil leaves into chicken in bowl or dish.
Cover top tightly with aluminum foil and
place in a steaming basket.

Heat remaining oil in wok, add snow peas,
and stir-fry 2 or 3 minutes or until just
tender. Transfer to a warmed serving plate.
Return chicken to wok. Add rice and
scallions. Heat about 1 minute, then transfer
to serving plate. Garnish with chopped
cilantro.

Makes 3 or 4 servings.

Cover with a lid. Position over a saucepan of
boiling water. Steam about 40 minutes or
until chicken is tender. Garnish with basil.

Makes 4 or 5 servings.

Note: In Thailand the curry is steamed on a
bed of lettuce and basil leaves, then wrapped
in a banana leaf.

THAI LEMONGRASS CHICKEN

1 (3-lb.) chicken, cut into 8 pieces
4 thick stalks lemongrass
4 scallions, chopped
4 black peppercorns, cracked
2 tablespoons vegetable oil
1 fresh green chili, seeded and thinly sliced
2 teaspoons fish sauce
fresh red chili, cut into thick slivers, to garnish

With the point of a sharp knife, cut slashes in each chicken piece; place in a shallow dish.

Bruise top parts of each lemongrass stalk and reserve. Chop lower parts, then pound with scallions and peppercorns using a mortar and pestle. Spread over chicken and into slashes. Cover and set aside 2 hours.

In a wok, heat oil, add chicken, and cook, turning occasionally, about 5 minutes or until lightly browned. Add green chili, bruised lemongrass stalks, and ¼ cup water. Cover wok and cook over low heat 25 to 30 minutes or until chicken is cooked through. Stir in fish sauce. Transfer chicken pieces to a warmed serving dish, spoon cooking juices on top, and sprinkle with red chili.

Makes 4 to 6 servings.

DUCK CURRY

⅓ cup coconut cream (see page 8)
⅓ cup Green Curry Paste (see page 230)
1 (3-lb.) duck, skinned if desired, trimmed of excess
  fat and divided into 8 portions
2½ cups coconut milk
1 tablespoon fish sauce
8 kaffir lime leaves, shredded
2 fresh green chilies, seeded and thinly sliced
12 Thai holy basil leaves
leaves from 5 cilantro sprigs
cilantro sprigs, to garnish

Heat coconut cream in a wok over a medium heat, stirring, until it thickens and oil begins to separate and bubble.

Stir in curry paste and cook about 5 minutes or until mixture darkens. Stir in duck pieces to coat with curry mixture. Lower heat, cover, and cook 15 minutes, stirring occasionally. If necessary, using a bulb baster, remove excess fat from surface, or carefully spoon it off. Stir in coconut milk, fish sauce, and lime leaves. Heat to just simmering point, then cook gently without boiling, turning duck over occasionally, 30 to 40 minutes or until meat is very tender. Remove surplus fat from surface, then stir in chilies.

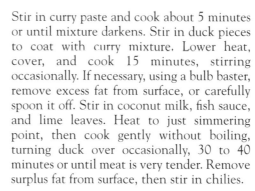

Cook an additional 5 minutes. Stir in basil and cilantro leaves and cook an additional 2 minutes. Garnish with cilantro sprigs.

Makes 4 servings.

CHICKEN WINGS IN SPICY SAUCE

8 to 12 chicken wings
salt and freshly ground black pepper
1 tablespoon sugar
1 tablespoon fish sauce
oil for deep-frying
1 cup Vietnamese Hot Sauce (see page 234)
⅓ cup chicken stock or water
1 tablespoon clear honey
lettuce leaves

Trim off tip of each chicken wing (these are known as "pinions"), which can be used for making stock.

In a bowl, marinate chicken wings with salt, pepper, sugar, and fish sauce at least 30 minutes, longer if possible. Heat oil in a wok or deep-fat fryer to 325°F and deep-fry chicken wings 2 or 3 minutes or until golden; remove and drain.

Heat Vietnamese Hot Sauce with chicken stock or water in a saucepan and add chicken wings. Bring to a boil and braise 5 or 6 minutes, stirring constantly until sauce is sticky. Add honey and blend well. Serve hot or cold on a bed of lettuce leaves.

Makes 4 to 6 servings.

CHICKEN & COCONUT CURRY

1 (2¼-lb.) chicken, cut into 10 to 12 pieces
salt and freshly ground black pepper
1 teaspoon sugar
1 tablespoon curry powder
3 or 4 tablespoons vegetable oil
3 red or white potatoes, peeled and cut into cubes
1 teaspoon chopped garlic
1 tablespoon chopped lemongrass
1 onion, cut into small pieces
1 cup Vietnamese Hot Sauce (see page 234)
2 cups stock or water
2 cups coconut milk
3 bay leaves and 1 carrot, sliced
2 tablespoons fish sauce
cilantro sprigs, to garnish

In a dish, marinate chicken pieces with salt, pepper, sugar, and curry powder at least 1 hour. Heat oil in a large pan and fry potatoes 3 or 4 minutes or until brown—it is not necessary to completely cook potatoes at this stage. Remove potatoes from pan and set aside.

In the same oil, stir-fry garlic, lemongrass, and onion about 30 seconds. Add chicken pieces and stir-fry 2 or 3 minutes, then add Vietnamese Hot Sauce, stock or water, coconut milk, and bay leaves. Bring to a boil and add parboiled potatoes, carrot slices, and fish sauce. Blend well, then cover and simmer 15 to 20 minutes, stirring now and then to make sure nothing is stuck on the bottom of the pan. Garnish with cilantro sprigs and serve.

Makes 4 to 6 servings.

BROILED CHICKEN DRUMSTICKS

VIETNAMESE CHICKEN STIR-FRY

1 or 2 cloves garlic, chopped
1 or 2 stalks lemongrass, chopped
2 shallots, chopped
1 or 2 small red or green chilies, chopped
1 tablespoon chopped cilantro leaves
¼ cup fish sauce
6 to 8 chicken drumsticks, skinned
lettuce leaves
Spicy Fish Sauce (see page 233), to serve

8 oz. chicken fillets, boned and skinned
2 teaspoons cornstarch
2 teaspoons fish sauce
salt and freshly ground pepper
2 or 3 tablespoons vegetable oil
½ teaspoon crushed garlic
1 teaspoon finely chopped lemongrass
1 teaspoon chopped fresh ginger
4 to 6 dried small red chilies
2 oz. snow peas, trimmed
½ red bell pepper, cored and cut into cubes
2 oz. sliced bamboo shoots, drained
1 teaspoon sugar
1 tablespoon rice vinegar
2 tablespoons oyster sauce
½ teaspoon sesame oil

Using a mortar and pestle, pound garlic, lemongrass, shallots, chilies, and cilantro to a paste.

In a mixing bowl, thoroughly blend pounded mixture with fish sauce to a smooth paste. Add drumsticks and coat well with paste, then cover the bowl and marinate 2 to 3 hours, turning drumsticks every 30 minutes or so.

Cut chicken into bite-size slices or cubes. Mix cornstarch with 1 tablespoon water. Place chicken in a bowl with cornstarch paste and fish sauce. Season with salt and pepper and marinate 20 to 25 minutes. Heat oil in a wok or skillet and stir-fry garlic, lemongrass, ginger, and chilies 30 seconds. Add chicken pieces and stir-fry about 1 minute until color of chicken changes.

Prepare grill or preheat broiler. Cook drumsticks over the grill or under the broiler 10 to 15 minutes, turning frequently and basting with marinade remaining in the bowl the first 5 minutes only. Serve hot on a bed of lettuce leaves with Spicy Fish Sauce as a dip.

Makes 4 to 6 servings.

Add snow peas, red bell pepper, and bamboo shoots, and cook 2 or 3 minutes, stirring constantly, then add sugar, vinegar, oyster sauce, and 3 or 4 tablespoons water. Blend well, bring to boil, and add sesame oil. Serve at once with flat rice noodles.

Makes 4 servings.

Variation: Use chicken stock instead of 3 or 4 tablespoons water.

CHICKEN HOT POT

1 lb. chicken thigh meat, boned and cut into small,
  bite-size pieces
salt and freshly ground pepper
2 teaspoons sugar
1 tablespoon each lime juice and fish sauce
1 tablespoon vegetable oil
2 cloves garlic, sliced, and 2 shallots, chopped
1 tablespoon dried small red chilies
2 tablespoons crushed yellow bean sauce
about 2 cups chicken stock
2 scallions, cut into short sections
cilantro sprigs, to garnish

Marinate chicken with salt, pepper, sugar,
lime juice, and fish sauce 1 to 2 hours.

Heat oil in a clay pot or flameproof casserole
and stir-fry garlic, shallots, and chilies about
1 minute, then add yellow bean sauce and
stir until smooth.

Add chicken pieces and stir-fry 1 or 2
minutes. Add chicken stock, blend well, and
bring to a boil, then reduce heat, cover, and
simmer gently 15 to 20 minutes. Uncover
and stir in scallions. Garnish with cilantro
sprigs and serve straight from the pot. Serve
with rice.

Makes 4 servings.

Note: The longer the chicken is marinated,
the better the flavor, so try to leave it
2 hours.

CHICKEN WITH LEMONGRASS

1 lb. boned and skinned chicken fillets, cut into
  bite-size slices or cubes
salt and freshly ground black pepper
1 teaspoon crushed garlic
2 tablespoons finely chopped lemongrass
1 tablespoon sugar
1 teaspoon chili sauce
3 tablespoons fish sauce
2 or 3 tablespoons vegetable oil
1 small onion, sliced
1 or 2 small red chilies, seeded and chopped

Mix chicken with salt, pepper, garlic,
lemongrass, sugar, chili sauce, and
1 tablespoon fish sauce and marinate
30 minutes.

Heat oil in a wok or skillet and stir-fry onion
slices about 1 minute until opaque. Add
chicken pieces, stir to separate them, then
add remaining fish sauce and cook 2 or 3
minutes or until color of chicken changes.

Add ¼ cup water to marinade bowl to rinse
out, then add to chicken. Bring to a boil and
cook 1 minute. Garnish with chopped
chilies and serve with rice noodles.

Makes 4 servings.

Variations: Firm white fish, pork, or cubes of
tofu can be cooked by the same method.
Chicken stock can be used to rinse out the
marinade bowl instead of water.

AROMATIC DUCK

2 half or 4 quarter portions duck
  (2 fillets and 2 legs)
salt and freshly ground black pepper
1 tablespoon five-spice powder
4 or 5 small pieces fresh ginger
3 or 4 scallions, cut into short sections
3 or 4 tablespoons Chinese rice wine or dry sherry
12 sheets dried rice paper, halved if large
fresh mint, basil, and cilantro leaves
Spicy Fish Sauce (see page 233), to serve

Rub salt, pepper, and five-spice powder all over duck portions.

In a shallow dish, mix ginger, scallions, and rice wine or sherry, add duck portions, and marinate at least 3 to 4 hours, turning duck pieces now and then. Steam duck portions with marinade in a hot steamer 2 to 3 hours. Remove duck portions from liquid and let cool. (Duck can be cooked up to this stage in advance, if desired.)

Preheat oven to 450°F and bake duck pieces, skin-side up, 10 to 15 minutes, then pull meat off the bone. Meanwhile, soften dried rice paper in warm water. Place about 2 tablespoons of meat in each half-sheet of rice paper, add a few mint, basil, and cilantro leaves, roll into a neat bundle, then dip roll in Spicy Fish Sauce before eating it.

Makes 4 to 6 servings.

VIETNAMESE ROAST DUCK

1 teaspoon crushed garlic
2 or 3 shallots, finely chopped
2 teaspoons five-spice powder
2 tablespoon sugar
¼ cup red rice vinegar
1 tablespoon fish sauce
1 tablespoon soy sauce
4 quarter portions duck (2 fillets and 2 legs)
1 cup coconut milk
salt and freshly ground black pepper
watercress, to serve
cilantro sprigs, to garnish

In a bowl, mix garlic, shallots, five-spice powder, sugar, vinegar, fish and soy sauces.

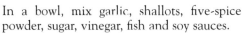
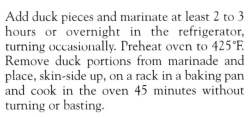

Add duck pieces and marinate at least 2 to 3 hours or overnight in the refrigerator, turning occasionally. Preheat oven to 425°F. Remove duck portions from marinade and place, skin-side up, on a rack in a baking pan and cook in the oven 45 minutes without turning or basting.

Remove duck and keep warm. Heat marinade with drippings in the baking pan, add coconut milk, bring to boil, and simmer 5 minutes. Season with salt and pepper, then pour sauce into a serving bowl. Serve duck portions on a bed of watercress, garnished with cilantro sprigs.

Makes 4 to 6 servings.

Note: The duck portions can be chopped through the bone into bite-size pieces for serving, if desired.

DUCK FILLETS IN SPICY SAUCE

4 duck fillets, boned but not skinned
salt and freshly ground black pepper
1 teaspoon chopped garlic
2 shallots or 1 small onion, finely chopped
1 tablespoon chopped lemongrass
1 tablespoon chopped fresh ginger
2 or 3 tablespoons vegetable oil
1 teaspoon sugar
2 tablespoons fish sauce
1 teaspoon chili sauce
½ cup chicken stock or water
2 teaspoons cornstarch
½ teaspoon sesame oil
1 or 2 small red chilies, seeded and shredded
cilantro sprigs, to garnish

Make a few shallow crisscross cuts on skin side of duck fillets. Rub salt and pepper all over and leave 15 to 20 minutes. Meanwhile, using a mortar and pestle, pound garlic, shallots or onion, lemongrass, and ginger to a paste.

Heat oil in a wok or pan and fry duck pieces, skin-side down, 2 or 3 minutes, then turn pieces over and cook an additional 2 minutes. Add garlic mixture and stir to coat well, then add sugar and fish and chili sauces. Cook, stirring, 1 minute. Add stock or water, bring to a boil, and braise 5 or 6 minutes, stirring. Mix cornstarch with 1 tablespoon water and stir into sauce. Blend in sesame oil. Slice duck, garnish with chilies and cilantro, and serve with rice vermicelli.

Makes 4 to 6 servings.

BROILED QUAIL

4 cleaned quail, each split down backbone and pressed flat
salt and freshly ground black pepper
1 teaspoon crushed garlic
1 tablespoon finely chopped lemongrass
1 teaspoon sugar
1 tablespoon fish sauce
1 tablespoon lime juice or vinegar
1 or 2 tablespoons vegetable oil
lettuce leaves
cilantro sprigs, to garnish
Spicy Fish Sauce (see page 233), to serve

Rub 4 quail all over with plenty of salt and pepper.

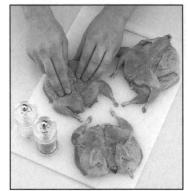

In a mixing bowl, blend garlic, lemongrass, sugar, fish sauce, and lime juice or vinegar. Add quail, turning to coat in mixture, then marinate 2 to 3 hours, turning over now and then.

Prepare a grill or preheat broiler. Brush quail with oil and cook over grill or under broiler 6 to 8 minutes on each side, basting with remaining marinade during first 5 minutes of cooking. Serve quail on a bed of lettuce leaves, garnished with cilantro sprigs, with Spicy Fish Sauce as a dip.

Makes 4 servings.

CHICKEN-ROLLED ASPARAGUS

4 boneless, skinless chicken fillets
¼ cup sake or white wine
salt and freshly ground black pepper
12 asparagus tips or 32 to 40 green beans, trimmed
vegetable oil for frying
1 cup dashi (see page 29) or chicken stock
2 cups spinach leaves, trimmed
MUSTARD SAUCE:
2 teaspoons mustard
3 tablespoons soy sauce

Cut chicken fillets in half along natural line and slice thickest half horizontally in two.

By making a few slits on thick parts, even out thickness to make 3 thin, flat pieces, about ¼ in. thick, from each chicken fillet. Sprinkle with a little sake and salt and pepper. Parboil asparagus (or green beans) in lightly salted water and drain. Place 1 asparagus tip (or 4 or 5 green beans) on a chicken piece, roll up, and secure with wooden toothpicks. If asparagus is too long, trim to length of chicken. Repeat with remaining chicken and asparagus or beans. Heat oil in a skillet and pan-fry chicken rolls until light golden.

Add remaining sake and dashi or stock to the pan, bring to a boil, then simmer 15 minutes. Cook spinach in boiling salted water 1 minute, drain, and chop into bite-size lengths. Dissolve mustard with soy sauce and add 2 or 3 tablespoons of cooking juices to make a sauce. Cut chicken rolls into bite-size pieces. Divide spinach between 4 individual serving plates, heaping it into a nest, pour sauce over the top, then arrange chicken pieces, cut-side up, on top.

Makes 4 servings.

CHICKEN & CABBAGE ROLLS

2 cups ground chicken
1 tablespoon miso
3 tablespoon soy sauce
1 tablespoon sugar
salt
4 large leaves Savoy cabbage
4 scallions, shredded
sake
cooked and shredded carrot, to garnish
1 or 2 teaspoons mustard

Mix ground chicken, miso, 1 tablespoon soy sauce, sugar, and a little salt, and grind to a smooth paste using the back of a tablespoon.

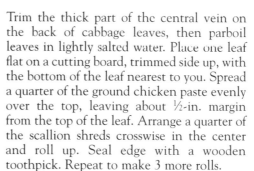

Trim the thick part of the central vein on the back of cabbage leaves, then parboil leaves in lightly salted water. Place one leaf flat on a cutting board, trimmed side up, with the bottom of the leaf nearest to you. Spread a quarter of the ground chicken paste evenly over the top, leaving about ½-in. margin from the top of the leaf. Arrange a quarter of the scallion shreds crosswise in the center and roll up. Seal edge with a wooden toothpick. Repeat to make 3 more rolls.

Place rolls on a large plate and sprinkle with sake. Place plate in a boiling steamer and steam rolls over high heat 15 minutes or until chicken meat is well cooked. Drain, remove toothpicks, and cut each roll diagonally into 4 or 5 pieces. Make a bed of shredded carrot on 4 individual serving plates and arrange pieces of roll on top. In a jug, mix mustard and remaining soy sauce with 2 or 3 tablespoons cooking juices. Pour over chicken and cabbage and serve at once.

Makes 4 servings as a starter.

BROILED SKEWERED CHICKEN

8 unskinned chicken thighs, boned and cut into
  1-in. pieces
8 scallions, white part only, cut into 1-in. lengths
24 okra, trimmed
lemon wedges, sansho bell peppers, and chili powder,
  to garnish
TARE SAUCE:
3 tablespoons sake
⅓ cup soy sauce
1 tablespoon each mirin and sugar

Mix ingredients for tare sauce in a saucepan
and bring to a boil. Remove from heat and
set aside.

If grilling, prepare grill. Thread 4 pieces of
chicken and 3 okra alternately onto an 8-in.
bamboo or stainless-steel skewer. Repeat
with another 7 skewers. Thread another
8 skewers with 4 pieces of chicken and
3 pieces of scallion. Thread any remaining
ingredients onto extra skewers. Cook on
grill, keeping skewer handles well away from
fire and turning them frequently. Brush with
tare sauce 2 or 3 times during cooking, until
chicken is well cooked and golden brown.

If broiling, preheat broiler. On a well-oiled
wire rack, spread chicken pieces well apart
and cook under broiler until both sides are
golden brown. Dip pieces in tare sauce, put
back on rack; broil another 30 seconds each
side. Set aside. Lightly broil scallions and
okra without dipping in sauce. Thread
4 chicken pieces alternately with 3 scallions
on 8 skewers and with okra on another
8 skewers. Serve on a platter, garnished with
lemon, bell peppers, and chili powder.

Makes 4 to 8 servings as a starter.

CHARBROILED YUAN CHICKEN

4 whole chicken legs, boned
8 large scallions, white part only
lime or lemon wedges, to garnish
MARINADE:
⅓ cup sake or white wine
⅓ cup mirin or 1 tablespoon sugar
⅓ cup soy sauce
zest of 1 lemon, in large pieces, not chopped
  or shredded

Place chicken legs on a cutting board, skin-
side up. Using a fork, pierce skin in a few
places. Cut scallions crosswise into 1½-in.
lengths.

In a dish, mix sake or wine, mirin or sugar,
soy sauce, and lemon zest, add chicken and
scallions, and marinate 30 minutes. If
grilling, prepare grill. Thread 3 or 4 stainless-
steel skewers through each chicken leg
parallel with skin in a fan shape. Charbroil
skin-side down, over high heat 6 or 7
minutes or until golden brown, then turn
and cook other side 3 or 4 minutes. Thread
scallions, 6 to 8 pieces to a skewer, and
charbroil. Remove skewers and serve
1 chicken leg and a quarter of the scallions
on each of 4 individual places.

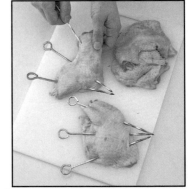

If broiling, preheat broiler. Lay chicken legs,
unskewered, flat on a wire rack, with skin
side facing heat first and broil about
10 minutes or until golden brown. Turn and
broil the other side 5 to 10 minutes or until
well cooked. Broil scallions until both sides
are golden brown. Cut chicken legs into
bite-size pieces and arrange chicken and
scallions on 4 individual plates. Serve hot,
garnished with lime or lemon wedges.

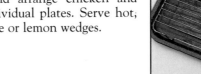

Makes 4 servings.

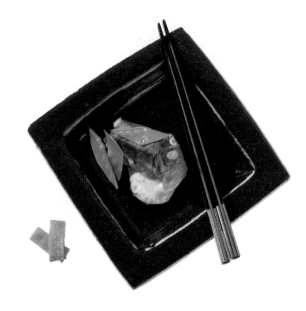

FRIED FISH-STUFFED CHICKEN

5- to 7-oz. cod fillet, skinned
salt and freshly ground black pepper
4 boneless, skinless chicken fillets
all-purpose flour for coating
1 egg, beaten
dried breadcrumbs for coating
vegetable oil for deep-frying
shredded lettuce, to serve
DIPPING SAUCE:
⅓ cup mayonnaise
1½ tablespoons soy sauce

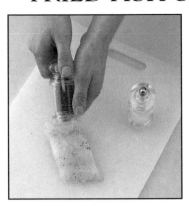

To make sauce, mix together mayonnaise and soy sauce. Set aside. Sprinkle cod fillet with a pinch of salt and pepper.

Separate one chicken fillet along its natural divide into 2 pieces and cut larger one crosswise into 4 pieces and smaller one into 2 pieces. Slice 2 thickest pieces horizontally in half to make 8 pieces of even thickness, about ¼ in. Repeat this with remaining 3 fillets. Make a deep slit horizontally in center of each piece to make chicken envelopes and stuff with small pieces of seasoned cod. The chicken should completely encase the fish.

Dust stuffed chicken with flour, dip into beaten egg, then roll in breadcrumbs and press gently to seal chicken envelope with breadcrumbs. Heat oil in a wok or deep skillet to 340°F and deep-fry chicken pieces, a few at a time, 5 or 6 minutes or until golden brown, turning frequently. Drain on a wire rack or absorbent paper towels. Make a bed of shredded lettuce on 4 individual plates. Arrange chicken on top. Serve at once with sauce.

Makes 4 servings.

COD ROE–STUFFED CHICKEN

4 chicken thighs, boned and skinned
5 oz. smoked cod roe
vegetable oil and butter for frying
sake or white wine
parboiled snow peas, to garnish
COD ROE MAYONNAISE:
¼ cup mayonnaise
1 tablespoon smoked cod roe, inside only
1 tablespoon mustard

Remove any fat from chicken thighs and place on a cutting board, skinned side down. Open up inner side by making several slits lengthwise and even out thickness.

Cut cod roe lengthwise into 5 strips and reserve one for making the sauce. Put a strip of cod roe on top of each chicken thigh, placing it lengthwise in the center. Roll into the original thigh shape and seal end with a wooden toothpick. Heat a skillet, add a little vegetable oil and a small piece of butter, and fry stuffed chicken thighs over high heat until both sides are golden brown. Drain on absorbent paper towels.

Transfer chicken to a large, deep plate or a shallow dish, and sprinkle generously with sake or white wine. Place chicken in a boiling steamer and steam vigorously 10 to 15 minutes or until well cooked. Mix mayonnaise, remaining cod roe, and mustard and place a quarter in the center of each of 4 individual plates. Remove chicken from steamer and drain. Remove toothpick and place chicken on mayonnaise. Garnish with snow peas and serve.

Makes 4 to 6 servings as a starter.

CHICKEN WITH ONION SAUCE

8 chicken thighs, boned
sake, soy sauce, and sesame oil
1 egg, beaten
1 cup broccoli florets
cornstarch for coating
vegetable oil for deep-frying
red bell pepper, shredded, to garnish
SCALLION SAUCE:
1 or 2 scallions, finely chopped
2 tablespoons each soy sauce and sake or white wine
2 tablespoons mirin or 2 teaspoons sugar
2 teaspoons sesame oil

Cut chicken, with skin on, into bite-size pieces and put in a large mixing bowl.

Sprinkle generously with sake, soy sauce, and sesame oil, and marinate about 15 minutes. Fold in beaten egg and leave another 15 minutes. Meanwhile, make scallion sauce by mixing together in a bowl scallions, soy sauce, sake (or white wine), mirin (or sugar), and sesame oil. Cook broccoli in lightly salted boiling water 3 minutes. Drain and keep warm. Roll chicken pieces in cornstarch and shake off excess.

Heat vegetable oil in a wok or deep skillet to 340°F and fry chicken pieces, several at a time, until well cooked and light golden, turning frequently. (Do not add too much chicken at a time—the pan should not be more than two-thirds full at any time.) Drain well on a wire rack or absorbent paper towels and arrange in the center of a serving platter along with broccoli. Pour sauce over the top, garnish with shredded red bell pepper, and serve at once.

Makes 4 servings.

CHICKEN WITH WASABI SAUCE

4 boneless, skinless chicken fillets
1 tablespoon sake
watercress sprigs and lemon slices, to garnish
WASABI SAUCE:
2 teaspoons wasabi paste or powder
3 tablespoons soy sauce
juice of ½ lemon
1 tablespoon sake or white wine
1 teaspoon chopped fresh chives

Inserting the knife blade diagonally, slice fillets crosswise into pieces ½ in. thick. Sprinkle with sake. To make wasabi sauce, mix wasabi paste, soy sauce, lemon juice, sake or white wine, and chopped chives. (If using wasabi powder, mix with an equal quantity of water to make a paste, then combine with other sauce ingredients.)

Cook chicken slices, a few at a time, in boiling water 2 minutes (do not overcook), then plunge into ice-cold water. Drain slices and serve on individual plates, garnished with watercress and lemon slices and accompanied by small individual bowls of wasabi sauce.

Makes 4 servings as a starter.

MEAT

BEEF

PORK

LAMB

BEEF-STUFFED CABBAGE

2 onions
⅓ cup vegetable oil
3 cloves garlic, crushed
2 fresh green chilies, seeded and chopped
3-in. piece fresh ginger, grated
2 cups lean ground beef
¼ teaspoon turmeric
2 teaspoons Garam Masala (see page 224)
1 Savoy cabbage
14½-oz. can diced tomatoes
2 tablespoons lemon juice
salt and pepper
lemon or lime slices, to garnish

Chop 1 onion and slice the other.

Heat 2 tablespoons oil in a heavy-bottomed pan, add chopped onion, and cook over a medium heat, stirring, about 8 minutes, until soft and golden brown. Add garlic, chilies, and one-third of the ginger and cook 1 minute, then remove with a slotted spoon and set aside.

Add beef to pan and cook, stirring, until browned and well broken up. Stir in turmeric and Garam Masala and cook 1 minute, then add onion mixture.

Cook, covered, 20 to 30 minutes, stirring occasionally, until cooking liquid is absorbed. Let cool. Remove core from cabbage with a sharp knife. Cook whole cabbage in boiling salted water 8 minutes, then drain and rinse in cold water. Leave until cool enough to handle, then carefully peel off 12 to 16 outside leaves, keeping them whole. Finely shred remaining cabbage.

To make sauce, heat remaining oil in a heavy-bottomed pan, add sliced onion, and cook, stirring frequently, 5 minutes or until soft but not brown. Add shredded cabbage, tomatoes, remaining ginger, lemon juice, and ⅔ cup water. Season with salt and pepper. Bring to a boil, then simmer uncovered, 5 minutes.

Preheat the oven to 375°F. Put about 2 tablespoons mince mixture on each cabbage leaf, fold sides in, and roll up neatly. Pour a little sauce into the bottom of an ovenproof casserole, add cabbage rolls, and pour remaining sauce on top. Cover and cook 40 to 50 minutes, until cabbage is tender. Serve hot, garnished with lemon or lime slices.

Makes 4 servings.

MADRAS MEAT CURRY

1½ lbs. braising steak
2 tablespoons vegetable oil
1 large onion, finely sliced
4 cloves
4 green cardamom pods, bruised
3 fresh green chilies, seeded and finely chopped
2 dried red chilies, seeded and crushed
1-in. piece fresh ginger, grated
2 cloves garlic, crushed
2 teaspoons ground coriander
2 teaspoons turmeric
¼ cup tamarind water (see page 11)
salt
lettuce leaves, to garnish

Cut beef into 1-in. cubes. Heat oil in a large, heavy-bottomed pan, add beef, and fry until browned all over. Remove with a slotted spoon and set aside. Add onion, cloves, and cardamom pods to pan and fry about 8 minutes, stirring until onion is soft and golden brown. Stir in chilies, ginger, garlic, cilantro, and turmeric, and fry 2 minutes. Return beef to pan, add ¼ cup water, and simmer, covered, 1 hour.

Stir in tamarind water and season with salt, re-cover, and simmer, covered, 15 to 30 minutes, until beef is tender. Serve garnished with lettuce leaves.

Makes 4 servings.

BEEF KABOBS

3 cups lean ground beef
1 onion, finely chopped
2-in. piece fresh ginger, grated
3 cloves garlic, crushed
1 teaspoon chili powder
1 tablespoon Garam Masala (see page 224)
1 tablespoon chopped cilantro leaves
1 tablespoon ground almonds
1 egg, beaten
¼ cup chickpea flour
⅓ cup plain yogurt
2 teaspoons vegetable oil
raw onion rings and thin lemon wedges, to garnish

In a large bowl, mix together beef, onion, ginger, garlic, chili powder, Garam Masala, cilantro, ground almonds, egg, and flour. Cover beef mixture and leave in a cool place up to 4 hours to allow flavors to blend. Shape into 16 to 20 long ovals and thread onto 4 long skewers. Mix together yogurt and oil and brush over kabobs.

Heat broiler. Cook kabobs 20 to 25 minutes, until well browned and no longer pink in centers. Baste kabobs with more yogurt and oil mixture and turn occasionally during cooking. Serve hot, garnished with onion rings and lemon wedges.

Makes 4 servings.

Note: The meatball mixture can be made up to 12 hours in advance and stored in the refrigerator.

GINGER BEEF WITH PINEAPPLE

1 lb. lean beef round or sirloin steak
salt and freshly ground black pepper
1 tablespoon sweet sherry
1-in. piece fresh ginger, peeled and finely chopped
1 clove garlic, finely chopped
1 teaspoon cornstarch
8 oz. fresh pineapple
1 tablespoon sunflower oil
2 red bell peppers, thinly sliced
4 scallions, chopped
2 tablespoons light soy sauce
1 piece candied ginger in syrup, drained and
   thinly sliced

STEAKS WITH CHILI SAUCE

4 lean beef fillet steaks, each weighing about 4 oz.
1 teaspoon dark soy sauce
1 clove garlic, finely chopped
1 teaspoon sesame oil
2 tablespoons chopped fresh chives, to garnish
CHILI SAUCE:
1 teaspoon sunflower oil
1 fresh green chili, seeded and finely chopped
1 shallot, finely chopped
1 teaspoon chili sauce
2 tablespoons red rice vinegar
¼ cup dry sherry
1 teaspoon brown sugar

Trim any visible fat from beef and cut into ¼-in. strips. Place in a bowl and season with salt and pepper. Add sherry, chopped ginger, garlic, and cornstarch, and mix well. Cover and chill 30 minutes. Meanwhile, peel and core pineapple and cut into 1-in. cubes.

Trim any fat from steaks. Tenderize lightly with a meat tenderizer or rolling pin. Preheat broiler. Place steaks on broiler rack. Mix together soy sauce, garlic, and sesame oil, and brush over steaks. Broil 3 or 4 minutes on each side, brushing with soy sauce mixture to keep steaks from drying out.

Heat oil in a wok, add beef mixture, and stir-fry 1 or 2 minutes or until beef is browned all over. Add bell peppers and stir-fry another minute. Add scallions, pineapple, and soy sauce, and simmer 2 or 3 minutes to heat through. Sprinkle with candied ginger and serve on a bed of noodles.

Makes 4 servings.

Meanwhile, make sauce. Heat oil in a wok and stir-fry chili and shallot over a low heat 1 minute. Add chili sauce, red rice vinegar, dry sherry, and brown sugar, and simmer 2 or 3 minutes. Drain cooked steaks on absorbent paper towels. Sprinkle with chives and serve with sauce and a salad.

Makes 4 servings.

MANGO BEEF WITH CASHEWS

1 lb. lean beef round or sirloin steak
1 clove garlic, finely chopped
1 tablespoon light soy sauce
1 tablespoon rice wine
1 teaspoon cornstarch
salt and freshly ground pepper
2 ripe mangoes
1 tablespoon sunflower oil
2 tablespoons chopped cilantro leaves
3 tablespoons unsalted cashews, coarsely crushed

ROAST HOISIN BEEF

1 to 1½ lbs. lean beef round
freshly ground pepper
2 cloves garlic, finely chopped
½-in. piece fresh ginger, peeled and finely chopped
2 teaspoons sesame oil
¼ cup hoisin sauce
2 cups Chinese Beef Stock (see page 16)
4 carrots
1 daikon
1 large green bell pepper
1 large yellow bell pepper
4 scallions, shredded
scallion rings, to garnish

Trim any fat from beef and cut into ¼-in. strips.

Place beef strips in a bowl and mix with garlic, soy sauce, rice wine, cornstarch, salt, and pepper. Cover and chill 30 minutes. Peel mangoes and slice flesh off large, flat pit in the center of each mango. Cut flesh into thick, even slices, reserving a few small strips for garnish.

Preheat oven to 350°F. Trim any fat from beef and place in nonstick baking pan. Season with pepper. Mix together garlic, ginger, sesame oil, and hoisin sauce, and spread over beef. Pour half the stock into the pan and roast 1 hour, basting occasionally to keep the beef from drying out.

Heat oil in a wok and stir-fry beef mixture 3 or 4 minutes or until beef is browned all over. Stir in sliced mango and cook over a low heat 2 or 3 minutes to heat through. Sprinkle with chopped cilantro and crushed cashews, garnish with reserved mango, and serve on a bed of rice.

Makes 4 servings.

Meanwhile, peel carrots and daikon. Halve carrots and slice lengthwise. Slice daikon crosswise. Quarter bell peppers. Arrange vegetables around beef, pour in remaining stock, and cook 45 to 60 minutes or until tender. Drain beef and vegetables. Slice beef and serve with vegetables, topped with shredded scallions and garnished with scallion rings.

Makes 4 servings.

BEEF WITH WATER CHESTNUTS

1 lb. lean beef round or sirloin steak
1 tablespoon dark soy sauce
1 tablespoon dry sherry
1 teaspoon chili sauce
2 teaspoons brown sugar
2 teaspoons cornstarch
1 cup broccoli florets
4-oz. can water chestnuts, drained
1 tablespoon sunflower oil
salt and freshly ground pepper
strips of fresh red chili, to garnish

Trim any fat from beef and cut into ¾-in. pieces.

Place beef in a bowl and mix with soy sauce, sherry, chili sauce, sugar, and cornstarch. Cover and chill 30 minutes. Bring a small saucepan of water to a boil and cook broccoli 3 minutes. Drain and rinse in cold water. Halve water chestnuts.

Heat oil in a wok. Add beef mixture and stir-fry 2 or 3 minutes. Add broccoli and water chestnuts, season with salt and pepper, and stir-fry 3 minutes. Garnish with red chili strips and serve with noodles.

Makes 4 servings.

SZECHUAN BEEF

1-lb. lean beef fillet
1 tablespoon sunflower oil
1 clove garlic, finely chopped
½-in. piece fresh ginger, peeled and finely chopped
4 scallions, finely chopped
1 tablespoon hoisin sauce
1 teaspoon Szechuan peppercorns, toasted and ground
4 oz. vegetables chow-chow
1 teaspoon sugar
shredded scallions, to garnish

Trim any fat and silver skin from beef. Cut beef into very thin slices.

Heat oil in a wok and stir-fry beef, garlic, ginger, and scallions 1 minute or until beef is browned.

Add hoisin sauce, Szechuan peppercorns, vegetables chow-chow, and sugar, and stir-fry 3 or 4 minutes or until beef is just cooked through. Garnish with shredded scallions and serve with rice.

Makes 4 servings.

BLACK-BEAN BEEF & RICE

1 tablespoon sunflower oil
2 shallots, chopped
2 cloves garlic, finely chopped
1 whole cinnamon stick, broken
2 star anise
8 oz. lean beef chuck, trimmed and cut into
  ¾-in. cubes
3 tablespoons fermented black beans
1¼ cups long-grain white rice, rinsed
3½ cups Chinese Beef Stock (see page 16)
salt and freshly ground pepper
2 tablespoons chopped fresh chives, to garnish

Heat oil in a wok and stir-fry shallots, garlic, cinnamon stick, star anise, beef, black beans, and rice 2 or 3 minutes or until beef is browned and rice is opaque.

Pour in stock and bring to a boil. Reduce heat and simmer 25 minutes or until liquid is absorbed and beef is tender. Discard cinnamon stick and star anise. Garnish with chives and serve with a salad.

Makes 4 servings.

STEAKS WITH SHERRY DIP

4 lean beef fillets, each weighing about 4 oz.
freshly ground pepper
1 tablespoon dry sherry
1-in. piece fresh ginger, peeled and finely chopped
1 teaspoon sesame oil
4 scallions, finely chopped, and scallion strips,
  to garnish
DIP:
2 teaspoons sunflower oil
4 scallions, finely chopped
½-in. piece fresh ginger, peeled and finely chopped
¼ cup dry sherry
2 tablespoons dark soy sauce

Trim any fat and silver skin from steaks and lightly tenderize with a meat tenderizer. Season both sides with pepper. Mix together sherry, ginger, and sesame oil. Preheat broiler. Place steaks on broiler rack and brush with sherry mixture. Broil 3 or 4 minutes on each side, basting to keep meat from drying out. Drain on absorbent paper towels.

Meanwhile, make dip. Heat oil in a wok and stir-fry scallions and ginger 2 minutes or until soft. Drain well on absorbent paper towels and place in a bowl. Mix in sherry and soy sauce. Garnish steaks with scallion and serve with dip and a salad.

Makes 4 servings.

BEEF WITH OYSTER SAUCE

GARLIC BEEF CASSEROLE

1 lb. lean beef round or sirloin steak, trimmed of fat
  and cut into ¼-in. strips
1 oz. dried Chinese mushrooms, soaked in hot water
  20 minutes
16 oyster mushrooms
1 tablespoon light soy sauce
1 tablespoon dry sherry
freshly ground pepper
2 tablespoons oyster sauce
1 tablespoon sunflower oil
2 tablespoons chopped fresh chives, to garnish

Drain soaked mushrooms, squeezing out
excess water. Discard stems and slice caps.
Slice oyster mushrooms.

Mix together soy sauce, sherry, pepper, and
oyster sauce, and set aside. Heat oil in a wok
and stir-fry beef and mushrooms 2 or 3
minutes or until beef is browned.

Stir soy sauce mixture into beef and stir-fry
2 or 3 minutes or until beef is tender.
Garnish with chives and serve on a bed of
noodles with freshly cooked vegetables.

Makes 4 servings.

1 lb. lean beef chuck, trimmed and cut into
  ¾-in. cubes
1 tablespoon peanut oil
2 shallots, chopped
4 cloves garlic, thinly sliced
2 large carrots, sliced
6 oz. baby corn, halved lengthwise
16 button mushrooms
1¼ cups Chinese Beef Stock (see page 16)
2 tablespoons dark soy sauce
1 tablespoon rice wine
2 teaspoons five-spice powder
2 tablespoons hoisin sauce
1 teaspoon chili sauce

Heat oil in a wok and stir-fry beef, shallots,
garlic, carrots, baby corn, and mushrooms
5 minutes. Add stock, soy sauce, rice wine,
five-spice powder, hoisin sauce, and chili
sauce, and bring to a boil. Reduce to a
simmer, cover, and simmer 1 hour.

Remove from heat and blot surface with
absorbent paper towels to absorb surface fat.
Increase heat and boil 10 minutes to reduce
and thicken sauce. Serve with rice.

Makes 4 servings.

BEEF IN CHILI SAUCE

8 dried red chilies, cored, seeded, and chopped
2 small onions, chopped
2-in. piece fresh ginger, chopped
1½ lbs. lean beef, cut into bite-size pieces
1 tablespoon ground coriander
1 tablespoon ground cumin
1 tablespoon tomato ketchup
2 teaspoons turmeric
2 teaspoons paprika
2 tablespoons vegetable oil
2 cloves garlic, crushed
1-in. stick cinnamon
seeds from 3 cardamom pods, crushed
sugar
salt
1 onion, sliced into thick rings

DRY BEEF WITH COCONUT

¼ cup vegetable oil
6 shallots, finely chopped
3 cloves garlic, finely chopped
1 fresh red chili, cored, seeded, and finely chopped
1½ lbs. lean beef, thinly sliced and cut into
  ½-in. strips
1 tablespoon light brown sugar
1½ teaspoons ground cumin
1 teaspoon ground coriander
squeeze of lime juice
salt
½ fresh coconut, shredded, or 2⅔ cups dried
  coconut

Put chilies in a small blender. Add ¼ cup hot water and leave until slightly softened. Add half of the small onions and half of the ginger to the blender and mix to a paste. Put beef in a large bowl. Add spice paste from blender, cilantro, cumin, tomato ketchup, turmeric, and paprika. Stir together. Cover and leave at least 1 hour to marinate.

In a wok or sauté pan, heat 1 tablespoon oil over medium heat. Add shallots, garlic, and chili, and fry about 5 minutes, stirring occasionally, until softened but not browned. Add beef, sugar, cumin, cilantro, lime juice, salt to taste, and ⅔ cup water. Cover pan tightly and simmer gently 30 minutes, stirring occasionally.

In a wok, heat oil over medium-high heat. Add remaining onion and ginger and garlic. Fry, stirring, 3 minutes or until lightly browned. Stir in cinnamon stick and cardamom and stir-fry 1 minute. Add meat and marinade and stir-fry 5 minutes. Add 1½ cups water, and sugar and salt to taste. Cover pan. Simmer very gently 1¼ hours or until beef is tender. Stir occasionally. Add onion rings and cook 3 to 5 minutes or until soft.

Makes 4 to 6 servings.

Uncover pan and stir in coconut until all liquid has been absorbed. Stir in remaining oil and continue stirring until coconut begins to brown.

Makes 6 servings.

SINGAPORE STEAMBOAT

6-oz. beef fillet, well chilled
6-oz. pork fillet or tenderloin, well chilled
6-oz. lamb fillet, well chilled
6-oz. boneless, skinless chicken fillet, well chilled
12 oz. rice vermicelli
4 oz. each snow peas, green beans, baby corn, oyster
   mushrooms, shiitake mushrooms, asparagus spears,
   cut into bite-size pieces

Thinly slice beef, pork, lamb, and chicken.
Cover with plastic wrap and set aside. Cook
noodles according to package directions.
Drain, then rinse under running cold water.
Drain again, cover, and set aside.

SHRIMP BALLS
12 oz. raw, peeled shrimp
1½ to 2½ teaspoons cornstarch
2 small scallions, finely chopped
1 small egg white, lightly beaten

Put shrimp and 1½ teaspoons cornstarch
into blender and mix until smooth. Mix in
scallion. Stir in egg white and more
cornstarch if necessary to bind mixture,
which should be firm enough to handle.
With wet hands, roll mixture into walnut-
size balls. Refrigerate until required.

CHILI VINEGAR
3 tablespoons rice vinegar
2 teaspoons sugar
½ or 1 fresh red chili, cored, seeded, and sliced
1½ tablespoons water

DIPPING SAUCE
2 tablespoons tomato paste
1 teaspoon soy sauce
1 teaspoon toasted sesame oil
1 fresh red chili, cored, seeded, and finely chopped
2 tablespoons water

In two bowls, mix together all ingredients for
chili vinegar and dipping sauce.

COCONUT SAUCE
2 teaspoons peanut oil
1 small onion, finely chopped
2-in. stalk lemongrass, bruised and thinly sliced
¼ teaspoon crushed coriander seeds
3-oz. piece creamed coconut
about 3 tablespoons stock

In a skillet or saucepan, heat oil. Add onion,
lemongrass, and coriander seeds, and fry
until onion has softened. Stir in coconut
cream until melted. Add enough stock to
make a dipping sauce.

STOCK
4 cups chicken or vegetable stock
1½ tablespoons chopped cilantro
2-in. lemongrass stalk (thick end), thinly sliced
2 scallions, thinly sliced

Place all stock ingredients in a saucepan and
bring to a boil, then pour into a warm fondue
pot or heavy, flameproof casserole set over a
burner. Diners serve themselves by dipping
meat, shrimp balls, and vegetables into stock
to cook, then transferring them to plates to
eat with sauces and chili vinegar.

When all meat, fish, and vegetables have
been eaten, either warm noodles in hot pot
or dunk them in a bowl or saucepan of
boiling water, then drain and divide them
among bowls. Ladle remaining stock, which
will have become concentrated, into bowls.

Makes 6 servings.

Note: Use fondue forks, chopsticks, Chinese
wire mesh baskets, or long wooden skewers
to serve.

STIR-FRIED BEEFSTEAK

SPICY BEEF STEW

8 oz. beefsteak, cut into small, thin slices about
    1 in. square
¼ teaspoon freshly ground black pepper
1 teaspoon sugar
1 tablespoon fish sauce
2 tablespoons vegetable oil
1 clove garlic, chopped
1 small onion, sliced
1 green bell pepper, cored and cut into cubes
4 oz. sliced bamboo shoots, drained
1 firm tomato, cut into 8 wedges
2 scallions, cut into short lengths
2 tablespoons soy or oyster sauce
2 teaspoons cornstarch

1 tablespoon vegetable oil
2 cloves garlic, chopped
1 onion, chopped
1 stalk lemongrass, chopped
1 lb. stewing beef, cut into bite-size cubes
2½ cups stock or water
⅓ cup soy or fish sauce
1 teaspoon chili sauce
2 teaspoons five-spice powder
1 tablespoon sugar
2 or 3 scallions, chopped
freshly ground black pepper
cilantro sprigs, to garnish

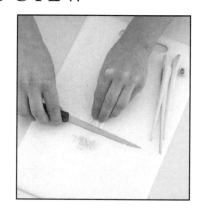

Mix beef with black pepper, sugar, and fish
sauce, and marinate 15 to 20 minutes. Heat
oil in a wok or skillet and stir-fry garlic and
onion about 1 minute. Add beef and stir-fry
1 minute.

Heat oil in a clay or flameproof casserole and
stir-fry garlic, onion, and lemongrass about
1 minute. Add beef and stir-fry 2 or 3
minutes or until color of meat changes. Add
stock or water, bring to a boil, then add soy
or fish sauce, chili sauce, five-spice powder,
and sugar. Blend well, then reduce heat,
cover, and simmer gently 45 to 50 minutes.

Add green bell pepper, bamboo shoots,
tomato, and scallions. Continue stir-frying
2 or 3 minutes, then blend in soy or oyster
sauce. Mix cornstarch with 1 tablespoon
water and stir into mixture. Cook, stirring,
until thickened. Serve with rice noodles.

Makes 4 servings.

Add scallions, season with pepper, and cook
an additional 5 minutes. Garnish with
cilantro sprigs and serve straight from the
pot.

Makes 4 servings.

Variation: Substitute curry powder for five-
spice powder to make beef curry.

BEEF & SEAFOOD HOT POT

8-oz. beef fillet, very thinly sliced
4-oz. firm white fish fillet, thinly sliced
4 oz. prepared squid
6 raw, peeled shrimp, cut in half lengthwise
1 tomato, thinly sliced
1 onion, thinly sliced
freshly ground black pepper
1 tablespoon sesame oil
2 teaspoons vegetable oil
1 clove garlic, chopped
2 shallots, chopped
1 tablespoon tomato paste
1 tablespoon sugar
1 teaspoon salt
2 tablespoons rice vinegar
3 cups stock or water

ACCOMPANIMENTS:
2 oz. bean thread vermicelli, soaked then cut into
    short lengths
6 to 8 Chinese dried mushrooms, soaked and cut
    in half or quartered
1 lb. 2 oz. tofu, cut into small cubes
about 1 cup shredded bok choy leaves
dried rice paper or lettuce leaves
fresh mint and cilantro leaves
Spicy Fish Sauce (see page 233)

Arrange vermicelli, mushrooms, tofu cubes, and bok choy on a serving platter in separate sections.

Arrange beef, fish, squid, and shrimp on a platter in separate sections. Place tomato and onion slices in the center and sprinkle pepper and sesame oil all over them. Set aside while you prepare the broth.

If using large sheets of rice paper, cut in half; if using lettuce leaves, separate them. Place on a serving dish. Place spicy sauce in individual small saucers for dipping. To serve, bring boiling broth in the hot pot or fondue pot to the table. Diners pick up a slice of beef or some seafood with vegetables and dip them into the broth to be cooked very briefly—usually no longer than 1 minute.

Heat vegetable oil in a saucepan and stir-fry garlic and shallots about 30 seconds, then add tomato paste, sugar, salt, and rice vinegar. Blend well, then add stock or water, bring to a boil, and transfer to a Chinese hot pot or fondue pot.

Meanwhile, they dip a piece of rice paper in hot water to soften it, then quickly remove food from broth and place in the center of the rice paper or a lettuce leaf. They can then add a few mint and cilantro leaves, then fold over to make a neat package, dipping package in Spicy Fish Sauce before eating it.

Makes 4 to 6 servings.

BEEF TATAKI

1 lb. lean sirloin steak
salt and vegetable oil for brushing
2 scallions, finely chopped
1-in. piece fresh ginger, peeled and grated
1 tablespoon wasabi paste
½ cucumber
lime slices and watercress, to garnish
DAIKON DIP:
3-in. daikon, peeled and shredded
3 tablespoons soy sauce
juice of ½ lime

Preheat broiler. Trim fat from meat, sprinkle with a pinch of salt, and brush with oil.

Quickly brown meat under a high broiler 2 or 3 minutes on each side. Remove from heat and immediately plunge into ice-cold water to stop further cooking. Traditionally, the meat should be golden brown outside but rare inside. Drain, pat dry, and set aside while preparing daikon dip. Mix shredded daikon, soy sauce, and lime juice in a serving bowl. Arrange chopped scallions, grated ginger, and wasabi in separate heaps on a small plate. Cut cucumber in half lengthwise, then slice crosswise into paper-thin half-moons.

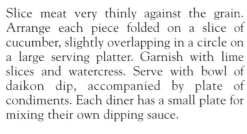

Slice meat very thinly against the grain. Arrange each piece folded on a slice of cucumber, slightly overlapping in a circle on a large serving platter. Garnish with lime slices and watercress. Serve with bowl of daikon dip, accompanied by plate of condiments. Each diner has a small plate for mixing their own dipping sauce.

Makes 4 to 6 servings.

SIMMERED BEEF & POTATOES

10-oz. piece lean beef
5 medium potatoes, peeled
2 Spanish onions
2 tablespoons vegetable oil
⅓ cup sugar
⅓ cup soy sauce
dashi (see page 29) or water
parboiled snow peas, to garnish

Put beef in the freezer about 1 hour to harden a bit, then slice very thinly against the grain into bite-size pieces.

Quarter each potato and boil until tender but still slightly hard in the center. Drain and set aside. Cut onions into thin half-moon slices. In a skillet or a shallow saucepan, heat a little vegetable oil and stir-fry beef slices over medium heat. When beef begins to change color, add potatoes and continue to stir. Add sugar and soy sauce to the pan and lightly fold in. Pour in enough dashi or water to just cover ingredients and bring to a boil. Skim the surface to remove any fat and lower the heat.

Place a small, wooden lid or a plate touching the ingredients inside the pan and simmer over medium heat 10 minutes. Add onion slices and continue to cook until all ingredients are tender and have absorbed the flavor. Serve in small individual bowls garnished with snow peas.

Makes 4 servings.

MIXED GRIDDLE

10-oz. beef sirloin or round, or 2 boneless, skinless
  chicken fillets
1 squid, cleaned (optional)
4 to 8 scallops or raw jumbo shrimp, peeled
4 to 8 fresh shiitake or button mushrooms,
  stalks removed
1 red or green bell pepper, seeded
2 cups bean sprouts, trimmed
1 lemon, cut into wedges
2 or 3 scallions, finely chopped
vegetable oil for frying
DIPPING SAUCE:
6-in. daikon, peeled
1 fresh or dried chili
soy sauce

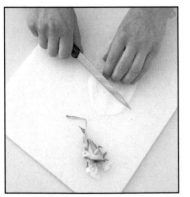

Prepare wafer-thin beef slices following the
method used for Sukiyaki, opposite. Skin
squid by holding two flaps together and
peeling down; cut in half lengthwise. Put
fillets on a cutting board, skinned-side up,
and make fine cross-slits on them with a
sharp knife. Cut fillets and flaps into 1-in.-
square pieces. Separate tentacles, if large.
Arrange meat and fish on separate platters. If
mushrooms are large, cut them in half. Slice
pepper into thin strips. Arrange all
vegetables on a platter.

Make "autumn maple leaf" relish following
method on page 145, or, alternatively, shred
daikon, finely chop fresh chili, and simply
mix together. Arrange daikon relish, lemon
wedges, and scallion in a serving bowl or on
a small plate. Place a hotplate in the center
of the dining table set with small individual
bowls. Serve meat, fish, and vegetable
platters and condiments: diners mix their
own sauce, adding soy sauce to taste, and fry
their portion themselves.

Makes 4 to 6 servings.

SUKIYAKI (PAN-COOKED BEEF)

1 lb. beef sirloin or round
2 leeks, white part only
8 fresh or dried shiitake or button mushrooms,
  stalks removed if fresh
sugar
9 oz. tofu
1 cup watercress, trimmed
2-in. square beef fat
⅓ cup sake or white wine
¼ cup soy sauce

Trim any fat from beef and cut beef into
3 x 1½-in. flat pieces.

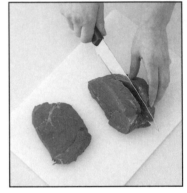

Place beef pieces in separate freezer bags and
freeze 1 to 2 hours. Remove from freezer and
leave until half-thawed. Cut beef into wafer-
thin slices and arrange in a circular fan on a
large platter. Slice leeks diagonally. If
shiitake mushrooms are large, cut in half. If
using dried shiitake, soak in warm water with
a pinch of sugar 45 minutes, then remove
stalks. Cut tofu into 16 cubes. Arrange all
vegetables and tofu on a large platter.

Place a cast-iron pan on a portable gas ring
or electric hotplate on the table together
with platters of raw ingredients, jugs of water
and soy sauce, sake, and a sugar pot. Melt
beef fat in the pan and move around to oil
the entire bottom. Cook a few slices
of beef first and sprinkle with about
2 tablespoons sugar. Pour in sake and soy
sauce and add water to taste. Diners serve
themselves using individual small bowls.

Makes 4 servings.

SHABUSHABU (BEEF HOT POT)

1 lb. beef sirloin or round
2 leeks, white part only
8 fresh or dried shiitake or 12 button mushrooms,
　stalks removed
9 oz. firm tofu
4 to 6 Chinese cabbage leaves
2½ cups spinach leaves, trimmed
4-in. piece dried konbu (kelp)
10 oz. udon noodles, cooked (optional)
finely chopped scallions, to garnish
CITRUS DIP:
½ daikon, peeled
1 dried or fresh red chili
2 scallions, finely chopped
juice of ½ lemon and ½ lime
½ cup soy sauce

SESAME DIP:
¼ cup sesame paste or smooth peanut butter
½ cup dashi (see page 29)
3 tablespoons soy sauce
1 tablespoon mirin or sweet sherry
1 tablespoon sugar
2 tablespoons sake or white wine
2 teaspoons chili oil or chili powder (optional)

Trim fat from beef and cut into 3 x 1½-in. flat pieces. Place in separate freezer bags and freeze 1 to 2 hours.

Remove from freezer and leave until half-thawed, then cut beef into wafer-thin slices and arrange in a circular fan on a large platter. Slice leeks diagonally. If shiitake mushrooms are large, cut in half. If using dried shiitake, soak in warm water with a pinch of sugar 45 minutes, then remove stalks before use. Cut tofu into 16 cubes. Cut Chinese cabbage and spinach into bite-size pieces. Arrange vegetables and tofu on a large platter.

To prepare citrus dip, first make "autumn maple leaf" relish by poking a chopstick into daikon to make a few holes lengthwise. Push in red chili strips and shred to make rust-colored daikon. (Alternatively, shred daikon very finely, chop chili, then mix together.) Put relish, chopped scallion, a mixture of lemon and lime juices, and soy sauce in separate small bowls. To make sesame dip, mix all ingredients together and stir until sesame paste (or peanut butter) is of a smooth, runny consistency. Divide between 4 to 6 individual dipping bowls.

Put konbu in a large pot (ideally a clay pot, an enamelled cast-iron casserole, or a copper-bottomed Mongolian hot pot) and fill two-thirds full with water. Bring to a boil and remove konbu. Put in some of the leek, Chinese cabbage, shiitake mushrooms, spinach, and tofu, and when it begins to come back to a boil, transfer the pot to a portable gas ring or electric hotplate on the dining table. Diners make their own citrus dip in individual dipping bowls by mixing 1 or 2 teaspoons each of relish, scallion, and citrus juice with some soy sauce.

Diners serve themselves by cooking meat in the pot, adding more vegetables, and eating them dipped in either of the sauces. When ingredients are finished, skim and season the soup with soy sauce and a little salt and sugar. If using noodles, warm them in the soup, seasoned with a little soy sauce to taste, so that diners can end the meal with plain noodles garnished with chopped scallion.

Makes 4 to 6 servings.

PORK IN SPINACH SAUCE

6 cups fresh spinach leaves, well rinsed
salt
1½ lbs. lean boneless pork
3 tablespoons vegetable oil
2 onions, finely sliced
4 cloves garlic, crushed
1-in. piece fresh ginger, grated
3 tablespoons Garam Masala (see page 224)
½ teaspoon turmeric
1 bay leaf
2 tomatoes, skinned and chopped
2 fresh chilies, seeded and chopped
⅔ cup plain yogurt
tomato slices and bay leaves, to garnish

Trim stems from spinach and cook leaves in boiling salted water 2 or 3 minutes, until tender. Drain thoroughly and rinse under cold running water. Put in a blender or food processor fitted with a metal blade and process to a smooth purée. Set aside. Preheat oven to 325°F. Cut pork into 1-in. cubes. Heat oil in a large skillet and fry pork until browned all over. Transfer to a casserole using a slotted spoon.

Add onions to skillet and cook, stirring, 10 or 15 minutes, until a rich brown. Add garlic, ginger, Garam Masala, turmeric, bay leaf, tomatoes, and chilies. Cook, stirring, 2 or 3 minutes, until tomatoes have softened. Add yogurt and ⅔ cup water and stir. Pour over pork, cover, and cook 1¼ to 1½ hours, until pork is cooked through. Remove bay leaf, stir in spinach and salt, re-cover, and cook an additional 10 minutes. Garnish and serve.

Makes 4 servings.

HOT SPICY RIBS

2 to 2½ lbs. meaty pork spareribs
3 tablespoons Hot Spice Mix (see page 224)
1 teaspoon turmeric
2-in. piece fresh ginger, grated
1 small onion, finely chopped
1 tablespoon white wine vinegar
1 tablespoon tomato paste
scallions and tomatoes, to garnish

Cut ribs into single rib pieces and chop into 3-in. lengths.

Place ribs in a large saucepan, cover with cold water, and bring to a boil, then simmer 15 minutes; drain. Put hot spice mix, turmeric, ginger, onion, vinegar, and tomato paste in a blender or food processor fitted with a metal blade. Add ⅓ cup water and process until smooth.

Place ribs in a nonmetallic dish, pour over spice mixture, and stir to coat well. Cover loosely and leave in a cool place 2 to 3 hours. Transfer ribs to a broiler pan. Heat broiler. Cook ribs about 15 minutes, turning occasionally and basting with any remaining marinade, until well browned and very tender. Serve hot, garnished with scallions and tomatoes.

Makes 4 servings.

HAM & SHRIMP BEAN SPROUTS

3 cups bean sprouts
1 tablespoon sunflower oil
4 oz. lean ham, trimmed and diced
4 oz. cooked, peeled large shrimp, thawed and dried
   if frozen
1 bunch scallions, finely chopped
1 green bell pepper, chopped
2 tablespoons light soy sauce
salt and freshly ground pepper
2 tablespoons chopped fresh chives, to garnish

Cook bean sprouts in boiling water a few seconds or until soft. Drain and rinse in cold water. Dry on absorbent paper towels.

Heat oil in a wok and stir-fry ham, shrimp, scallions, and bell pepper 2 or 3 minutes or until lightly golden.

Add soy sauce, bean sprouts, salt, and pepper, and stir-fry 2 minutes to heat through. Garnish with chopped chives and serve with rice.

Makes 4 servings.

HOT SWEET PORK

12-oz. lean pork fillet
1 tablespoon light soy sauce
1 tablespoon rice wine
freshly ground pepper
1 tablespoon cornstarch
1 tablespoon sunflower oil
2 fresh red chilies, seeded and chopped
1 clove garlic, finely chopped
1 red bell pepper, diced
1 large zucchini, diced
4-oz. can bamboo shoots, drained
2 tablespoons red rice vinegar
2 tablespoons brown sugar
large pinch salt
1 tablespoon sesame seeds
strips of fresh red chili, to garnish

Trim any fat and silver skin from pork fillet. Cut into ½-in. strips. Place in a bowl and mix with soy sauce, rice wine, pepper, and cornstarch. Cover and chill 30 minutes.

Heat oil in a wok and stir-fry pork mixture 1 or 2 minutes or until pork is browned. Add chilies, garlic, red bell pepper, zucchini, bamboo shoots, rice vinegar, sugar, and salt, and stir-fry 4 or 5 minutes or until vegetables are just cooked through. Sprinkle with sesame seeds, garnish with chili strips, and serve with noodles.

Makes 4 servings.

BROILED CITRUS PORK CHOPS

PORK WITH WALNUTS

4 lean pork chops, each weighing about 4 oz.
grated zest and juice of 1 lime, 1 small lemon, and
  1 small orange
1 teaspoon sesame oil
2 tablespoons dry sherry
2 tablespoons light soy sauce
1 tablespoon sugar
large pinch ground white pepper
1 teaspoon cornstarch mixed with 2 teaspoons water
lime, lemon, and orange slices and strips of zest,
  to garnish

Trim fat from chops and score in a crisscross pattern. Place in a shallow dish, sprinkle with citrus zests, and top with juices.

Cover and chill 30 minutes. Drain chops well, reserving juices. Preheat broiler. Place chops on broiler rack and brush lightly with sesame oil. Broil 3 or 4 minutes on each side or until cooked through. Drain on absorbent paper towels and keep warm. Place reserved juices in a small saucepan with sherry, soy sauce, sugar, pepper, and cornstarch mixture. Bring to a boil, stirring until thickened.

Slice pork chops and arrange on serving plates with lime, lemon, and orange slices. Top with sauce and garnish with strips of citrus zest to serve.

Makes 4 servings.

1-lb. lean pork fillet
1 tablespoon rice wine
1 tablespoon light soy sauce
1 teaspoon cornstarch
1 bunch scallions
2 teaspoons sunflower oil
1 teaspoon sugar
salt and freshly ground pepper
¼ cup walnut pieces

Trim any fat and silver skin from pork and cut fillet into ¼-in. strips. Place in a bowl and mix in rice wine, soy sauce, and cornstarch. Cover and chill 30 minutes.

Trim scallions, discarding any damaged outer leaves. Cut scallions into 2-in. pieces.

Heat oil in a wok and stir-fry pork mixture 2 or 3 minutes or until browned. Add scallions, sugar, salt, and pepper, and stir-fry 3 minutes. Sprinkle with walnut pieces and serve with noodles.

Makes 4 servings.

DRY PORK CURRY

12 oz. lean boneless pork, trimmed and cut into
  ¾-in. cubes
1 tablespoon light brown sugar
2 or 3 medium potatoes
2 or 3 medium carrots
13 shallots
1 tablespoon sunflower oil
1-in. piece fresh ginger, peeled and finely chopped
2 tablespoons Madras curry paste
⅔ cup coconut milk
1¼ cups Chinese Chicken Stock (see page 16)
salt and freshly ground pepper
2 tablespoons chopped cilantro leaves

ROAST PORK WITH HONEY

1-lb. piece lean pork fillet
¼ cup chopped cilantro leaves
GLAZE:
1 teaspoon Szechuan peppercorns, toasted and ground
1 tablespoon honey
2 teaspoons brown sugar
1 tablespoon dark soy sauce
1-in. piece fresh ginger, peeled and finely chopped
1 clove garlic, finely chopped

Preheat oven to 375°F. Trim any fat and
silver skin from pork and place fillet on a
rack in a baking pan. Pour in enough water
to cover bottom of pan.

In a bowl, mix together pork and brown
sugar and set aside. Cut potatoes and carrots
into ¾-in. chunks. Peel and halve shallots.

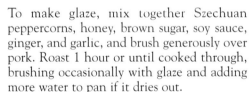

To make glaze, mix together Szechuan
peppercorns, honey, brown sugar, soy sauce,
ginger, and garlic, and brush generously over
pork. Roast 1 hour or until cooked through,
brushing occasionally with glaze and adding
more water to pan if it dries out.

Heat oil in a wok and stir-fry pork, ginger,
potatoes, carrots, and shallots 2 or 3 minutes
or until lightly browned. Blend curry paste
with coconut milk, stock, salt, and pepper.
Stir into pork mixture and bring to a boil.
Reduce heat and simmer 40 minutes.
Sprinkle with cilantro and serve on a bed of
rice.

Makes 4 servings.

Remove cooked pork from rack and sprinkle
with chopped cilantro until coated all over.
Slice and serve with rice and vegetables.

Makes 4 servings.

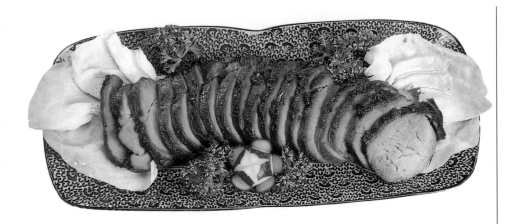

CHAI SUI ROAST PORK

2 tablespoons rice wine or dry sherry
3 tablespoons brown sugar
3 tablespoons groundnut (peanut) oil
1 tablespoon yellow bean paste
2 tablespoons dark soy sauce
2 tablespoons red fermented tofu
450 g (1 lb) pork fillet

In a bowl, mix together rice wine or dry sherry, brown sugar, groundnut oil, yellow bean paste, soy sauce and fermented tofu.

Spoon sauce over pork and leave to marinate at room temperature for 1 hour. Meanwhile, pre-heat oven to 200C (400F/Gas 6).

Put pork fillet on a rack in a roasting tin and roast for 15-20 minutes until juices run clear and outside is richly coloured.

Serves 4.

PORK WITH CASHEW NUTS

1 teaspoon rice wine or dry sherry
1 teaspoon sea salt
1 teaspoon sugar
1 tablespoon cornflour
450 g (1 lb) pork tenderloin, cubed
550 ml (20 fl oz/2½ cups) groundnut (peanut) oil
115 g (4 oz/¾ cup) cashew nuts
3 cloves garlic, finely chopped
2 spring onions, coarsely chopped
4 dried winter mushrooms, soaked in hot water for 25 minutes, drained
½ red pepper and ½ green pepper, seeded and diced
1 teaspoon light soy sauce
¼ teaspoon ground white pepper
70 ml (2½ fl oz/⅓ cup) Chinese Chicken Stock (see page 16)

In a bowl, mix together rice wine or dry sherry, ½ teaspoon of sea salt, sugar and 2 teaspoons of cornflour. Stir in pork to coat evenly. Leave for 30 minutes. In a wok, heat oil until very hot, add pork and deep-fry for 3-4 minutes until cooked through. Using a slotted spoon, lift out pork and drain on absorbent kitchen paper. Place cashew nuts in a small wire basket, lower into oil and deep-fry for a few seconds until lightly coloured. Drain on absorbent kitchen paper.

Pour oil from wok, leaving 1 tablespoonful. Add garlic, fry briefly, then add spring onions, mushrooms and red and green pepper. Continue cooking for 3-4 minutes. In a bowl, mix together soy sauce, ground white pepper, stock and remaining ½ teaspoon of salt and 1 teaspoon of cornflour. Stir into wok and simmer until sauce has thickened. Stir in pork and heat through gently.

Serves 4.

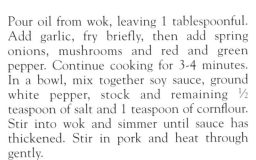

SWEET AND SOUR PORK

SZECHUAN PORK

2 teaspoons rice wine or dry sherry
1 large egg, beaten
½ teaspoon sea salt
1 lb. belly pork, cubed
1 cup cornstarch
2½ cups peanut oil
3 scallions, thinly sliced
3-oz. can bamboo shoots, drained, thinly sliced
1 green bell pepper, seeded and thinly sliced
2 cloves garlic, finely chopped
1 teaspoon sesame oil
SAUCE:
2 tablespoons brown sugar
1 tablespoon vegetable oil
3 tablespoons malt vinegar
1 teaspoon cornstarch

3 tablespoons vegetable oil
6 oz. Szechuan preserved cabbage, soaked 1 hour, drained and shredded
1 lb. pork tenderloin, very thinly sliced
3 scallions, finely chopped
3 slices fresh ginger, peeled and finely chopped
1 fresh red chili, seeded and very finely sliced
1 red bell pepper, seeded and cut into strips
1 tablespoon light soy sauce
2 tablespoons rice wine or dry sherry
½ teaspoon brown sugar

In a bowl, mix together rice wine or dry sherry, egg, and salt. Stir in pork to coat evenly. Remove pork and roll in cornstarch to coat evenly. In a wok, heat peanut oil until smoking and deep-fry pork about 5 minutes or until crisp and well cooked. Using a slotted spoon, lift pork from oil and drain on absorbent paper towels. Pour oil from wok, leaving just 2 tablespoonsful. Add scallions, bamboo shoots, green bell pepper, and garlic, and stir-fry 3 minutes. Stir in pork and mix thoroughly.

In a wok, heat oil, add cabbage and pork, and stir-fry 2 minutes or until pork changes color. Stir in scallions, ginger, chili, and pepper.

To make sauce, in a saucepan, stir together brown sugar, vegetable oil, malt vinegar, and cornstarch, and place over a moderate heat 4 minutes, stirring continuously until hot and well blended. Pour over pork and briefly heat together. Sprinkle with sesame oil and serve.

Makes 4 servings.

In a small bowl, mix together soy sauce, rice wine or dry sherry, and brown sugar. Stir into wok and cook 2 minutes.

Makes 4 servings.

MIXED SATAY

12-oz. pork fillet, chilled, thinly sliced
12-oz. steak, chilled, thinly sliced
½ lime
2 teaspoons ground coriander
2 teaspoons ground cumin
1 teaspoon ground turmeric
1 tablespoon light brown sugar
¼ cup coconut milk
12 large raw shrimp, peeled, tails left on, deveined
oil for brushing
Satay Sauce (see page 227)

Lay each pork slice between sheets of plastic wrap and beat with a rolling pin until fairly thin. Cut slices into 1-in.-wide strips.

Cut steak into strips about the same size as pork. Put meats into a nonreactive bowl and squeeze lime juice on top. In a small bowl, mix together cilantro, cumin, turmeric, sugar, and coconut milk to make a fairly dry paste. Add shrimp to dish with meat and spoon coconut mixture over to coat thoroughly. Cover and marinate 1 hour or overnight in a refrigerator.

Prepare grill or preheat broiler. Soak bamboo skewers in water 20 to 30 minutes. Thread pork strips, steak strips, and shrimp onto separate skewers. Brush with oil and cook at a very high heat 10 minutes, turning frequently. Shrimp should have turned opaque with bright pink tails, pork should be cooked through, and beef still be pink in the center. Meanwhile, heat satay sauce. Serve sauce with skewers.

Makes 6 servings.

PORK WITH TAMARIND

4 dried red chilies, cored and seeded
1 large onion, chopped
4 candlenuts or cashews
2 tablespoons vegetable oil
1½ lbs. pork shoulder, cut into large, bite-size pieces
2 tablespoons tamarind paste (see page 11)
2 tablespoons dark soy sauce
1 tablespoon yellow bean sauce
1 tablespoon light brown sugar
sliced fresh chilies, to garnish (optional)

Put chilies in a blender. Add ¼ cup hot water and leave until slightly softened. Add onion and nuts; mix to a smooth paste.

In a sauté pan, preferably nonstick, heat oil over medium-high heat. Add meat in batches and fry until an even light brown. Using a slotted spoon, transfer to absorbent paper towels to drain.

Add chili paste to pan and fry about 5 minutes. Stir in pork, tamarind paste, soy sauce, yellow bean sauce, sugar, and 1½ cups water. Bring to a simmer, cover pan, then cook gently 30 to 40 minutes, stirring occasionally, until pork is very tender. Serve garnished with sliced fresh chilies, if desired.

Makes 4 servings.

PORK WITH WATER CHESTNUTS

1½ tablespoons vegetable oil
4 cloves garlic, chopped
2 fresh red chilies, seeded and finely chopped
12 oz. lean pork, cubed
10 canned water chestnuts, chopped
1 teaspoon fish sauce
freshly ground black pepper
3 tablespoons chopped cilantro leaves
6 scallions, chopped
3 or 4 scallion brushes (see page 14), to garnish

GRILLED SPARERIBS

2 tablespoons chopped cilantro stalks
3 cloves garlic, chopped
1 teaspoon black peppercorns, cracked
1 teaspoon grated kaffir lime zest
1 tablespoon Green Curry Paste (see page 230)
2 teaspoons fish sauce
1½ teaspoons crushed palm sugar
¾ cup coconut milk
2 lbs. pork spareribs, trimmed
scallion brushes (see page 14), to garnish

In a wok, heat oil, add garlic and chilies, and cook, stirring occasionally, until garlic becomes golden.

Using a mortar and pestle or small blender, pound or mix together cilantro, garlic, peppercorns, lime zest, curry paste, fish sauce, and sugar. Stir in coconut milk. Place spareribs in a shallow dish and pour over spiced coconut mixture. Cover and leave in a cool place 3 hours, basting occasionally.

Stir in pork and stir-fry about 2 minutes or until almost cooked through. Add water chestnuts, heat 2 minutes, then stir in fish sauce, ¼ cup water, and plenty of black pepper. Stir in cilantro and scallions. Serve garnished with scallion brushes.

Makes 3 or 4 servings.

Prepare grill or heat broiler. Cook ribs about 5 minutes a side, over moderate heat, until cooked through and brown, basting occasionally with coconut mixture. Garnish with scallion brushes.

Makes 4 to 6 servings.

Note: The ribs can also be cooked on a rack in a baking pan in an oven preheated to 400°F, 45 to 60 minutes. Baste occasionally.

STIR-FRIED PORK & BEANS

2 tablespoons vegetable oil
6 cloves garlic, chopped
12 oz. lean pork, finely chopped
12 oz. long beans or green beans
12 water chestnuts
4 oz. cooked, peeled shrimp
1 tablespoon fish sauce
½ teaspoon crushed palm sugar
freshly ground black pepper

In a wok, heat oil, add garlic, and fry, stirring occasionally, until golden.

Add pork and beans and stir-fry 2 minutes, then add water chestnuts. Stir 1 minute.

Add shrimp, fish sauce, sugar, plenty of black pepper, and about 3 tablespoons water. Simmer a minute or two, then transfer to a warmed serving plate.

Makes 4 servings.

THAI PORK CURRY

½ cup coconut cream (see page 8)
1 onion, chopped
1 clove garlic, finely crushed
2 tablespoons Fragrant Curry Paste (see page 231)
2 teaspoons fish sauce
½ teaspoon crushed palm sugar
12 oz. lean pork, diced
3 kaffir lime leaves, shredded
25 Thai holy basil leaves
1 long fresh red chili, seeded and cut into strips, and Thai holy basil sprig, to garnish

In a wok, heat ⅓ cup coconut cream until oil begins to separate. Stir in onion and garlic and cook, stirring occasionally, until lightly browned. Stir in curry paste and continue to stir about 2 minutes. Stir in fish sauce and sugar, then pork to coat. Cook 3 or 4 minutes.

Add lime and basil leaves and cook an additional 1 minute. If necessary, add a little water, but final dish should be dry. Serve garnished with a trail of remaining coconut cream, chili strips, and basil sprig.

Makes 3 servings.

PORK WITH SCALLIONS

2½ cups coconut milk
1 lb. lean pork, cut into 1-in. cubes
1 tablespoon fish sauce
½ teaspoon crushed palm sugar
⅔ cup skinned peanuts
3 fresh red chilies, seeded and chopped
1¼-in. piece galangal, chopped
4 cloves garlic
1 stalk lemongrass
¼ cup coconut cream (see page 8)
8 scallions, chopped
8 cups young spinach leaves
warmed coconut cream (see page 8) and dry-roasted
  peanuts, to serve

In a wok, heat coconut milk until just simmering; adjust heat so liquid barely moves. Add pork and cook about 25 minutes or until very tender. Meanwhile, using a small blender or food processor, mix fish sauce, sugar, peanuts, chilies, galangal, garlic, and lemongrass to a paste. In another wok or a skillet, heat coconut cream until oil separates. Add scallions and peanut paste and cook, stirring frequently, 2 or 3 minutes.

Stir in milk from pork and boil until lightly thickened. Pour over pork, stir, and cook an additional 5 minutes. Rinse spinach leaves, then pack into a saucepan with just the water left on them. Gently cook about 3 minutes or until just beginning to wilt. Arrange on a warmed serving plate. Spoon pork and sauce onto center. Trickle coconut cream on top and sprinkle with dry-roasted peanuts.

Makes 4 to 6 servings.

MIXED VEGETABLES & PORK

8 oz. lean pork, finely chopped
freshly ground black pepper
2 tablespoons vegetable oil
3 cloves garlic, finely chopped
1 lb. prepared mixed vegetables, such as snow peas,
  broccoli florets, red bell pepper, and zucchini
1 tablespoon fish sauce
½ teaspoon crushed palm sugar
3 scallions, finely chopped

In a bowl, mix together pork and plenty of black pepper. Set aside 30 minutes.

In a wok or skillet, heat oil, add garlic, and cook, stirring occasionally, 2 or 3 minutes, then stir in pork. Stir briefly until pork changes color.

Stir in mixed vegetables, then fish sauce, sugar, and ½ cup water. Stir 3 or 4 minutes or until snow peas are bright green and vegetables still crisp. Stir in scallions. Heat through and serve.

Makes 4 servings.

SPICY PORK HOT POT

1 tablespoon vegetable oil
2 cloves garlic, chopped
2 shallots, chopped
1 lb. lean pork, cut into bite-size pieces
3 tablespoons sugar
3 tablespoons fish sauce
1 teaspoon five-spice powder
1 cup stock or water
salt and freshly ground black pepper
2 or 3 scallions, cut into short sections, to garnish
snow peas and bell peppers, to serve (optional)

Heat oil in a clay pot or flameproof casserole and stir-fry garlic and shallots about 1 minute until fragrant.

Add pork pieces and stir-fry about 2 minutes or until pork turns almost white in color.

Add sugar, fish sauce, and five-spice powder, stir 1 minute, then add stock or water. Bring to a boil, reduce heat, cover, and simmer 15 to 20 minutes. Adjust seasoning, garnish with scallions, and serve, with snow peas and bell peppers if desired.

Makes 4 servings.

Variation: Chicken, lamb, veal, or beef can all be cooked in the same way; increase the cooking time by 10 to 15 minutes for lamb and veal, 20 to 25 minutes for beef.

SPICY PORK & LEMONGRASS

1 clove garlic, chopped
2 shallots, chopped
3 tablespoons chopped lemongrass
1 tablespoon sugar
1 tablespoon fish sauce
salt and freshly ground black pepper
12-oz. pork fillet, cut into small, thin slices
2 or 3 tablespoons vegetable oil
2 or 3 stalks celery, thinly sliced
6 to 8 straw mushrooms, halved lengthwise
4 small red chilies, seeded and shredded
2 scallions, shredded
1 tablespoon soy sauce
¼ cup stock or water
2 teaspoons cornstarch
cilantro sprigs, to garnish

Using a mortar and pestle, pound garlic, shallots, and lemongrass to a paste. Transfer to a mixing bowl and add sugar, fish sauce, salt, and pepper. Blend well, then add pork slices, turning to coat them with mixture, and marinate 25 to 30 minutes.

Heat oil in a wok or skillet and stir-fry pork slices 2 minutes. Add celery, straw mushrooms, chilies, scallions, and soy sauce, and stir-fry 2 or 3 minutes. Use stock to rinse out marinade bowl and add to pork. Bring to a boil. Mix cornstarch with 1 tablespoon water and add to sauce to thicken it. Garnish with cilantro sprigs and serve at once, with a mixture of rice and wild rice.

Makes 4 servings.

PORK WITH VEGETABLES

8-oz. pork fillet, thinly shredded
salt and freshly ground black pepper
3 tablespoons vegetable oil
2 shallots, finely chopped
1 teaspoon chopped fresh ginger
2 cups bean sprouts
1 small red bell pepper, cored and thinly sliced
2 or 3 scallions, shredded
2 tablespoons soy sauce
cilantro sprigs, to garnish

In a bowl, season pork with salt and pepper and leave 10 to 15 minutes.

Heat oil in a wok or skillet and stir-fry shallots and ginger about 1 minute. Add pork and stir-fry 2 or 3 minutes, until shreds are separated and pork turns almost white in color.

Add beans sprouts, red bell pepper, scallions, and soy sauce, and stir-fry an additional 2 or 3 minutes. Garnish with cilantro sprigs and serve at once.

Makes 4 servings.

STIR-FRIED PORK

1 teaspoon crushed garlic
2 shallots, finely chopped
½ teaspoon chopped fresh ginger
1 teaspoon sugar
1 tablespoon fish sauce
salt and freshly ground black pepper
1-lb. pork fillet, cut into small slices or cubes
2 or 3 tablespoons vegetable oil
4 oz. sliced bamboo shoots, drained
2 small red chilies, seeded and chopped
2 scallions, chopped
2 tablespoons oyster sauce
¼ cup stock or water
2 teaspoons cornstarch
½ teaspoon sesame oil
cilantro sprigs and cucumber slices, to serve

In a bowl, mix garlic, shallots, ginger, sugar, fish sauce, and salt and pepper. Add pork and marinate 25 to 30 minutes.

Heat oil in a wok or skillet and stir-fry pork pieces 2 minutes, then add bamboo shoots, chilies, scallions, and oyster sauce, and stir-fry 4 or 5 minutes. Rinse out marinade bowl with stock or water and add to pork mixture. Bring to a boil. Mix cornstarch with 1 tablespoon water and stir into sauce. Cook, stirring, until thickened. Add sesame oil, garnish with cilantro sprigs, and serve with halved cucumber slices.

Makes 4 servings.

FRIED PORK CUTLETS

4 pork loin cutlets or boneless chops
salt and freshly ground black pepper
all-purpose flour for coating
2 eggs, beaten
dried breadcrumbs for coating
vegetable oil for deep-frying
shredded cabbage and lemon wedges, to garnish
TONKATSU SAUCE:
¼ cup tomato ketchup
1 tablespoon soy sauce
2 teaspoons Worcestershire sauce
2 teaspoons mustard, plus extra for serving

Make a few slits in the fat of the cutlets or chops to prevent curling when cooked.

Sprinkle both sides of pork cutlets with salt and pepper and dredge with flour, shaking off any excess. Dip in beaten egg, then coat in breadcrumbs. Heat oil in a wok or deep skillet to 350°F. Gently slide in pork cutlets, 1 or 2 at a time, and deep-fry 5 to 7 minutes or until golden brown, turning once or twice. Drain on absorbent paper towels. In between each batch, clean oil with a mesh ladle. Meanwhile, mix together tomato ketchup, soy sauce, Worcestershire sauce, and mustard in a small serving bowl.

When all cutlets have been cooked, place them on a cutting board and cut each one crosswise into 1-in. lengths. Arrange on 4 individual plates and garnish with very finely shredded raw cabbage and lemon wedges. Serve with sauce and extra mustard, if desired.

Makes 4 servings.

Note: This dish is called *Tonkatsu* in Japanese.

GINGER PORK

1 lb. pork fillets or boneless chops
2-in. piece fresh ginger, peeled and grated
¼ cup soy sauce
boiled rice and lightly cooked snow peas, to serve

Inserting the blade of a knife diagonally, slice pork fillets crosswise into very thin, 1-in.-diameter discs. If using chops, discard fat and cut roughly 2 x 1-in. thin pieces.

Place pork slices on a large plate, spreading as widely apart as possible, and sprinkle all over with grated ginger, together with its juice, and soy sauce. Leave to marinate 15 minutes.

Heat a skillet, add 2 or 3 tablespoons vegetable oil, and fry pork slices 2 or 3 minutes on each side until they are well cooked and both sides are golden brown. Arrange a quarter of the cooked pork slices on a bed of boiled rice, garnish with snow peas, and serve at once.

Makes 4 servings.

BROILED PORK WITH MISO

PORK WITH CITRUS SOY SAUCE

4 pork loin steaks
lemon wedges, to garnish
MISO SAUCE:
3 tablespoons red miso
3 scallions, finely chopped
2 teaspoons sake
2 teaspoons fresh ginger juice

Remove any fat from pork. If pork is more than ⅔ in. thick, slice in half horizontally.

Preheat broiler. Heat a well-oiled wire rack under hot broiler and place pork steaks on it. Gently broil pork 3 or 4 minutes on each side or until both sides are golden brown and well cooked.

Meanwhile, in a bowl, make miso sauce by mixing red miso, scallions, sake, and ginger juice. Lower heat and remove rack from broiler. Spoon miso sauce evenly onto the center of the pork steaks and put back under a medium-hot broiler 1 minute, until miso sauce is fairly dry. Transfer steaks to 4 individual plates, garnish with lemon wedges, and serve.

Makes 4 servings.

1-lb. pork loin
3 scallions, cut in half
2-in. piece fresh ginger, peeled and cut into
   3 or 4 pieces
CITRUS SOY SAUCE:
juice of ½ lemon
1 tablespoon lime juice
1 tablespoon rice vinegar
2 tablespoons soy sauce
½ tablespoon mirin
2 scallions, finely chopped
1-in. piece fresh ginger, peeled and finely chopped

Put pork, scallions, ginger, and a pinch of salt in a large pot and cover with water.

Bring to a boil, cover pot, and simmer gently 2 hours. Drain meat, put it in a bowl of ice-cold water, and refrigerate until chilled. Remove pork from water, pat dry, and then slice it crosswise against the grain as thinly as possible. Arrange slices, fanning them out around the edge of a large serving platter.

To make citrus soy sauce, mix together lemon and lime juices, rice vinegar, soy sauce, mirin, scallions, and ginger, and stir well. Transfer to a serving bowl or a ramekin and place in the center of the pork circle. Serve cold.

Makes 4 servings.

LAMB TIKKA

2 lbs. boneless leg of lamb, trimmed of fat and cut
    into 1¼-in. cubes
1 teaspoon ground cumin
¾ teaspoon turmeric
salt
⅓ cup plain yogurt
½ small onion, finely chopped
2-in. piece fresh ginger, grated
2 cloves garlic, crushed
few drops of red food coloring (optional)
1 teaspoon Garam Masala (see page 224)

Put lamb in a bowl and add cumin, turmeric,
salt, yogurt, onion, ginger, and garlic.

Mix together well, then, if desired, add
enough coloring to give mixture a red tint.
Cover and refrigerate 4 to 6 hours to
marinate. Drain lamb from marinade and
thread cubes onto 8 short skewers, pressing
cubes closely together.

Heat broiler. Cook kabobs 15 to 20 minutes,
basting with any remaining marinade and
turning occasionally during cooking, until
well browned and done to taste. Sprinkle
with Garam Masala and serve at once.

Makes 4 servings.

Note: These kabobs can be cooked on a grill
using metal skewers. Cooking time depends
on heat of grill.

KASHMIR MEATBALL CURRY

3 cups ground lamb
¼ cup chickpea flour
3 tablespoons Garam Masala (see page 224)
¼ teaspoon cayenne pepper
⅓ cup plain yogurt
salt
2 tablespoons vegetable oil
3-in. cinnamon stick
6 green cardamom pods, bruised
2 fresh bay leaves
6 whole cloves
2-in. piece fresh ginger, grated
2 tablespoons chopped cilantro leaves, to garnish

Put lamb, chickpea flour, Garam Masala,
cayenne, and 3 tablespoons of yogurt in a
bowl. Season with salt and mix together
well. Shape into 16 long ovals. Heat oil
in a shallow, heavy-bottomed pan, add
cinnamon, cardamom pods, bay leaves, and
cloves. Stir-fry a few seconds, then add
meatballs and fry until lightly browned on all
sides. Add ginger and fry an additional few
seconds. Stir remaining 3 tablespoons of
yogurt into 1 cup cold water and pour over
meatballs.

Cover pan and bring to a boil. Reduce heat
and simmer about 30 minutes, stirring gently
2 or 3 times, until meatballs are cooked and
almost all the sauce has been absorbed.
Sprinkle with cilantro and serve at once.

Makes 4 servings.

Note: If meatballs release a lot of fat during
initial frying, drain it off before adding
yogurt liquid.

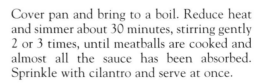

LAMB KORMA

1½ lbs. boneless leg of lamb
¼ cup vegetable oil
1 large onion, finely chopped
1 quantity Cashew Masala (see page 224)
2 tablespoons Garam Masala (see page 224)
3 dried red chilies, seeded and crushed
1-in. piece fresh ginger, grated
1 tablespoon chopped cilantro leaves
1 cup light cream
salt
2 teaspoons lemon juice
cilantro leaves and lemon wedges, to garnish

Wipe lamb, trim off excess fat, and cut into 2-in. cubes.

Heat oil in a heavy-bottomed pan, add lamb, and fry until browned all over. Add onion and cook about 5 minutes, stirring frequently, until soft. Stir in masala, chilies, and ginger, and cook an additional 2 minutes.

Add chopped cilantro, cream, ⅓ cup water, and season with salt. Bring to a boil and simmer, covered, about 1 hour or until lamb is tender. Stir in lemon juice and serve hot, garnished with cilantro and lemon wedges.

Makes 4 servings.

RED LAMB & ALMOND CURRY

1½ lbs. boneless leg of lamb
¼ cup vegetable oil
6 green cardamom pods, bruised
1 teaspoon turmeric
1 teaspoon chili powder
1 teaspoon ground cumin
1 tablespoon paprika
1 teaspoon ground coriander
1 small piece rattan jog (type of bark that stains food red), optional
1 quantity Almond Masala (see page 224)
⅔ cup plain yogurt
14½-oz. can diced tomatoes
1 large onion, finely chopped

Trim excess fat from lamb and cut lamb into 1½-in. cubes. Heat oil in a heavy-bottomed pan, add cardamom pods, turmeric, chili powder, cumin, paprika, cilantro, rattan jog (if using), and Almond Masala. Fry, stirring, 2 or 3 minutes, then stir in yogurt and tomatoes and bring to a boil. Add onion and cook 3 or 4 minutes. Add lamb cubes, stir well, and cover.

Bring to a boil again, then reduce heat and cook 40 to 50 minutes, stirring occasionally, until lamb is tender and liquid makes a thick sauce.

Makes 4 servings.

Note: On special occasions, this dish can be garnished with real silver leaf, available from Indian stores. Just before serving, place a sheet, silver-side down, on top and peel off backing paper.

LAMB WITH ONIONS

1½ lbs. shoulder of lamb, boned
1 teaspoon turmeric
1 teaspoon ground cumin
1 teaspoon ground coriander
1-in. piece fresh ginger, grated
2 cloves garlic, crushed
3 tablespoons vegetable oil
1 tablespoon superfine granulated sugar
4 large onions, sliced into thin rings
3 medium potatoes, cut into large chunks
salt and cayenne pepper
1 teaspoon Garam Masala (see page 224)
rosemary sprig, to garnish

Wipe lamb, trim, and cut into cubes.

Put lamb in a glass or china bowl. Mix together turmeric, cumin, cilantro, ginger, and garlic, and add to lamb. Stir well, then cover loosely and leave in a cool place 2 to 3 hours. Heat oil in heavy-bottomed pan until smoking. Stir in sugar, then add onions and cook over a medium to high heat for 10 minutes, stirring frequently, until a rich brown. Remove onions with a slotted spoon and set aside.

Add lamb to pan and fry until browned all over. Add potatoes and fry, stirring, for 2 minutes. Return onions to pan, add 1 cup water, and season with salt and pepper. Bring to a boil and simmer, covered, 1¼ hours or until lamb is tender, stirring occasionally. Stir in Garam Masala and serve, garnished with rosemary sprigs.

Makes 4 servings.

LEG OF LAMB & PISTACHIOS

3½ to 4 lbs. leg of lamb, boned, rolled, and tied
2 cloves garlic, crushed
1-in. piece fresh ginger, grated
1 teaspoon ground cumin
2 teaspoons Murghal Masala (see page 224)
salt and cayenne pepper
¾ cup shelled pistachio nuts
2 tablespoons lemon juice
2 tablespoons soft brown sugar
½ cup plain yogurt
2 pinches saffron threads
2 tablespoons boiling water
1 tablespoon cornstarch
2 tablespoons shelled pistachio nuts, sliced,
  to garnish

Prick lamb all over with the point of a knife and place in a large glass bowl. Put garlic, ginger, cumin, masala, salt and cayenne pepper to taste, pistachio nuts, lemon juice, sugar, and yogurt in a blender or food processor fitted with a metal blade and process until smooth. Pour over lamb and marinate 24 hours, turning lamb occasionally. Preheat oven to 350°F. Transfer lamb to a flameproof casserole, add ⅔ cup water, and bring to a boil.

Cover tightly and cook in the oven for 1½ hours. Reduce heat to 275°F and cook an additional 30 minutes. Turn off oven and leave 30 minutes. Soak saffron in water 20 minutes, then blend in cornstarch. Remove lamb and keep warm. Skim excess fat from sauce, add saffron mixture, and boil, stirring, until thick. Slice lamb, pour a little sauce on top, and garnish with nuts. Serve remaining sauce separately.

Makes 6 to 8 servings.

LAMB IN GARLIC SAUCE

1 lb. lamb tenderloin, very thinly sliced
3 tablespoons dark soy sauce
⅓ cup peanut oil
2 tablespoons rice wine or dry sherry
½ teaspoon ground Szechuan pepper
½ teaspoon sea salt
2 cloves garlic, chopped
8 scallions, chopped
1 tablespoon rice vinegar
2 tablespoons sesame oil

In a shallow dish, combine lamb with 1 tablespoon soy sauce, 2 tablespoons oil, rice wine or dry sherry, pepper, and salt.

Leave meat to marinate 30 minutes. In a wok, heat remaining 3 tablespoons peanut oil until smoking, then add garlic and lamb. Stir-fry 2 minutes or until lamb just changes color; remove from wok. Pour oil from wok, leaving just 1 tablespoonful. Add scallions and stir-fry 2 minutes. Add remaining 2 tablespoons soy sauce and rice vinegar.

Continue stir-frying another minute, then add lamb slices and sesame oil. Stir-fry 1 minute, making sure lamb and sauce are thoroughly combined.

Makes 4 servings.

LAMB WITH SCALLIONS

1 egg white
½ cup cornstarch
1 teaspoon sea salt
1 tablespoon rice wine or dry sherry
1-lb. lamb fillet, cut into strips
1¼ cups vegetable oil
10 scallions, chopped
½-in. piece fresh ginger, peeled and finely chopped
2 cloves garlic, finely chopped
1 teaspoon brown sugar
2 teaspoons dark soy sauce
¼ teaspoon ground white pepper
1 teaspoon sesame oil to serve

In a bowl, mix together egg white, cornstarch, ½ teaspoon salt, and rice wine or dry sherry. Stir in lamb strips to coat thoroughly. In a wok, heat oil until smoking, add lamb in small batches, keeping strips separate, and stir-fry 2 minutes.

Using a slotted spoon, remove lamb from wok, drain on absorbent paper towels, and keep warm. Pour oil from wok, leaving just 1 tablespoonful. Stir in scallions, ginger, garlic, remaining ½ teaspoon salt, sugar, soy sauce, and pepper. Add lamb and heat through completely. Serve sprinkled with sesame oil.

Makes 4 servings.

RED-COOKED LAMB FILLET

1-lb. lean lamb fillet
3 tablespoons dry sherry
½-in. piece fresh ginger, peeled and chopped
2 cloves garlic, thinly sliced
1 teaspoon five-spice powder
3 tablespoons dark soy sauce
1¼ cups Chinese Vegetable Stock (see page 17)
2 teaspoons sugar
2 teaspoons cornstarch mixed with 4 teaspoons water
salt and freshly ground pepper
shredded scallions, to garnish

Trim any excess fat and silver skin from lamb and cut lamb into ¾-in. cubes.

Cook lamb in a saucepan of boiling water 3 minutes. Drain well. Heat a wok and add lamb, sherry, ginger, garlic, five-spice powder, and soy sauce. Bring to a boil, reduce heat, and simmer 2 minutes, stirring. Pour in stock, return to a boil, then simmer 25 minutes.

Add sugar, cornstarch mixture, salt, and pepper, and stir until thickened. Simmer 5 minutes. Garnish with shredded scallions and serve on a bed of rice.

Makes 4 servings.

STIR-FRIED MEATBALLS

1 eggplant, weighing about 1 lb.
¼ cup salt
1 tablespoon sunflower oil
2 tablespoons rice wine
4-oz. can bamboo shoots, drained and cut into strips
4 scallions, finely chopped, to garnish
MEATBALLS:
1½ cups lean ground lamb
4 scallions, finely chopped
2 cloves garlic, finely chopped
2 tablespoons chopped fresh chives
salt and ground white pepper
1 teaspoon ground cinnamon
2 teaspoons cornstarch
1 egg white

Cut eggplant into ¼-in. slices and layer in a bowl, sprinkling generously with salt. Set aside 30 minutes. Meanwhile, make meatballs by mixing together ground lamb, scallions, garlic, chives, salt, pepper, cinnamon, cornstarch, and egg white. Divide mixture into 24 portions and roll into balls, flouring hands with extra cornstarch. Set aside. Transfer eggplant to a colander and rinse well under cold running water, pressing gently to remove all salt. Drain well and pat dry with absorbent paper towels.

Heat oil and rice wine in a wok and stir-fry eggplant 2 or 3 minutes or until softened. Add meatballs and carefully stir-fry 5 minutes. Add bamboo shoots and stir-fry 2 minutes. Remove meatballs and vegetables with a slotted spoon. Garnish with chopped scallions and serve with a salad.

Makes 4 servings.

YELLOW BEAN LAMB

4 oz. rice vermicelli
12 oz. lean boneless lamb
1 tablespoon peanut oil
1 clove garlic, finely chopped
2 scallions, finely chopped
4 oz. snow peas, sliced
2 tablespoons yellow bean sauce
freshly ground pepper
2 tablespoons chopped fresh chives, to garnish

Bring a saucepan of water to a boil. Remove from heat and add noodles. Leave to soak 2 or 3 minutes or until soft, then drain well and set aside.

Trim any fat from lamb and cut into ½-in. strips. Heat oil in a wok and stir-fry lamb, garlic, scallions, and snow peas 2 or 3 minutes or until lamb is browned.

Stir in yellow bean sauce and noodles, season with pepper, and stir-fry 3 minutes. Garnish with chopped chives and serve with a mixed salad.

Makes 4 servings.

STIR-FRIED SESAME LAMB

12-oz. lean lamb fillet
1 tablespoon sunflower oil
7 shallots, sliced
1 red bell pepper, sliced
1 green bell pepper, sliced
1 clove garlic, finely chopped
1 tablespoon light soy sauce
1 teaspoon white rice vinegar
1 teaspoon sugar
freshly ground black pepper
2 tablespoons sesame seeds

Trim any fat and silver skin from lamb fillet. Cut fillet into ¼-in. cubes.

Heat oil in a wok and stir-fry lamb 1 or 2 minutes or until browned. Remove with a slotted spoon and set aside. Stir-fry shallots, bell peppers, and garlic 2 minutes or until just softened.

Return lamb to wok with soy sauce, rice vinegar, sugar, and black pepper. Stir-fry 2 minutes. Sprinkle with sesame seeds and serve with rice and vegetables.

Makes 4 servings.

LAMB WITH SPICY HOT SAUCE

10-oz. lamb steak, thinly sliced
salt and freshly ground black pepper
1 teaspoon crushed garlic
1 teaspoon chopped fresh ginger
1 tablespoon fish sauce
3 tablespoons vegetable oil
2 cups spinach leaves or 8 oz. any green vegetable
1 tablespoon oyster sauce
2 or 3 tablespoons Vietnamese Hot Sauce (see page 234)
about 2 or 3 tablespoons stock or water
½ teaspoon sesame oil
fresh mint and/or cilantro sprigs, to garnish

Marinate lamb slices with salt, pepper, garlic, ginger, and fish sauce 2 to 3 hours.

Heat about half of the oil in a wok or pan and stir-fry spinach (or other green vegetable) about 2 minutes. Blend in oyster sauce, then place on a warmed serving dish.

Wipe clean the wok or pan and add remaining oil. When hot, add lamb slices and Vietnamese Hot Sauce and stir-fry 2 minutes. Rinse out remaining marinade with stock or water and add to lamb. Bring to a boil and cook 2 or 3 minutes, stirring all the time. Add sesame oil, then spoon lamb over spinach or green vegetable. Garnish with mint and/or cilantro sprigs and serve at once.

Makes 4 servings.

MALAYSIAN LAMB CURRY

2 onions, chopped
3 cloves garlic, crushed
4 fresh red chilies, cored, seeded, and chopped
1 stalk lemongrass, chopped
1½ tablespoons chopped fresh ginger
2 teaspoons ground coriander
1 teaspoon ground cumin
3½ cups coconut milk
2¼ lbs. lean mature lamb or mutton shoulder, cut into 2-in. cubes
juice of 1 lime
1½ teaspoons light brown sugar
salt

Put onions, garlic, chilies, lemongrass, ginger, cilantro, and cumin in a blender. Add about ⅔ cup of the coconut milk and mix together well. Pour into a large saucepan. Stir in 1¼ cups coconut milk and 3 cups plus 2 tablespoons water and bring to a simmer. Add lamb and lime juice. Simmer gently, uncovered, stirring occasionally, about 2 hours until meat is tender and liquid has evaporated.

Add a little boiling water if liquid evaporates too quickly. Stir in remaining coconut milk and sugar. Add salt to taste and simmer about 5 minutes. Serve with boiled rice.

Makes 4 to 6 servings.

VEGETABLES

MIXED VEGETABLE CURRY

CARROTS WITH FRESH DILL

3 tablespoons vegetable oil
1 onion, sliced
1 teaspoon ground cumin
1 teaspoon chili powder
2 teaspoons ground coriander
1 teaspoon turmeric
1 or 2 medium potatoes, diced
1 cup cauliflower florets
4 oz. green beans, sliced
2 medium carrots, diced
4 tomatoes, skinned and chopped
1¼ cups hot vegetable stock
onion rings, to garnish

5 or 6 medium carrots
1 tablespoon vegetable oil
2 tablespoons butter or ghee
¾ teaspoon cumin seeds
pinch ground asafoetida
½-in. piece fresh ginger, finely chopped
2 fresh green chilies, seeded and finely sliced
1 teaspoon ground coriander
¼ teaspoon turmeric
¼ cup chopped fresh dill
salt
dill sprigs, to garnish

Cut carrots into ⅛ x 1-in. sticks and set aside.

Heat oil in a large saucepan, add onion, and fry 5 minutes, until softened. Stir in cumin, chili powder, cilantro, and turmeric, and cook 2 minutes, stirring occasionally. Add potatoes, cauliflower, green beans, and carrots, tossing them in spices until coated.

Heat oil and butter or ghee in a heavy-bottomed pan and fry cumin seeds about 30 seconds, until they begin to pop. Add asafoetida, ginger, chilies, cilantro, and turmeric, and fry 2 minutes. Stir in carrots and ⅓ cup water.

Add tomatoes and stock and cover. Bring to a boil, then reduce heat and simmer 10 to 12 minutes or until vegetables are just tender. Serve hot, garnished with onion rings.

Makes 4 servings.

Variation: Use any mixture of vegetables to make a total of 1½ lbs.—turnips, rutabaga, zucchini, eggplant, parsnips, and leeks are all suitable for this curry.

Cook over a medium heat, covered, for 5 minutes or until carrots are just tender. Uncover, add chopped dill, season with salt, and cook over a high heat about 2 minutes to evaporate any excess liquid. Serve hot, garnished with dill sprigs.

Makes 4 servings.

Note: This recipe is also delicious chilled and served as a salad.

TAMIL NADU VEGETABLES

⅔ cup red split lentils
½ teaspoon turmeric
1 small eggplant
¼ cup vegetable oil
⅓ cup dried coconut
1 teaspoon cumin seeds
½ teaspoon mustard seeds
2 dried red chilies, crushed
1 red bell pepper, seeded and sliced
½ large or 1 small zucchini, thickly sliced
3 oz. green beans, cut into ¾-in. pieces
⅔ cup vegetable stock
salt
red bell pepper strips, to garnish

Wash lentils and put into a large saucepan with turmeric and 2½ cups water. Bring to a boil, then reduce heat and simmer, covered, 15 to 20 minutes, until lentils are soft. Meanwhile, cut eggplant into ½-in. dice. Heat oil in a large, shallow pan, add coconut, cumin, mustard seeds, and chilies.

Fry 1 minute, then add eggplant, red bell pepper, zucchini, green beans, stock, and salt. Bring to a boil, then simmer, covered, 10 to 15 minutes, until vegetables are just tender. Stir in lentils and any cooking liquid and cook an additional 5 minutes. Serve hot, garnished with red bell pepper strips.

Makes 4 servings.

SPICED BROWN LENTILS

1¼ cups whole brown lentils
1¼ cups coconut milk (see page 224)
¼ teaspoon chili powder
½ teaspoon turmeric
2 tablespoons vegetable oil
1 onion, finely chopped
4 curry leaves
½ stalk lemongrass
3-in. cinnamon stick
sprigs of lemon thyme, to garnish

Wash lentils, put in a bowl, cover with cold water, and let soak 6 hours or overnight.

Drain lentils and put them in a large saucepan with coconut milk, chili powder, and turmeric. Bring to a boil, then simmer, covered, 30 minutes or until just tender. Heat oil in a separate pan, add onion, curry leaves, lemongrass, and cinnamon, and fry over a medium heat, stirring, 8 minutes or until onion is soft and golden brown.

Stir into lentil mixture and simmer an additional 10 minutes or until liquid has evaporated and lentils are soft but not broken up. Remove whole spices and serve hot, garnished with thyme sprigs.

Makes 4 servings.

Note: Substitute a few sprigs of lemon thyme if lemongrass is unavailable.

MUSHROOM CURRY

30 button mushrooms
2 fresh green chilies, seeded
2 teaspoons ground coriander
1 teaspoon ground cumin
½ teaspoon chili powder
2 cloves garlic, crushed
1 onion, cut into wedges
⅔ cup coconut milk (see page 224)
salt
2 tablespoons butter or ghee
bay leaves, to garnish

Wipe mushrooms and trim stalks, then set aside.

Put chilies, ground coriander, cumin, chili powder, garlic, onion, coconut milk, and salt to taste in a blender or food processor fitted with a metal blade and blend until smooth.

Melt butter in a saucepan, add mushrooms, and fry 3 or 4 minutes, until golden brown. Pour over spicy coconut milk and simmer, uncovered, 10 minutes or until mushrooms are tender. Serve hot, garnished with bay leaves.

Makes 4 servings.

BELL PEPPERS & CAULIFLOWER

¼ cup vegetable oil
1 large onion, sliced
2 cloves garlic, crushed
2 green chilies, seeded and chopped
1 cauliflower, divided into small florets
½ teaspoon turmeric
1 teaspoon Garam Masala (see page 224)
1 green bell pepper
1 red bell pepper
1 orange or yellow bell pepper
salt and pepper
1 tablespoon chopped cilantro leaves, to garnish

Heat oil in a large saucepan, add onion, and fry over a medium heat 8 minutes or until soft and golden brown. Stir in garlic, chilies, and cauliflower, and fry 5 minutes, stirring continuously. Stir in turmeric and Garam Masala and fry 1 minute.

Reduce heat, add ¼ cup water, and cook, covered, 10 to 15 minutes, until cauliflower is almost tender. Cut bell peppers in half lengthwise, remove stalks and seeds, then slice bell peppers finely. Add to pan and cook an additional 3 to 5 minutes, until softened. Season with salt and pepper. Serve hot, garnished with chopped cilantro.

Makes 4 servings.

SPICY OKRA

DRY POTATO CURRY

12 oz. okra
2 tablespoons vegetable oil
1-in. piece fresh ginger, grated
1 teaspoon turmeric
½ teaspoon chili powder
1 teaspoon chickpea flour
salt
1¼ cups plain yogurt
2 tablespoons chopped cilantro leaves, to garnish

Wash okra and pat dry with absorbent paper towels, then cut into thick slices.

3 medium waxy potatoes
salt
2 tablespoons vegetable oil
1 teaspoon mustard seeds
1 onion, finely sliced
2 cloves garlic, crushed
1-in. piece fresh ginger, grated
1 fresh green chili, seeded and chopped
1 teaspoon turmeric
½ teaspoon cayenne pepper
1 teaspoon ground cumin
green bell pepper strips, to garnish (optional)

Cut potatoes into ¾-in. chunks.

Heat oil in a saucepan, add okra, and fry, stirring continuously, 4 minutes. Stir in ginger, turmeric, chili powder, and chickpea flour. Season with salt and fry an additional 1 minute.

Cook potatoes in boiling salted water 6 to 8 minutes, until just tender, then drain and set aside. Heat oil in a large saucepan, add mustard seeds, and fry 30 seconds or until they begin to pop. Add onion and fry 5 minutes, until soft but not brown. Stir in garlic and ginger and fry an additional 1 minute.

Stir in 3 tablespoons water, then cover and cook gently 10 minutes or until okra is tender. Stir in yogurt and reheat gently. Serve hot, sprinkled with cilantro.

Makes 4 servings.

Note: Choose okra pods that are about 4 in. long—larger pods are tough and stringy to eat.

Add potatoes, chili, turmeric, cayenne, and cumin, and stir well. Cook, covered, 3 to 5 minutes, stirring occasionally, until potatoes are very tender and coated with spices. Serve hot, garnished with green bell pepper strips.

Makes 4 servings.

VEGETARIAN EIGHT TREASURE

2 tablespoons vegetable oil
4 scallions, sliced
1 clove garlic, finely chopped
½ small green bell pepper, seeded and diced
½ small red bell pepper, seeded and diced
2 fresh hot green chilies, seeded and sliced
4 oz. canned water chestnuts, diced
1 lb. 2 oz. spiced tofu
6 dried black winter mushrooms, soaked in hot
   water 25 minutes, drained
½ small cucumber, diced
2 tablespoons black bean paste
1 teaspoon red bean paste
1 teaspoon rice wine or dry sherry
1 teaspoon dark soy sauce
1 teaspoon brown sugar
¼ teaspoon ground white pepper
4 oz. deep-fried gluten balls (see Note), if desired
1 teaspoon sesame oil, to serve

In a wok, heat vegetable oil, add scallions and garlic, and stir-fry 3 or 4 minutes or until just beginning to color. Add pepper, chilies, and water chestnuts; stir-fry 1 minute.

Stir in mushrooms, cucumber, black and red bean pastes, rice wine, soy sauce, brown sugar, white pepper, deep-fried gluten balls (if using), and 2 tablespoons water, and cook 3 minutes. Sprinkle with sesame oil and serve.

Makes 4 servings.

Note: Deep-fried gluten balls are available in packets in Asian markets and specialty delicatessens.

VEGETARIAN NEW YEAR

2½ cups vegetable oil
2¼ lbs. tofu, cut into bite-size pieces
6 pieces white ji stick (see Note), if desired
2 oz. dried cloud mushrooms, soaked in hot water
   20 minutes, drained
2 oz. dried black winter mushrooms, soaked in hot
   water 25 minutes, drained
3-oz. can bamboo shoots, drained and sliced
3-oz. can water chestnuts, drained and sliced
2 oz. golden needles (see Note), soaked in warm
   water 10 minutes, drained
⅓ cup shelled ginko nuts or skinned almonds
9 oz. red tofu
1 teaspoon brown sugar
1 tablespoon dark soy sauce

In a wok, heat vegetable oil until smoking, add tofu and ji sticks (if using), and fry 3 or 4 minutes or until golden and puffy. Remove and drain on absorbent paper towels. Pour oil from wok, leaving just 4 tablespoonsful. Add mushrooms, bamboo shoots, water chestnuts, and golden needles, and stir-fry 5 minutes. Add nuts, stir-fry 1 minute, then stir in a few tablespoons water to keep vegetables from drying out. Reduce heat and simmer 4 minutes. Add ji sticks.

In a bowl, mix together red tofu, sugar, and soy sauce, then stir into wok. Cover and simmer 10 minutes; if mixture begins to dry out, add a little more water. Stir in deep-fried tofu to heat through.

Makes 4 servings.

Note: Ji sticks are strips of tofu. Golden needles are dried lilies (they may also be called "tiger lilies"), and add a subtle flavor.

SESAME GARLIC VEGETABLES

1 cup broccoli florets
1 large green bell pepper
2 small zucchini
8 to 10 asparagus spears
2 cloves garlic, thinly sliced
2 teaspoons sesame oil
1 tablespoon sesame seeds
soy sauce for dipping

Cut pepper into 8 sections. Slice zucchini into 1-in. pieces and halve. Trim away tough ends from asparagus and slice into 2-in. pieces. Place vegetables in a colander and rinse well.

Bring a wok or large saucepan of water to a boil. Arrange vegetables on a layer of nonstick baking parchment in a steamer and place over water. Sprinkle with garlic and sesame oil. Cover and steam 10 minutes.

Remove vegetables from steamer and place on warmed serving plates. Sprinkle with sesame seeds and serve with soy sauce for dipping.

Makes 4 servings.

Note: This makes an ideal accompaniment to Five-Spice Salmon Steaks (see page 73).

RED-ROAST VEGETABLES

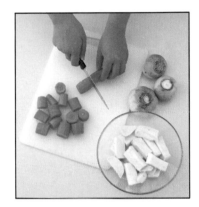

1 lb. sweet potatoes, cut into 2 x ½-in. pieces
2 medium turnips, cut into 1-in. pieces
3 large carrots, cut into 1-in. pieces
1 tablespoon sunflower oil
2 fresh red chilies, seeded and chopped
1 clove garlic, finely chopped
½-in. piece fresh ginger, peeled and chopped
2 tablespoons hoisin sauce
¼ cup dark soy sauce
⅓ cup Chinese Vegetable Stock (see page 17)
strips of fresh ginger, to garnish

Preheat oven to 400°F. Bring a large saucepan of water to a boil, add prepared vegetables, and cook 5 minutes. Drain well. Place drained vegetables in a nonstick baking pan.

In a small bowl, mix together oil, chilies, garlic, ginger, hoisin sauce, soy sauce, and stock, and spoon over vegetables. Stir thoroughly to coat vegetables and roast 30 minutes, basting occasionally, until tender. Garnish with strips of ginger and serve.

Makes 4 servings.

Note: This makes an ideal accompaniment to roast meats such as Roast Pork with Honey (see page 149).

SPICY STIR-FRIED CABBAGE

GARLIC EGGPLANT

1 lb. bok choy
½ head Chinese cabbage
1 tablespoon peanut oil
2 cloves garlic, finely chopped
1 tablespoon light soy sauce
1 teaspoon five-spice powder
1 teaspoon chili sauce
salt and freshly ground pepper
sliced fresh red chili, to garnish

Discard outer leaves of bok choy and Chinese cabbage. Break bok choy leaves from stem, rinse, and dry on absorbent paper towels. Discard stem at base of leaves and shred finely.

Bring a large saucepan of water to a boil and cook bok choy a few seconds until just wilted. Drain well, then rinse in cold water. Drain thoroughly and pat dry with absorbent paper towels. Remove core from Chinese cabbage and shred finely.

Heat oil in a wok and stir-fry bok choy and garlic 2 minutes. Add Chinese cabbage, soy sauce, five-spice powder, chili sauce, and salt and pepper, and stir-fry 2 minutes. Garnish with sliced red chili and serve immediately.

Makes 4 servings.

Note: This makes an ideal accompaniment to Beef with Oyster Sauce (see page 138).

1 eggplant
¼ cup salt
1 tablespoon sunflower oil
2 cloves garlic, thinly sliced
3 tablespoons dark soy sauce
⅓ cup rice wine
1 tablespoon yellow bean sauce
freshly ground pepper
4 scallions, finely chopped
shredded and sliced scallions, to garnish

Halve eggplant lengthwise. Halve again and cut into ½-in.-thick pieces.

Layer eggplant in a bowl with salt and leave 30 minutes. Rinse well and dry on absorbent paper towels. Heat oil in a wok and stir-fry eggplant and garlic 2 or 3 minutes or until lightly browned.

Add soy sauce, rice wine, yellow bean sauce, and pepper. Bring to a boil, reduce heat, and simmer 5 minutes or until softened. Stir in chopped scallions, garnish with shredded and sliced scallions, and serve.

Makes 4 servings.

Note: This makes an ideal accompaniment to Stir-fried Sesame Lamb (see page 165).

CHILI ROAST BELL PEPPERS

1 large red bell pepper
1 large orange pepper
1 large green bell pepper
1 large yellow bell pepper
1 tablespoon dark soy sauce
1 teaspoon chili sauce
1 tablespoon sunflower oil
freshly ground pepper
2 tablespoons chopped fresh chives

Halve bell peppers lengthwise, remove core and seeds, then halve again. Place in a baking pan.

Preheat oven to 375°F. In a small bowl, mix together soy sauce, chili sauce, oil, and ground pepper, and spoon over bell peppers, turning to make sure they are well coated. Roast 30 minutes or until softened, basting occasionally.

Transfer roast bell peppers to warmed serving plates, sprinkle with chives, and serve.

Makes 4 servings.

Note: This makes an ideal accompaniment to Ginger Chicken Patties (see page 102).

PAN-COOKED VEGETABLES

1 oz. dried Chinese mushrooms, soaked in hot water
  20 minutes
1 tablespoon peanut oil
1 whole cinnamon stick, broken
7 shallots, quartered
8 oz. baby corn
½ cup small broccoli florets
2 tablespoons dark soy sauce
¼ cup dry sherry
1 tablespoon brown sugar
4 oz. snow peas
4-oz. can water chestnuts, rinsed
4-oz. can bamboo shoots, drained and sliced
salt and freshly ground pepper

Drain mushrooms and squeeze out any excess water. Discard stems and thinly slice caps. Heat oil in a wok and stir-fry mushrooms, cinnamon, shallots, baby corn and broccoli 2 or 3 minutes or until lightly browned.

Add soy sauce, sherry, and sugar, and bring to a boil. Reduce heat and simmer 5 minutes. Add snow peas, water chestnuts, bamboo shoots, and salt and pepper, mix well, and cook 3 minutes. Discard cinnamon and serve with noodles.

Makes 4 servings.

STIR-FRIED SUGAR SNAP PEAS

VEGETABLE STIR-FRY

8 oz. sugar snap peas
1½ tablespoons vegetable oil
6 cloves garlic with skins on, lightly bruised
4 oz. raw, peeled medium shrimp
2 tablespoons light soy sauce
1½ tablespoons oyster sauce
1 teaspoon rice wine
½ cup fish stock or water mixed with 1 teaspoon
 cornstarch
freshly ground black pepper (optional)

Add sugar snap peas to a pan of boiling
water. Boil for 5 seconds, then drain
thoroughly.

Heat oil in a wok or large skillet over high
heat. Add garlic and stir-fry a few seconds.
Add shrimp and stir-fry until they turn pink.
Add sugar snap peas, soy sauce, oyster sauce,
and rice wine. Stir-fry 30 seconds.

Stir in cornstarch mixture and bring to a
boil, stirring. Add black pepper, if desired,
and serve.

Makes 4 servings.

2 tablespoons peanut oil
2 fresh red chilies, cored, seeded, and finely chopped
1-in. piece fresh ginger, grated
2 cloves garlic, crushed
1 carrot, cut into matchsticks
4 oz. green beans
½ cup broccoli florets
4 oz. baby corn, halved
1 red bell pepper, cut into fine strips
1 small bok choy, coarsely chopped
4 scallions, including some green, sliced
1 tablespoon hot curry paste
1¼ cups coconut milk
2 tablespoons Satay Sauce (see page 227)
2 tablespoons soy sauce
1 teaspoon light brown sugar
¼ cup chopped cilantro leaves
whole roasted peanuts, to garnish

In a wok or sauté pan, heat oil. Add chilies,
ginger, and garlic. Stir-fry 1 minute. Add
carrot, green beans, broccoli, corn, and
pepper, and stir-fry over high heat 3 or 4
minutes. Stir in bok choy, scallions, and
curry paste, and stir-fry 1 or 2 minutes longer.

Stir in coconut milk, satay sauce, soy sauce,
and sugar. Bring to a boil, then simmer
1 or 2 minutes or until vegetables are just
tender. Add cilantro, then serve garnished
with peanuts.

Makes 4 to 6 servings.

OKRA IN SPICE SAUCE

2 tablespoons dried shrimp
3 fresh red chilies, cored, seeded, and chopped
4 cloves garlic, chopped
1½ teaspoons shrimp paste
3 shallots, chopped
3 tablespoons vegetable oil
8 oz. fresh okra, trimmed
1 tablespoon lime juice
freshly ground black pepper

Soak dried shrimp in hot water 10 minutes. Drain and put in a blender. Add chilies, garlic, shrimp paste, and shallots. Mix to a paste, adding water if necessary.

In a wok or skillet, heat oil over medium-high heat. Add okra and stir-fry about 5 minutes. Remove with a slotted spoon and set aside.

Add spice paste to skillet and stir-fry 1 minute. Lower heat and return okra to skillet with lime juice, ¼ cup water, and plenty of black pepper. Bring to a simmer, then cook gently, stirring occasionally, 5 minutes or until okra is tender.

Makes 3 or 4 servings as a side dish.

SPICED BROILED SQUASH

2 small butternut squash, quartered and seeded
2 cloves garlic, finely chopped
2 teaspoons ground cumin
2 or 3 tablespoons vegetable oil
½ lime
salt and freshly ground black pepper

Using a small, sharp knife, make shallow crisscross cuts in flesh of each squash quarter.

In a bowl, mix together garlic, cumin, oil, a good squeeze of lime juice, and salt and pepper to taste. Brush over flesh side of each piece of squash, working it well into cuts.

Preheat grill or broiler. Cook squash quarters 10 to 15 minutes, until lightly browned and flesh is tender. Brush occasionally with any remaining cumin mixture.

Makes 4 servings as a side dish.

COCONUT MILK & VEGETABLES

1½ teaspoons tamarind
2 tablespoons peanut oil
2 small onions, chopped
2 cloves garlic, chopped
2 fresh red chilies, cored, seeded, and chopped
¼ teaspoon ground turmeric
6 oz. green beans, cut in 2-in. lengths
1¼ cups coconut milk
2½ cups shredded Chinese cabbage
2 tomatoes, peeled, seeded, and chopped
salt

Soak tamarind in 1½ tablespoons hot water. Strain through a fine sieve, extracting as much liquid as possible. Reserve liquid.

In a wok or sauté pan, heat oil over medium heat. Add onion, garlic, and chilies, and cook about 4 minutes or until softened but not colored. Stir in turmeric.

Add beans and ¾ cup coconut milk to pan. Bring to a boil and simmer 5 minutes. Add Chinese cabbage and cook an additional 4 minutes or until vegetables are just tender. Stir in tamarind liquid, tomatoes, and remaining coconut milk. Heat, stirring, for 1 or 2 minutes. Season with salt to taste.

Makes 4 servings as a side dish.

SPINACH WITH SESAME

1½ tablespoons oyster sauce
4 cups young spinach leaves
1½ tablespoons vegetable oil
2 cloves garlic, thinly sliced
1 teaspoon sesame oil
toasted sesame seeds, to garnish

Mix oyster sauce with 1 tablespoon boiling water. Set aside. Bring a large saucepan of water to a boil. Quickly add spinach and return to a boil, 30 seconds. Drain very well.

Transfer spinach to a warm serving dish. Trickle oyster sauce mixture over spinach. Keep warm.

Meanwhile, in a wok or small skillet, heat oil. Add garlic and fry until just turning golden. Sprinkle over spinach and trickle a little sesame oil on top. Sprinkle sesame seeds on top and serve.

Makes 4 servings as a side dish.

VEGETARIAN STIR-FRY

8 dried Chinese black mushrooms
8 oz. firm tofu, rinsed
1 tablespoon cornstarch
3 tablespoons peanut oil
3 cloves garlic, finely chopped
1 fresh red chili, cored, seeded, and chopped
8 oz. long beans or green beans, cut into
  2-in. lengths
2 carrots, thinly sliced diagonally
½ cauliflower, divided into florets
6 oz. snow peas
3 tablespoons soy sauce
2 teaspoons dark sesame oil
2 teaspoons light brown sugar

Soak mushrooms in ½ cup warm water for 30 minutes. Drain through cheesecloth; reserve liquid. Slice mushroom caps and discard stalks. Pat tofu dry. Cut tofu into 1-in. cubes. Put cornstarch on a plate and dip tofu in to coat evenly; press cornstarch in firmly. In a wok or skillet, heat oil; add tofu and fry 6 to 8 minutes or until browned on all sides. Using a slotted spoon, transfer to absorbent paper towels to drain.

Add garlic, chili, beans, carrots, and cauliflower to skillet and stir-fry 1 minute. Add snow peas and stir-fry an additional 1 minute. Add black mushrooms and reserved mushroom liquid. Stir-fry about 5 minutes or until vegetables are tender. Stir soy sauce, sesame oil, and sugar into vegetables. Add fried tofu and toss gently until hot and coated with liquid.

Makes 4 servings.

GREEN BEANS IN SPICED SAUCE

2 cloves garlic, chopped
1 stalk lemongrass, chopped
6 shallots, chopped
3 tablespoons vegetable oil
2 strips lime zest
2 fresh red chilies, cored, seeded, and finely chopped
2 scallions, thickly sliced diagonally
1½ lbs. green beans, cut into 1½-in. lengths
1 cup coconut milk
salt

Put garlic, lemongrass, and shallots in a blender. Add 2 tablespoons water and mix to a paste.

In a large skillet, heat oil over medium-high heat. Add spice paste from blender and fry, stirring, 5 minutes or until paste is lightly browned. Add lime zest, chilies, and scallions. Stir an additional minute, then add beans and coconut milk.

Pour in 1 cup water. Bring to a boil. Lower heat, cover, and simmer gently for about 20 minutes or until beans are tender. Add salt to taste.

Makes 4 to 6 servings as a side dish.

STUFFED EGGPLANTS

2 small eggplants, each weighing about 8 oz.
2 cloves garlic, finely chopped
2 stalks lemongrass, chopped
2 tablespoons vegetable oil
1 small onion, finely chopped
6-oz. boneless, skinless chicken fillet, finely chopped
2 teaspoons fish sauce
25 Thai holy basil leaves
freshly ground black pepper
Thai holy basil leaves, to garnish

Preheat broiler. Place eggplants under broiler and cook, turning as necessary, for about 20 minutes or until evenly charred.

Meanwhile, using a mortar and pestle, pound together garlic and lemongrass; set aside. Heat oil in a wok, add onion, and cook, stirring occasionally, until lightly browned. Stir in garlic mixture, cook 1 or 2 minutes, then add chicken. Stir-fry 2 minutes. Stir in fish sauce, basil leaves, and plenty of black pepper.

Using a sharp knife, slice each charred eggplant in half lengthwise. Using a teaspoon, carefully scoop eggplant flesh into a bowl; keep skins warm. Using kitchen scissors, chop flesh. Add to wok and stir ingredients together about 1 minute. Place eggplant skins on a large warmed plate and divide chicken mixture between them. Garnish with basil leaves.

Makes 4 servings.

STIR-FRIED SNOW PEAS

2 tablespoons vegetable oil
3 cloves garlic, finely chopped
4 oz. lean pork, very finely chopped
1 lb. snow peas
½ teaspoon crushed palm sugar
1 tablespoon fish sauce
2 oz. cooked, peeled shrimp, chopped
freshly ground black pepper

In a wok, heat oil over a medium heat, add garlic, and fry until lightly colored. Add pork and stir-fry 2 or 3 minutes.

Add snow peas and stir-fry about 3 minutes or until cooked but still crisp.

Stir in sugar, fish sauce, shrimp, and black pepper. Heat briefly and serve.

Makes 4 to 6 servings.

VEGETABLES WITH SAUCE

1 small eggplant, weighing about 8 oz.
4 oz. long beans or green beans
½ cup cauliflower florets
2 cups coconut milk
2 red shallots, chopped
2 cloves garlic, chopped
4 cilantro roots, chopped
2 dried red chilies, seeded and chopped
1 stalk lemongrass, chopped
1¼-in. piece galangal, chopped
grated zest of 1 kaffir lime
¼ cup coconut cream (see page 8)
1½ tablespoons ground roasted peanuts
3 tablespoons tamarind water (see page 11)
1 tablespoon fish sauce
2 teaspoons crushed palm sugar

Cut eggplant into 1½-in. cubes; cut beans into 2-in. lengths. Put eggplant, beans, and cauliflower into a saucepan, add coconut milk, and bring to a boil. Cover and simmer 10 minutes or until vegetables are tender. Remove from heat, uncover, and set aside. Using a mortar and pestle or small blender, pound or mix together shallots, garlic, cilantro roots, chilies, lemongrass, galangal, and lime zest.

Mix in ¼ cup liquid from vegetables. Place in a small, heavy skillet, stir in coconut cream, and heat, stirring, until oil is released and paste is thick. Stir into vegetables with peanuts, tamarind water, fish sauce, and sugar. Heat through gently about 1 minute.

Makes 6 servings.

SPICED CABBAGE

14 black peppercorns
2 tablespoons coconut cream (see page 8)
2 shallots, chopped
4 oz. lean pork, very finely chopped
1 small white cabbage, finely sliced
1¼ cups coconut milk
1 tablespoon fish sauce
1 fresh red chili, seeded and very finely chopped

In a wok, heat peppercorns about 3 minutes or until aroma changes. Stir in coconut cream, heat 2 or 3 minutes, then stir in shallots.

Stir-fry an additional 2 or 3 minutes, then stir in pork and cabbage. Cook, stirring occasionally, 3 minutes, then add coconut milk and bring just to a boil. Cover and simmer 5 minutes.

Uncover and cook about 10 minutes or until cabbage is tender but retains some bite. Stir in fish sauce. Serve sprinkled with finely chopped chili.

Makes 4 or 5 servings.

TOSSED GREENS

2 tablespoons peanut oil
8 oz. boneless, skinless chicken fillets, very
  finely chopped
6 cloves garlic, finely chopped
6 cups spinach leaves, torn into large pieces
  if necessary
1½ tablespoons fish sauce
freshly ground black pepper
1½ tablespoons dry-fried unsalted peanuts, chopped
fresh red chili, seeded and thinly sliced, to garnish

In a wok, heat oil, add chicken, and stir-fry
2 or 3 minutes. Using a slotted spoon,
transfer to absorbent paper towels; set aside.

Add garlic to wok and fry until just colored.
Using a slotted spoon, transfer half to
absorbent paper towels; set aside. Increase
heat beneath wok so oil is lightly smoking.
Quickly add all spinach and stir briefly to
coat with oil and garlic.

Spread chicken on top and sprinkle with fish
sauce and pepper. Reduce heat, cover wok,
and simmer 2 or 3 minutes. Sprinkle with
peanuts and reserved garlic and garnish with
sliced chili. Serve immediately.

Makes 4 servings.

MUSHROOMS & BEAN SPROUTS

2 tablespoons vegetable oil
2 fresh red chilies, seeded and thinly sliced
2 cloves garlic, chopped
12 to 16 shiitake mushrooms, sliced
1 cup bean sprouts
4 oz. cooked, peeled shrimp
2 tablespoons lime juice
2 red shallots, sliced into rings
1 tablespoon fish sauce
½ teaspoon crushed palm sugar
1 tablespoon ground browned rice (see page 10)
6 cilantro sprigs, stalks and leaves finely chopped
10 Thai mint leaves, shredded
Thai mint leaves, to garnish

In a wok, heat oil, add chilies and garlic, and
cook, stirring occasionally, 2 or 3 minutes.
Add mushrooms and stir-fry 2 or 3 minutes.

Add bean sprouts and shrimp, stir-fry for
1 minute, then stir in lime juice, shallots, fish
sauce, and sugar. When hot, remove from
heat and stir in rice, cilantro, and mint.
Serve garnished with mint leaves.

Makes 4 servings.

FRIED GREEN BEANS

2 tablespoons vegetable oil
1 clove garlic, chopped
1 small onion, sliced
1 lb. green beans, topped, tailed, and halved
about 2 tablespoons stock or water
2 or 3 small red chilies, seeded and shredded
2 firm tomatoes, cut into wedges
salt and freshly ground black pepper
½ teaspoon sugar
chopped cilantro leaves, to garnish (optional)

ZUCCHINI WITH GINGER

2 tablespoons vegetable oil
small piece fresh ginger, peeled and sliced
1 teaspoon crushed garlic
3 medium zucchini, peeled and cut into small wedges
1 small carrot, sliced
2 or 3 tablespoons stock or water
4 straw mushrooms, halved lengthwise
1 tomato, sliced
2 scallions, cut into short lengths
salt and freshly ground pepper
½ teaspoon sugar
1 tablespoon fish sauce

Heat oil in a wok or skillet and stir-fry garlic and onion about 1 minute.

Add green beans and stir-fry 2 or 3 minutes, adding a little stock or water if beans seem to be too dry.

Heat oil in a wok or skillet and stir-fry ginger and garlic about 30 seconds until fragrant. Add zucchini and carrot and stir-fry about 2 minutes, then add stock or water to create steam, and continue stirring another 1 or 2 minutes.

Add chilies and tomatoes and stir-fry an additional 1 minute, then add salt, pepper, and sugar, and blend well. Serve beans hot or cold, garnished with chopped cilantro if desired.

Makes 4 servings.

Add straw mushrooms, tomato, and scallions with salt, pepper, and sugar. Blend well and cook an additional 1 or 2 minutes. Sprinkle with fish sauce and serve at once.

Makes 4 servings.

Variation: Other fresh, delicate vegetables, such as asparagus, snow peas, green bell peppers, or cucumber, can also be cooked in this way.

EGGPLANT IN SPICY SAUCE

SPICY TOFU

1 eggplant, cut into small strips, like potato chips
2 or 3 tablespoons vegetable oil
1 clove garlic, chopped
2 shallots, finely chopped
salt and freshly ground black pepper
½ teaspoon sugar
2 or 3 small hot red chilies, seeded and chopped
2 tomatoes, cut into wedges
1 tablespoon soy sauce
1 teaspoon chili sauce
1 tablespoon rice vinegar
about ½ cup vegetable stock
2 teaspoons cornstarch
½ teaspoon sesame oil
cilantro sprigs, to garnish

vegetable oil for deep-frying
1 lb. 2 oz. tofu, cut into small cubes
1 clove garlic, chopped
2 shallots, chopped
2 or 3 small red chilies, seeded and chopped
2 leeks, sliced
about ½ oz. black fungus, soaked and cut into small pieces
salt and freshly ground black pepper
½ teaspoon sugar
1 tablespoon rice vinegar
1 tablespoon crushed black bean sauce
about ¼ cup stock or water
2 teaspoons cornstarch
½ teaspoon sesame oil
chopped scallions, to garnish

Stir-fry eggplant in a dry wok or skillet 3 or 4 minutes or until soft and a small amount of natural juice has appeared. Remove and set aside. Heat oil and stir-fry garlic and shallots about 30 seconds. Add eggplants, salt, pepper, sugar, and chilies, and stir-fry 2 or 3 minutes.

Heat oil in a wok or deep-fat fryer and deep-fry tofu cubes until browned on all sides. Remove and drain. Pour off excess oil, leaving about 1 tablespoon in the wok. Add garlic, shallots, and chilies, and stir-fry about 30 seconds, then add leeks and stir-fry for 2 or 3 minutes.

Add tomatoes, soy sauce, chili sauce, rice vinegar, and stock, blend well, and bring to a boil. Reduce heat and simmer 3 or 4 minutes. Mix cornstarch with 1 tablespoon water and stir into sauce to thicken it. Blend in sesame oil, garnish, and serve at once.

Makes 4 servings.

Variation: For nonvegetarians, fish sauce or shrimp paste can be used instead of soy sauce. Chicken stock can be used instead of vegetable stock.

Add tofu, black fungus, salt, and pepper. Stir-fry 1 minute, then blend in sugar, vinegar, black bean sauce, and stock or water. Bring to a boil and simmer 1 or 2 minutes. Mix cornstarch with 1 tablespoon water and stir into mixture with sesame oil. Serve garnished with chopped scallions.

Makes 4 servings.

Note: For a nonvegetarian dish, add about 6 oz. chopped beef with leeks in step 2 and increase seasonings by half.

STIR-FRIED VEGETABLES

2 tablespoons vegetable oil
1 clove garlic, chopped
1 teaspoon chopped fresh ginger
1 carrot, sliced
4 oz. baby corn, halved
1 or 2 young leeks, sliced
1 or 2 bok choy, cut into small pieces
4 oz. snow peas
1 cup bean sprouts
salt and freshly ground black pepper
1 tablespoon soy sauce
2 teaspoons cornstarch
½ teaspoon sesame oil (optional)

Heat oil in a wok or skillet and stir-fry garlic and ginger about 30 seconds. Add carrot, baby corn, leeks, bok choy, and snow peas, and stir-fry about 2 minutes.

Add bean sprouts and continue stir-frying 1 minute. Add salt, pepper, and soy sauce, and stir-fry an additional 2 minutes. Mix cornstarch with 1 tablespoon water and stir into gravy to thicken it. Finally blend in sesame oil, if using, then serve vegetables hot or cold.

Makes 4 to 6 servings.

Variation: Fish or oyster sauce can be used instead of soy sauce for nonvegetarians.

VEGETABLES IN SPICY SAUCE

2 or 3 tablespoons vegetable oil
9 oz. tofu, cut into small cubes
½ teaspoon crushed garlic
2 shallots, sliced
1 tablespoon curry powder
2 tablespoons soy sauce
1 tablespoon chopped lemongrass
1 tablespoon chopped fresh ginger
1 teaspoon chili sauce (optional)
1 cup coconut milk
1 tablespoon sugar
2 small carrots, sliced
1 onion, sliced
½ cup cauliflower florets
8 oz. green beans, trimmed and cut in half
2 firm tomatoes, cut into wedges

Heat oil in a wok or large skillet and fry tofu until browned on all sides. Remove and drain. Stir-fry garlic and shallots in the same oil about 1 minute, then add curry powder, soy sauce, lemongrass, ginger, and chili sauce, if using, and continue cooking an additional minute. Add coconut milk, sugar, and ½ teaspoon salt, and bring to a boil.

Add carrots, onion, cauliflower, beans, and tofu, and stir-fry 3 or 4 minutes, then add tomatoes. Blend well and cook an additional 2 minutes. Serve at once.

Makes 4 to 6 servings.

Variation: For nonvegetarians, either fish sauce or oyster sauce can be used instead of soy sauce for this dish.

GREEN BEANS KINPIRA

8 oz. green beans, trimmed, or 3 carrots or
    parsnips, peeled
1 dried or fresh red chili
2 tablespoons vegetable oil
2 tablespoons sake
2 tablespoons soy sauce
1 tablespoon sugar

Cut green beans diagonally into thin strips.
If using carrots or parsnips, cut them into
2-in. pieces, slicing lengthwise and then
cutting into strips.

If using dried chili, soak it in warm water
10 to 15 minutes or until outer skin is soft.
To seed fresh or dried chili, cut it lengthwise
and scrape out seeds with the back of the
knife blade. Chop chili very finely.

Heat a wok or a large skillet, add oil, and tilt
the pan to spread it over the bottom. Stir in
chili and green beans, or carrot or parsnip
strips, and stir-fry over high heat about
3 minutes or until vegetable strips begin to
soften. Lower heat and sprinkle with sake,
soy sauce, and sugar. Stir-fry over moderate
heat until liquid is almost completely
absorbed. Serve hot or at room temperature
in one deep serving dish or in small, deep
individual dishes.

Makes 4 servings.

BROILED EGGPLANTS

4 eggplants, stems removed
vegetable oil for frying
GINGER SAUCE:
⅓ cup dashi (see page 29)
2 tablespoons soy sauce
2 tablespoons mirin or 2 teaspoons sugar
2 tablespoons sake
1½ to 2-in. piece fresh ginger, peeled
8 fresh mint leaves
SESAME SAUCE:
3 tablespoons white sesame seeds
3 tablespoons dashi
1½ tablespoons soy sauce
½ tablespoon sugar
salt

To make ginger sauce, put dashi, soy sauce,
mirin or sugar, and sake in a saucepan and
boil 1 minute. Remove from heat and set
aside. Grate ginger with a Japanese daikon
grater or a cheese grater. Finely shred mint
leaves. To make sesame sauce, toast sesame
seeds in a small, dry saucepan, then grind
them to a paste using a mortar and pestle.
Mix in dashi and soy sauce. Season with
sugar and a pinch of salt. Slice eggplants
lengthwise into quarters and fry, in batches,
in a little oil over high heat 1 or 2 minutes
on each side.

Place 2 slices on each of 8 small plates.
Arrange grated ginger and mint slices on top
of 4 of the plates and add ginger sauce. Pour
sesame sauce over eggplant slices on the
other 4 plates. Serve one of each type to
each person.

Makes 4 servings.

Note: This dish is also excellent cooked on
a grill.

186

SALADS

SWEET & SOUR FISH SALAD

8 oz. trout fillets
8 oz. cod fillets
1¼ cups Chinese Vegetable Stock (see page 17)
2 tablespoons dry sherry
2 shallots, sliced
2 pineapple slices, chopped
1 small red bell pepper, diced
1 bunch watercress
pineapple pieces and watercress leaves, to garnish
DRESSING:
2 teaspoons sunflower oil
1 tablespoon red rice vinegar
pinch chili powder
1 teaspoon honey
salt and freshly ground black pepper

Rinse and pat dry trout and cod fillets and place in a wok. Add stock and sherry. Bring to a boil and simmer 7 or 8 minutes or until fish just begins to flake. Let cool in cooking liquid. Drain, remove skin, and flake flesh into a bowl.

Carefully mix flaked fish with shallots, pineapple, and pepper. Arrange watercress on 4 serving plates and top with fish mixture. Mix together oil, vinegar, chili powder, honey, salt, and pepper, and pour over salad. Garnish with pineapple pieces and watercress leaves and serve.

Makes 4 servings.

SZECHUAN SHRIMP SALAD

1 teaspoon chili oil
1 teaspoon Szechuan peppercorns, toasted
  and ground
pinch salt
1 tablespoon white rice vinegar
1 teaspoon sugar
12 oz. cooked, peeled large shrimp, thawed and
  dried if frozen
½ large cucumber
1 tablespoon sesame seeds
½ head Chinese cabbage, shredded
fresh red chili strips and lemon wedges, to garnish

In a large bowl, mix together chili oil, peppercorns, salt, vinegar, and sugar.

Add shrimp and mix well. Cover and chill 30 minutes. Thinly slice cucumber and slice each piece into thin strips. Pat dry with absorbent paper towels and mix into shrimp with sesame seeds.

Arrange Chinese cabbage on 4 serving plates and top with shrimp mixture. Garnish with chili strips and lemon wedges and serve immediately.

Makes 4 servings.

CORIANDER CHICKEN

2 teaspoons sunflower oil
1 clove garlic, finely chopped
1 shallot, finely chopped
12 oz. lean cooked skinless chicken, diced
1 teaspoon ground coriander
2 teaspoons dark soy sauce
freshly ground pepper
2 tablespoons chopped cilantro leaves
1 cup bean sprouts
1 large carrot, shredded
¾ cup cilantro leaves
2 nectarines, sliced
2 bananas, halved, sliced, and tossed in juice of
   1 small lemon

Heat oil in a wok and stir-fry garlic and shallot 1 minute. Add chicken, coriander, soy sauce, and pepper, and stir-fry 2 or 3 minutes or until chicken is lightly browned. Remove from heat and stir in chopped cilantro.

Mix together bean sprouts, shredded carrot, and cilantro leaves. Place on serving plates and top with warm chicken mixture. Arrange nectarine and banana slices around edge of each salad and serve immediately.

Makes 4 servings.

EIGHT-TREASURE SALAD

12 oz. lean cooked skinless turkey
1 red, 1 green, and 1 yellow bell pepper
4 oz. snow peas
4 oyster mushrooms
1 bunch scallions
⅓ cup salted cashews, crushed, to garnish
DRESSING:
2 teaspoons sesame oil
1 tablespoon white rice vinegar
1 teaspoon honey
freshly ground pepper

Cut turkey into ¼-in. slices and arrange in the center of 4 serving plates.

Halve and seed bell peppers. Cut into thin slices and arrange around turkey. Diagonally slice snow peas. Shred oyster mushrooms and scallions. Arrange on serving plates.

Mix together sesame oil, vinegar, honey, and pepper. Pour dressing over each salad, garnish with cashews, and serve.

Makes 4 servings.

BEEF & ORANGE SALAD

1 tablespoon peanut oil
4 lean beefsteaks, each weighing about 4 oz.,
  trimmed
3 tablespoons dark soy sauce
3 tablespoons dry sherry
1 teaspoon ground cinnamon
1 tablespoon brown sugar
freshly ground pepper
1½ cups fresh young spinach leaves
4-oz. can water chestnuts, rinsed and sliced
1 bunch scallions, shredded
2 oranges, peeled and segmented
strips of orange zest, to garnish

Heat oil in a wok and fry beefsteaks 2 minutes on each side. Drain on absorbent paper towels and wipe out wok. Mix together soy sauce, dry sherry, cinnamon, brown sugar, and pepper. Return steaks to wok; add water chestnuts and soy sauce mixture. Bring to a boil, reduce heat, and simmer 5 or 6 minutes, turning steaks halfway through.

Arrange spinach leaves on serving plates and top each with a steak, water chestnuts, and sauce. Sprinkle with scallions and top with orange segments. Garnish with strips of orange zest and serve immediately.

Makes 4 servings.

HOISIN BEEF SALAD

12 oz. lean roast beef, thinly sliced
½ head Chinese cabbage
2 large carrots
8 oz. daikon
¼ cup chopped fresh chives
carrot and daikon flowers (see page 14), to garnish
DRESSING:
2 tablespoons hoisin sauce
1 teaspoon brown sugar
1 tablespoon red rice vinegar
1 teaspoon sesame oil

Trim any fat from beef slices and cut into ½-in. strips.

Discard damaged outer layer of Chinese cabbage and cut out center core. Shred leaves finely and arrange on 4 serving plates. Peel and shred carrot and daikon and arrange on top of Chinese cabbage.

Arrange beef strips in the center and sprinkle each plate with chives. In a small bowl, mix together hoisin sauce, sugar, vinegar, and oil, and drizzle over beef. Garnish with carrot and daikon flowers and serve.

Makes 4 servings.

SUMMER NOODLE SALAD

3 nests dried egg noodles
1 teaspoon sesame oil
2 tablespoons crunchy peanut butter
2 tablespoons light soy sauce
2 teaspoons sugar
pinch chili powder
3 or 4 tomatoes, thinly sliced
1 bunch scallions, finely chopped
1 cup bean sprouts
1 large carrot, shredded
8 pitted dates, finely chopped

Cook noodles in boiling water 4 or 5 minutes or until tender but firm to the bite. Drain well, rinse in cold water, and set aside.

Mix together sesame oil, peanut butter, soy sauce, sugar, and chili powder. Drain noodles well, place in a large bowl, and mix in peanut sauce. Arrange tomato slices on a serving plate.

Using chopsticks or 2 forks, toss scallions, bean sprouts, shredded carrot, and dates into noodles and mix well. Pile on top of sliced tomato and serve.

Makes 4 servings.

STIR-FRIED TOFU SALAD

12 oz. tofu, drained and rinsed
2 tablespoons dark soy sauce
2 tablespoons rice wine
4 oz. snow peas
4 oz. baby corn
2 small red bell peppers, quartered
2 tablespoons ground almonds
2 cloves garlic, finely chopped
2 tablespoons cornstarch
salt and freshly ground pepper
1 tablespoon sunflower oil
2 tablespoons chopped fresh chives, to garnish

Cut tofu into ½-in. cubes; spoon soy sauce and wine on top. Cover and chill 1 hour.

Bring a saucepan of water to a boil. Add snow peas, baby corn, and bell peppers, and cook 2 minutes. Drain well and rinse in cold water. Leave in cold water until needed. Remove tofu from soy sauce mixture and drain well. On a plate, mix together ground almonds, garlic, cornstarch, salt, and pepper. Toss tofu in almond mixture.

Heat oil in a wok and stir-fry tofu 4 or 5 minutes or until golden. Drain well on absorbent paper towels. Drain vegetables and arrange on serving plates. Top with tofu, garnish with chives, and serve.

Makes 4 servings.

MIXED VEGETABLE SALAD

3 large carrots, cut into thin, 3-in.-long sticks
10 long beans or 3 oz. green beans, cut into
  2-in. pieces
½ small cauliflower, cut into florets
1 cucumber, peeled, halved, seeded, and cut
  into matchsticks
½ green cabbage, cored and shredded
2 cloves garlic, crushed
6 candlenuts or cashews, chopped
2 fresh red chilies, cored, seeded, and chopped
6 shallots, chopped
1½ teaspoons ground turmeric
¼ cup vegetable oil
½ cup (tightly packed) light brown sugar
¼ cup roasted unsalted peanuts

Bring a large saucepan of water to a boil.
Add carrots, beans, and cauliflower. Simmer
2 or 3 minutes or until tender but still crisp.
Add cucumber and cabbage and simmer
1 minute longer. Drain, rinse under cold
running water, and drain again thoroughly.
Put garlic, nuts, chilies, shallots, and
turmeric in a blender. Mix to a paste.

Heat oil in a wok or skillet over medium
heat. Add spice paste and cook, stirring,
3 or 5 minutes or until slightly thickened
and spices are fragrant. Add sugar, vinegar,
and salt to taste. Bring to a boil. Add
vegetables to skillet. Stir and toss to coat
thoroughly. Transfer to a bowl. Cover tightly
and leave at room temperature about 1 hour.
To serve, mound vegetables in a serving dish
and sprinkle peanuts on top.

Makes 8 to 10 servings.

BEAN SPROUT SALAD

salt
5 cups bean sprouts
1 tablespoon sesame seeds
1 fresh red chili, cored, seeded, and chopped
2 cloves garlic, finely chopped
2 tablespoons sesame oil
4 scallions, including green parts, very thinly sliced

Bring a large saucepan of salted water to a
boil. Add bean sprouts all at once. Cover the
pan and quickly return to a boil. Uncover
the pan and boil 30 seconds.

Tip bean sprouts into a colander and rinse
under running cold water. Press bean sprouts
gently to squeeze out surplus water. Transfer
bean sprouts to a bowl. Heat a small, heavy
skillet. Add sesame seeds and dry-fry,
stirring, until fragrant and lightly browned.
Add to bean sprouts.

Add chili, garlic, sesame oil, and scallions to
bowl with bean sprouts. Toss to mix the
ingredients thoroughly.

Makes 4 servings as a side dish.

TOFU & PEANUT SALAD

8 oz. firm tofu
3 large carrots, cut into 3-in.-long sticks
10 long beans or 3 oz. green beans, cut into
  2-in. pieces
1 cucumber, peeled, seeded, and cut into matchsticks
2 cups bean sprouts
PEANUT DRESSING:
2 cloves garlic, crushed
6 shallots, chopped
2 fresh red chilies, cored, seeded, and chopped
½ cup roasted unsalted peanuts
3 tablespoons peanut oil
2 tablespoons light brown sugar
¼ cup rice vinegar
1 tablespoon soy sauce
juice of 1 lime

Half-fill a saucepan with water. Bring to a boil. Add tofu and simmer, turning once, 10 minutes. Drain, cool on absorbent paper towels, then cut into ½-in. cubes. Bring a large saucepan of water to a boil. Add carrots and beans. Simmer 2 minutes or until tender but still crisp. Add cucumber and simmer an additional 1 minute. Drain, rinse under cold running water, and drain thoroughly. To make dressing, put garlic, shallots, chilies, and nuts in a blender. Mix to a paste.

Heat oil in a wok or skillet over medium heat. Add spice paste and cook, stirring, for 3 to 5 minutes or until slightly thickened and fragrant. Add sugar, vinegar, soy sauce, lime juice, and ¼ cup water. Bring to a boil. Remove from heat. Arrange bean sprouts on a serving plate. Top with other vegetables and tofu. Spoon some dressing on top. Cover and chill 1 hour. Serve remaining dressing separately.

Makes 4 servings.

CUCUMBER & PINEAPPLE SALAD

5 oz. peeled pineapple
1 small cucumber, peeled
2 shallots, thinly sliced
½ or 1 thin fresh red chili, cored, seeded, and
  thinly sliced
15 to 20 mint leaves, torn into small pieces
2 tablespoons lime juice
1¼ teaspoons light brown sugar
salt

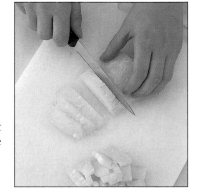

Cut pineapple and cucumber into about 2-in.-long strips. Put into a nonreactive bowl.

Add shallots, chili, mint leaves, lime juice, and sugar to bowl. Stir together.

Season salad with salt to taste. Adjust levels of chili, mint, lime juice, and sugar to taste if necessary.

Makes 4 to 6 servings.

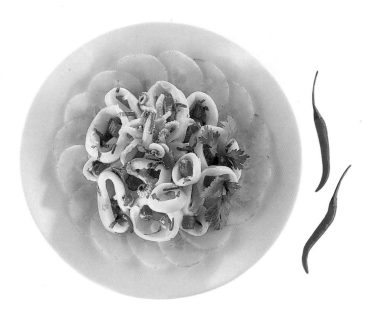

SQUID SALAD

1 lb. small or medium squid
2 tablespoons vegetable oil
½ small red bell pepper, seeded and halved
  lengthwise
1 tablespoon fish sauce
3 tablespoons lime juice
1 teaspoon crushed palm sugar
2 cloves garlic, very finely crushed
1 stalk lemongrass, very finely chopped
1 fresh red chili, seeded and thinly sliced
10 Thai mint leaves, cut into strips
2 tablespoons chopped cilantro leaves
2 scallions, chopped
1 cucumber, peeled if desired, thinly sliced
cilantro sprigs, to garnish

Heat oil in a wok, add squid, and fry gently, stirring occasionally, about 10 to 15 minutes or until tender. Using a slotted spoon, transfer to absorbent paper towels to drain.

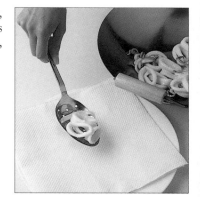

Clean squid. Holding head just below eyes, gently pull away from body pouch. Discard soft innards that come away with it. Carefully remove ink sac; retain if desired. Pull quill-shaped pen free from pouch and discard. Slip your fingers under skin on body pouch and slip it off.

Meanwhile, preheat broiler, then broil red bell pepper, turning frequently, 8 to 10 minutes or until evenly charred. Leave until cool enough to handle, then remove skin. Seed and roughly chop.

Cut off edible fins on either side of pouch. Cut off tentacles just below eyes; discard head. Squeeze out beak-like mouth from in between tentacles and discard. Rinse tentacles, pouch, and fins thoroughly. Dry well, then slice into rings.

In a bowl, mix together fish sauce, lime juice, sugar, and garlic. Add squid and mix together, then toss with lemongrass, chili, red bell pepper, mint, cilantro, and scallions. Arrange cucumber slices on a plate. Place squid salad on cucumber and garnish with cilantro sprigs.

Makes 3 or 4 servings.

Variation: Instead of cucumber, serve with small celery leaves.

CHICKEN & WATERCRESS SALAD

SHRIMP SALAD WITH MINT

2 cloves garlic, finely chopped
1¼-in. piece galangal, finely chopped
1 tablespoon fish sauce
3 tablespoons lime juice
1 teaspoon crushed palm sugar
2 tablespoons peanut oil
8 oz. boneless, skinless chicken fillets, finely
    chopped
about 25 dried shrimp
1 bunch watercress, weighing about 4 oz., coarse
    stalks removed
3 tablespoons chopped dry-roasted peanuts
2 fresh red chilies, seeded and cut into fine strips

16 to 20 raw large shrimp, peeled and deveined
juice of 2 limes
2 teaspoons vegetable oil
2 teaspoons crushed palm sugar
2 tablespoons tamarind water (see page 11)
1 tablespoon fish sauce
2 teaspoons Red Curry Paste (see page 230)
2 stalks lemongrass, very finely chopped
¼ cup coconut cream (see page 8)
10 Thai mint leaves, shredded
5 kaffir lime leaves, shredded
1 small crisp lettuce, divided into leaves
1 small cucumber, thinly sliced
That mint leaves, to garnish

Using a mortar and pestle, pound together garlic and galangal. Mix in fish sauce, lime juice, and sugar; set aside. In a wok, heat oil, add chicken, and stir-fry about 3 minutes or until cooked through. Using a slotted spoon, transfer to absorbent paper towels to drain. Put into a serving bowl and set aside.

Put shrimp in a bowl, cover with lime juice, and leave 30 minutes. Remove shrimp, allow excess liquid to drain into bowl; reserve liquid. Heat oil in a wok, add shrimp, and stir-fry 2 or 3 minutes or until just cooked (marinating in lime juice partially "cooks" them).

Chop half of the dried shrimp and add to bowl. Mix in watercress, peanuts, and half of chilies. Pour over garlic mixture and toss to mix. Sprinkle with remaining chilies and shrimp.

Makes 3 or 4 servings.

Meanwhile, stir sugar, tamarind water, fish sauce, curry paste, lemongrass, coconut cream, mint, and lime leaves into reserved lime liquid. Stir in cooked shrimp. Set aside until cold. Make a bed of lettuce on a serving plate and add a layer of cucumber slices. Spoon shrimp and dressing on top. Garnish with mint leaves.

Makes 3 or 4 servings.

THAI BEEF SALAD

12 oz. lean beef, very finely chopped
1 tablespoon fish sauce
2 tablespoons lime juice
2 teaspoons crushed palm sugar
1½ tablespoons long-grain white rice, browned and
  coarsely ground (see page 10)
2 fresh green chilies, seeded and finely chopped
2 cloves garlic, finely chopped
8 Thai mint leaves
4 kaffir lime leaves, torn
8 Thai holy basil leaves
lettuce leaves, to serve
chopped scallions and a chili flower (see page 14),
  to garnish

Heat a wok, add beef, and dry-fry about 2 minutes or until tender. Transfer to a bowl. In a small bowl, mix together fish sauce, lime juice, and sugar. Pour over warm beef, add rice, and toss together. Cover and leave until cold.

Add chilies, garlic, mint, lime, and basil leaves to bowl and toss ingredients together. Line a plate with lettuce leaves and spoon beef mixture into center. Sprinkle with scallions and garnish with a chili flower.

Makes 3 or 4 servings.

PORK & BAMBOO SHOOT SALAD

3 tablespoons vegetable oil
3 cloves garlic, chopped
1 small onion, thinly sliced
8 oz. lean pork, very finely chopped
1 egg, beaten
8-oz. can bamboo shoots, drained and cut into strips
1 tablespoon fish sauce
1 teaspoon crushed palm sugar
3 tablespoons lime juice
freshly ground black pepper
lettuce leaves, to serve

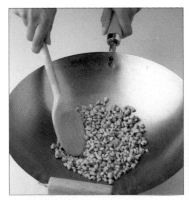

In a wok, heat 2 tablespoons oil, add garlic and onion, and cook, stirring occasionally, until lightly browned. Using a slotted spoon, transfer to absorbent paper towels to drain; set aside. Add pork to wok and stir-fry about 3 minutes or until cooked through. Using a slotted spoon, transfer to absorbent paper towels; set aside. Using absorbent paper towels, wipe out wok.

Heat remaining oil, pour in egg to make a thin layer, and cook 1 or 2 minutes or until just set. Turn egg over and cook an additional 1 minute. Remove egg from wok and roll up. Cut across into strips. In a bowl, toss together pork, bamboo shoots, and egg. In a small bowl, stir together fish sauce, sugar, lime juice, and pepper. Pour over pork mixture and toss. Serve on lettuce leaves and sprinkle with garlic and onion.

Makes 3 or 4 servings.

BEAN SALAD

2 tablespoons lime juice
2 tablespoons fish sauce
½ teaspoon crushed palm sugar
1½ tablespoons Nam Prik (see page 232)
2 tablespoons ground roasted peanuts
2 tablespoons vegetable oil
3 cloves garlic, chopped
3 shallots, thinly sliced
¼ dried red chili, seeded and finely chopped
2 tablespoons coconut cream (see page 8)
8 oz. green beans, very thinly sliced

HOT BAMBOO SHOOT SALAD

1 tablespoon fish sauce
2 tablespoons tamarind water (see page 11)
½ teaspoon crushed palm sugar
1 clove garlic, chopped
1 small fresh red chili, seeded and finely chopped
6 oz. bamboo shoots, cut into fine strips
1 tablespoon coarsely ground browned rice
  (see page 10)
2 scallions, including some green parts, sliced
cilantro leaves, to garnish

In a small bowl, mix together lime juice, fish sauce, sugar, nam prik, peanuts, and 2 tablespoons water; set aside. In a small saucepan, heat oil, add garlic and shallots, and cook, stirring occasionally, until beginning to brown. Stir in chili and cook until garlic and shallots are browned. Using a slotted spoon, transfer to absorbent paper towels and set aside.

In a saucepan, heat fish sauce, tamarind water, sugar, garlic, chili, and 2 tablespoons water to a boil. Stir in bamboo shoots and heat 1 or 2 minutes.

In a small saucepan over a low heat, warm coconut cream, stirring occasionally. Bring a saucepan of water to a boil, add beans, return to a boil, and cook about 30 seconds. Drain and rinse under cold running water. Drain well. Transfer to a serving bowl and toss with shallot mixture and contents of small bowl. Spoon over warm coconut cream.

Makes 3 or 4 servings.

Stir in rice, then turn into a warmed dish, sprinkle with scallion, and garnish with cilantro leaves.

Makes 2 or 3 servings.

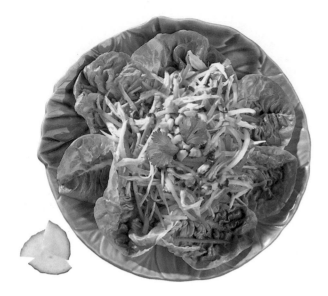

SPICY CHICKEN SALAD

8 to 10 oz. cooked chicken meat, shredded
½ cucumber, thinly shredded
1 carrot and 1 small onion, thinly shredded
salt and freshly ground black pepper
a few lettuce leaves
2 small red chilies, seeded and shredded
1 tablespoon roasted peanuts, crushed
cilantro sprigs, to garnish
DRESSING:
1 clove garlic, chopped
1 teaspoon chopped fresh ginger
1 or 2 small red or green chilies, chopped
1 tablespoon sugar
2 tablespoons fish sauce
2 tablespoons lime juice
1 tablespoon sesame oil

In a bowl, mix together chicken, cucumber, carrot, and onion, and season with salt and pepper. Arrange a bed of lettuce leaves on a serving dish or plate and spoon chicken mixture on top.

To make dressing, using a mortar and pestle, pound garlic, ginger, chilies, and sugar to a fine paste. Blend paste with fish sauce, lime juice, and sesame oil. Pour dressing all over salad just before serving and garnish with chilies, peanuts, and cilantro sprigs.

Makes 4 to 6 servings.

Note: Do not toss and mix salad with dressing until just before serving.

VIETNAMESE SALAD

4 to 6 soft lettuce leaves
½ cucumber, cut into thin strips lengthwise
1 or 2 carrots, peeled and cut into thin strips
1 small onion, thinly shredded
2 firm tomatoes, cut into wedges
2 or 3 small red chilies, seeded and chopped
fresh mint leaves
cilantro leaves
Spicy Fish Sauce or Vegetarian Dipping Sauce
  (see page 233), to serve

Line a serving platter with lettuce leaves.

Arrange separate sections of cucumber and carrot strips, shredded onion, and tomato wedges on the bed of lettuce leaves.

Arrange separate mounds of chopped red chilies and mint and cilantro leaves on top of vegetables. Serve with either Spicy Fish Sauce or Vegetarian Dipping Sauce poured over the salad at the table.

Makes 4 servings.

Note: At Vietnamese meals this vegetable platter is served either as a starter or as a side dish, and vegetables can be varied according to seasonal availability.

CHINESE CABBAGE & KIMCHEE

TRICOLOR SALAD

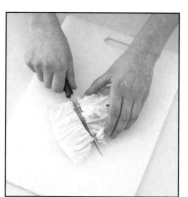

20 Chinese cabbage leaves
1 or 2 fresh red or green chilies, seeded
2 teaspoons salt
2 tablespoons kimchee dressing (Korean chili
  and garlic dressing)
finely grated lemon zest, to garnish

Wash and trim Chinese cabbage. Cut in half lengthwise, then crosswise into 2-in. pieces. Chop chili into fine half-rings.

Put a quarter of the Chinese cabbage in a freezer bag and sprinkle with one quarter of the salt and chili. Add another quarter of the leaves on top and sprinkle with another quarter of the salt and chili. Repeat this two more times with remaining ingredients and shake the bag to spread salt and chili pieces evenly throughout leaves. Tie the bag almost airtight and leave in the refrigerator at least 1 to 2 days, preferably 1 week.

Keeping leaves in the bag, squeeze out the water, then turn out leaves into a mixing bowl. Add kimchee dressing, mix well, and arrange on a serving dish. Garnish with lemon zest and serve.

Makes 4 to 8 servings.

Note: Kimchee dressing is available in jars at Asian markets.

1 carrot
3½-in. piece large daikon, peeled
5 oz. snow peas, trimmed
DRESSING:
1 tablespoon soy sauce
3 tablespoons vegetable oil
2 tablespoons rice vinegar
⅓ teaspoon salt
freshly ground black pepper

Chop carrot and daikon separately into 1½-in. shreds. Put them in 2 large mixing bowls and sprinkle each with a pinch of salt. Leave 15 minutes.

Cook snow peas in salted boiling water for 1 or 2 minutes or until tender but still crisp. Drain and immediately rinse under cold running water. Slice each snow pea on a slight diagonal into 3 pieces. Arrange different vegetable shreds on a serving dish, each occupying one third of the dish.

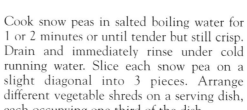

In a bowl, mix soy sauce, oil, and vinegar. Add salt and a pinch of pepper. Blend vigorously with a whisk and pour into a serving bowl or a gravy boat. Vegetables and dressing are served separately and mixed together at the table before eating.

Makes 4 servings.

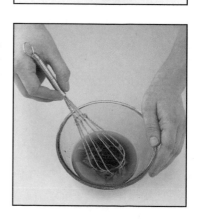

NAMASU SALAD

6-in. piece daikon, peeled
1 or 2 carrots
1 teaspoon salt
⅓ cup rice vinegar
3 tablespoons sugar
finely shredded lime zest, to garnish

Cut the daikon and carrots into three 2-in. pieces, slice each piece very thinly lengthwise, then shred them into thin matchsticks.

Place daikon and carrot matchsticks in a mixing bowl and sprinkle with salt. Using your hand, gently squash them, then leave 15 to 20 minutes. Lightly squeeze out water between your hands (do not press too hard) and put in another mixing bowl.

Mix rice vinegar and sugar and stir well until sugar has dissolved. Pour mixture into daikon and carrot shreds and gently fold in to mix the colors evenly. Heap it on a serving dish and garnish with finely shredded lime zest.

Makes 4 servings.

Note: The Japanese regard the combination of red and white as celebration colors, so this dish is considered essential for a New Year's Day brunch table.

SQUID & CUCUMBER SALAD

1 lb. 2 oz. squid, cleaned (see page 194)
½ cucumber
salt
DRESSING:
1 teaspoon mustard
2 tablespoons soy sauce
1 teaspoon sake
1 teaspoon sesame oil

Peel the outer skin off the squid, then cut squid in half lengthwise. Wash inside well and parboil, with the tentacles, 1 minute. Drain and immediately rinse under cold running water to prevent overcooking.

Cut the body parts in half lengthwise and then crosswise into ¼-in. strips. Separate the tentacles and chop each into 1½ to 2-in. pieces. Put the squid in a large mixing bowl.

Halve the cucumber lengthwise. Using a tablespoon, scoop out the seeds. Slice the cucumber into thick half-moons and sprinkle with a pinch of salt. Lightly squash with your hand to squeeze out the water, then add to squid in the bowl. In a small cup, mix mustard, soy sauce, sake, and sesame oil, and pour into the squid and cucumber mixture. Toss the squid and cucumber in the dressing and serve in small individual dishes.

Makes 4 servings as a starter.

RICE

SWEET SAFFRON RICE

1¼ cups basmati rice
1 teaspoon saffron threads
3 tablespoons boiling water
3 tablespoons vegetable oil
6 cloves
6 green cardamom pods, bruised
3-in. cinnamon stick
½ cup raisins
3 tablespoons sugar
salt
parsley sprigs, to garnish

Place rice in a sieve and wash under cold running water until water runs clear.

Put rice in a bowl with 2½ cups water and soak 30 minutes. Put saffron in a small bowl, add boiling water, and let soak 5 minutes. Heat oil in a heavy-bottomed saucepan, add cloves, cardamom pods, and cinnamon, and fry 1 minute. Drain rice and reserve soaking water. Add rice to the pan and fry 2 or 3 minutes, until opaque and light golden.

Stir in reserved water, saffron and its soaking water, raisins, and sugar, and season with salt. Bring to a boil, then lower the heat and simmer, covered, 12 to 15 minutes, stirring once or twice, until liquid is absorbed and rice is very tender. Serve hot, garnished with parsley.

Makes 4 servings.

Note: The whole spices in the rice are not meant to be eaten.

FRAGRANT FRIED RICE

1 cup basmati rice
3 tablespoons vegetable oil
8 cloves
4 black cardamom pods, bruised
1 bay leaf
3-in. cinnamon stick
1 teaspoon black peppercorns
1 teaspoon cumin seeds
1 teaspoon coriander seeds
1 onion, sliced into rings
1 small cauliflower, cut into small florets
salt
onion rings and bay leaves, to garnish

Place rice in a sieve and wash under cold running water until water runs clear. Put in a bowl with 2½ cups water and soak for 30 minutes. Heat oil in a heavy-bottomed saucepan, add cloves, cardamom pods, bay leaf, cinnamon, peppercorns, and cumin and coriander seeds, and fry 1 minute. Add onion and cook 5 minutes, until softened. Drain rice and reserve soaking water.

Add rice to the pan and fry 2 or 3 minutes, until opaque and light golden. Stir in reserved water and cauliflower and season with salt. Bring to a boil, lower heat, and simmer, covered, 12 to 15 minutes, stirring once or twice, until liquid is absorbed and rice and cauliflower are tender. Serve hot, garnished with onion rings and bay leaves.

Makes 4 servings.

Note: Do not eat the whole spices.

EGG FRIED RICE

¾ cup long-grain white rice
3 eggs, beaten
2 tablespoons vegetable oil
1 clove garlic, chopped
3 scallions, finely chopped
¾ cup peas, cooked, or frozen and thawed
1 tablespoon light soy sauce
1 teaspoon sea salt

Cook rice in boiling water 15 minutes or until tender but still firm. Drain and rinse with boiling water. In a small saucepan, cook eggs over moderately low heat, stirring until lightly scrambled. Remove and keep warm.

In a wok, heat oil, add garlic, scallions, and peas, and stir-fry 1 minute. Stir in rice to mix thoroughly.

Add soy sauce, eggs, and salt. Stir to break up egg and mix thoroughly.

Makes 4 servings.

YANGCHOW FRIED RICE

¾ cup long-grain white rice
3 tablespoons peanut oil
2 medium onions, finely sliced
3 slices fresh ginger, peeled and finely chopped
½ cup ground pork
1 tablespoon light soy sauce
1 teaspoon brown sugar
½ teaspoon sea salt
2 eggs, beaten
3 dried black winter mushrooms, soaked in hot water 25 minutes, then drained and squeezed
2 large tomatoes, peeled, seeded, and chopped
½ cup peas, cooked, or frozen and thawed

Cook rice in plenty of boiling water for 15 minutes or until tender but still firm to the bite. Drain and rinse with boiling water. In a wok, heat oil, add onion and ginger, and stir-fry 2 minutes. Stir in pork, continue stirring 3 minutes or until crisp, then add soy sauce and sugar. Stir-fry 1 minute, then stir in rice.

Remove to a warmed dish and keep warm. Pour eggs into wok, season with salt and pepper, then cook, stirring, 2 or 3 minutes or until just beginning to set. Stir in mushrooms, tomatoes, and peas. Cook 2 or 3 minutes, then stir in rice mixture.

Makes 4 servings.

GREEN RICE

1¼ cups long-grain white rice, rinsed
3½ cups Chinese Vegetable Stock (see page 17)
1 cup small broccoli florets
2 cups fresh spinach leaves, tough ribs removed
1 tablespoon peanut oil
2 cloves garlic, finely chopped
1 fresh green chili, seeded and chopped
1 bunch scallions, finely chopped
1½ cups frozen green peas
2 tablespoons light soy sauce
salt and freshly ground black pepper
¼ cup chopped fresh chives
fresh chives, to garnish

CILANTRO TURKEY RICE

1 tablespoon sunflower oil
2 shallots, chopped
2 cloves garlic, finely chopped
1 oz. prosciutto, trimmed and cut into strips
1¼ cups long-grain white rice, rinsed
1 teaspoon ground coriander
salt and freshly ground black pepper
4 cups Chinese Chicken Stock (see page 16)
4 or 5 asparagus spears, cut into 1-in. pieces,
    blanched
1½ cups frozen green peas
8 oz. cooked turkey, skinned and diced
¼ cup chopped cilantro leaves

Place rice and stock in a large saucepan, bring to a boil, reduce heat, and simmer 25 minutes or until rice is cooked and liquid has been absorbed. Cook broccoli in a saucepan of boiling water 2 minutes. Drain and set aside. Blanch spinach in a saucepan of boiling water a few seconds or until just wilted. Drain well, shred, and set aside.

Heat oil in a wok and stir-fry shallots, garlic, ham, rice, and ground coriander 2 minutes. Season with salt and pepper.

Heat oil in a wok and stir-fry garlic, chili, scallions, and broccoli 1 minute. Add cooked rice, spinach, frozen peas, and soy sauce. Season with salt and pepper and simmer 5 minutes. Stir in chopped chives. Garnish with chives to serve.

Makes 4 servings.

Pour in stock and bring to a boil. Reduce heat and simmer 20 minutes. Gently stir in asparagus, peas, turkey, and cilantro, and cook over low heat 5 minutes or until heated through, stirring to prevent sticking. Serve immediately.

Makes 4 servings.

SPICED RICE

2-in. cinnamon stick
1 tablespoon coriander seeds, lightly crushed
seeds from 1 green cardamom pod, lightly crushed
2 whole star anise
1 small onion, chopped
2 cloves garlic, chopped
¾-in. piece fresh ginger, chopped
1 tablespoon vegetable oil
1¼ cups long-grain white rice, rinsed
1 teaspoon dark soy sauce
1 tablespoon candlenuts or cashews
2 tablespoons raisins

Put cinnamon, cilantro, cardamom seeds, and star anise in a saucepan.

Add 3½ cups water and simmer, uncovered, until reduced to 2 cups. Set aside to cool, then strain. Put onion, garlic, and ginger in a blender and mix to a paste, adding a little spiced water if necessary. In a saucepan, heat oil over medium-high heat. Add paste and fry 3 or 4 minutes, stirring occasionally.

Stir in rice. Add strained spiced water and soy sauce and bring to a boil. Stir, cover, and simmer until rice is tender and liquid has been absorbed. Add nuts and raisins and fluff up rice with chopsticks or a fork.

Makes 4 servings as a side dish.

MALAYSIAN FRIED RICE

1¼ cups long-grain white rice, rinsed
3 tablespoons vegetable oil
2 eggs, beaten
1 onion, chopped
2 fresh red chilies, cored, seeded, and chopped
2 cloves garlic, crushed
1 teaspoon shrimp paste
6 oz. boneless, skinless chicken fillets, cut into thin strips
4 oz. raw, large shrimp, peeled and deveined
2 tablespoons dark soy sauce
1 tablespoon light brown sugar
2 scallions, including some green parts, sliced diagonally

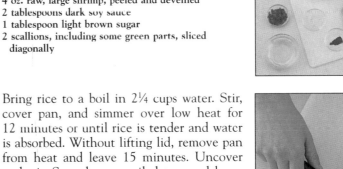

Bring rice to a boil in 2¼ cups water. Stir, cover pan, and simmer over low heat for 12 minutes or until rice is tender and water is absorbed. Without lifting lid, remove pan from heat and leave 15 minutes. Uncover and stir. Spread on an oiled tray and leave 30 to 60 minutes. Heat 1 tablespoon oil in a wok. Add eggs to make an omelette. When cool, roll up and slice. Mix onion, chilies, garlic, and shrimp paste into a paste in a blender. Heat remaining oil in wok over medium-high heat. Add paste and cook 30 seconds.

Increase heat to high. Add chicken and stir-fry 2 or 3 minutes or until opaque. Add shrimp and stir-fry 1 or 2 minutes or until just pink. Transfer chicken and shrimp to absorbent paper towels. Lower heat to medium; add rice and stir 1 or 2 minutes. Cover and cook 3 minutes, stirring twice. Add soy sauce, sugar, and scallions. Stir-fry 1 minute. Return chicken and shrimp to wok. Add egg strips and cook over high heat 2 or 3 minutes.

Makes 4 servings.

RICE, SHRIMP, & TOFU

1 cup long-grain white rice
3 tablespoons vegetable oil
3 cloves garlic, chopped
1 small onion, chopped
4 oz. tofu, drained and cut into ½-in. cubes
2 small fresh red chilies, seeded and finely chopped
1 tablespoon fish sauce
6 oz. peeled shrimp
1 shallot, thinly sliced
chili flower (see page 14), shrimp in their shells, and cilantro leaves, to garnish

SPICY FRIED RICE

1 cup long-grain white rice
2 tablespoons vegetable oil
1 large onion, finely chopped
3 cloves garlic, chopped
2 fresh green chilies, seeded and finely chopped
2 tablespoons Red Curry Paste (see page 230)
2 oz. lean pork, very finely chopped
3 eggs, beaten
1 tablespoon fish sauce
2 oz. cooked peeled shrimp
finely sliced red chili, shredded cilantro leaves, and scallion brushes (see page 14), to garnish

Rinse rice several times in cold running water. Put into a heavy saucepan with 1¼ cups water, cover, and bring quickly to a boil. Uncover and stir vigorously until water has evaporated. Reduce heat to very low, cover pan, and steam 20 minutes or until rice is tender, light, and fluffy. In a wok, heat oil, add garlic and onion, and cook, stirring occasionally, 3 or 4 minutes or until lightly browned. Add tofu and fry about 3 minutes or until browned. Add chilies and stir-fry briefly. Stir in fish sauce and rice 2 or 3 minutes, then stir in shrimp.

Cook rice following method for Rice, Shrimp, & Tofu (opposite). In a wok, heat oil, add onion, garlic, and chilies, and cook, stirring occasionally, until onion has softened. Stir in curry paste and continue to stir 3 or 4 minutes. Add pork and stir-fry 2 or 3 minutes. Stir in rice to coat with ingredients, then push to sides of wok.

Add shallot, stir quickly to mix, then transfer to a warmed serving plate. Garnish with chili flower and shrimp in their shells and sprinkle cilantro leaves over rice mixture.

Makes 4 servings.

Pour eggs into center of wok. When just beginning to set, mix evenly into the rice, adding fish sauce at the same time. Stir in shrimp, then transfer to a shallow, warmed serving dish. Garnish with chili, cilantro, and scallion brushes.

Makes 4 servings.

THAI FRIED RICE

1 cup long-grain white rice
4 oz. long beans or green beans, cut into
  1-in. lengths
3 tablespoons vegetable oil
2 onions, finely chopped
3 cloves garlic, crushed
3 oz. lean pork, very finely chopped
3 oz. boneless, skinless chicken fillets, very finely
  chopped
2 eggs, beaten
2 tablespoons Nam Prik (see page 232)
1 tablespoon fish sauce
3 oz. cooked peeled shrimp
cilantro leaves, sliced scallions, and lime wedges,
  to garnish

Cook rice following method on page 206. Add beans to a saucepan of boiling water and cook 2 minutes. Drain and rinse under cold running water. Drain well. In a wok, heat oil, add onions and garlic, and cook, stirring occasionally, until softened. Stir in pork and chicken and stir-fry 1 minute. Push to side of wok.

Pour eggs into center of wok, leave until just beginning to set, then stir in pork mixture followed by Nam Prik, fish sauce, and rice. Stir 1 or 2 minutes, then add beans and shrimp. Serve garnished with cilantro leaves, scallions, and lime wedges.

Makes 4 servings.

CHICKEN & MUSHROOM RICE

1 cup long-grain white rice
2 tablespoons vegetable oil
1 small onion, finely chopped
2 cloves garlic, finely chopped
2 fresh red chilies, seeded and cut into slivers
8 oz. boneless, skinless chicken fillets, finely
  chopped
3 oz. bamboo shoots, chopped or cut into
  matchstick strips
8 pieces dried Chinese black mushrooms, soaked
  30 minutes, then drained and chopped
2 tablespoons dried shrimp
1 tablespoon fish sauce
about 25 Thai holy basil leaves
Thai holy basil sprig, to garnish

Cook rice following method on page 206. In a wok, heat oil, add onion and garlic, and cook, stirring occasionally, until golden. Add chilies and chicken and stir-fry 2 minutes.

Stir in bamboo shoots, mushrooms, dried shrimp, and fish sauce. Continue to stir 2 minutes, then stir in rice and basil. Serve garnished with basil sprig.

Makes 4 servings.

STEAMED CHICKEN & RICE

salt and freshly ground black pepper
1 teaspoon each sugar and sesame oil
1 tablespoon fish sauce
2 teaspoons chopped garlic
10 oz. chicken thigh meat, boned and skinned, cut
  into bite-size pieces
3 tablespoons vegetable oil
4 shallots, finely chopped
2½ cups long-grain white rice
2½ cups chicken stock
8 dried Chinese mushrooms, soaked and cut into
  small pieces
4 oz. canned straw mushrooms, drained
1 tablespoon each soy sauce and oyster sauce
2 scallions, chopped
cilantro sprigs, to garnish

In a bowl, mix salt, pepper, sugar, sesame oil, fish sauce, and half the garlic. Add chicken and marinate 25 to 30 minutes. Heat about 2 tablespoons vegetable oil in a clay pot or flameproof casserole and stir-fry remaining garlic and half of the chopped shallots about 1 minute. Add rice and stir-fry about 5 minutes, then add stock. Stir and bring to a boil, then reduce the heat to very low, cover, and cook gently 8 to 10 minutes.

Heat remaining oil in a wok or saucepan and stir-fry remaining shallots until opaque. Add chicken pieces and stir-fry 2 or 3 minutes. Add mushrooms and soy sauce and continue stirring about 5 minutes. Uncover rice and fluff up with a fork. Spoon chicken and mushroom mixture on top of rice, add oyster sauce and scallions, cover, and cook an additional 5 minutes. Garnish with cilantro sprigs and serve at once.

Makes 4 to 6 servings.

SEAFOOD FRIED RICE

1¼ cups long-grain white rice
3 tablespoons vegetable oil
1 clove garlic, chopped
2 shallots, chopped
4 oz. small cooked peeled shrimp
4 oz. crabmeat, flaked
salt and freshly ground black pepper
2 or 3 eggs, beaten
2 tablespoons fish or soy sauce
chopped scallions, to garnish

The day before, cook rice following method on page 206, then refrigerate it, so that it is cold and dry when needed.

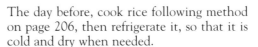

Heat about 1 tablespoon oil in a wok or skillet and stir-fry garlic and shallots about 30 seconds, then add shrimp and crabmeat with salt and pepper. Stir-fry 2 or 3 minutes, remove from pan, and set aside.

Heat remaining oil in the pan and lightly scramble beaten eggs. When just beginning to set hard, add rice and stir-fry mixture 2 or 3 minutes. Add shrimp and crabmeat with fish or soy sauce and blend well. Garnish with chopped scallions and serve at once.

Makes 4 servings.

RICE BALLS

2 cups Japanese rice
salt
5½-oz. salmon steak
2 oz. smoked cod roe, skinned
2 teaspoons sake
red chili powder (optional)
2 tablespoons black or white sesame seeds
1 or 2 sheets nori (wafer-thin dried seaweed),
   optional

Boil rice following the method given opposite. Heavily salt salmon and leave at least 30 minutes. Preheat broiler.

Wipe off salt from salmon with absorbent paper towels and broil salmon under high heat until both sides are lightly burned. Remove skin and break flesh into rough flakes. Put cod roe in a small bowl, sprinkle with sake, and make into a paste. Add a pinch of chili powder if desired. Put sesame seeds in a small saucepan and quickly toss over high heat. Place a sheet of nori over low heat and swiftly turn over a few times to bring out the flavor. Using kitchen scissors, cut it into 8 pieces. Repeat if using a second sheet.

Put 2 tablespoons rice into each of 4 wet teacups. Make a hole in center of each, put 1 teaspoonful salmon into each one, and press to cover with rice. Wet hands and rub with salt. Put rice in your hand and squeeze, shaping it into a round. Sprinkle with sesame seeds and partly wrap with nori. Make 4 more with cod roe inside but without sesame seeds. Mix rest of the rice with remaining ingredients to make 4 or 5 rice balls.

Makes about 12.

BOILING RICE & SUMESHI

2 cups Japanese rice
VINEGARY SUMESHI:
⅓ cup rice vinegar
1 tablespoon sugar
1 teaspoon salt

Wash rice thoroughly, changing the water several times until it becomes clear.

Put the rice in a deep 5 or 6-in. saucepan with 25 percent more cold water than rice. To do this, first cover rice with water, then add another 1 cup water—the water level should be about ¾ in. above rice. Leave 1 hour. Place the pan, covered, over high heat 5 minutes or until you hear a sizzling noise. Reduce heat and simmer gently for 10 minutes. To make sumeshi, put vinegar, sugar, and salt in a jug and mix until sugar and salt have dissolved.

Transfer rice to a large bowl and gradually fold in vinegar mixture using a wooden spatula. Do not stir. Cool rice to room temperature using a fan—this will make it shiny. It is now ready to make sushis.

Makes 4 servings.

Variation: To make sweet sumeshi, add 1 tablespoon mirin to rice cooking water. Mix ¼ cup rice vinegar, 1½ tablespoons sugar, and ½ tablespoon salt. Fold into the cooked rice, as above.

BABY CLAM RICE

3 cups Japanese rice
2 tablespoons sake or white wine
2 tablespoons soy sauce
1 teaspoon sugar
9 oz. canned baby clams, drained
⅔ teaspoon salt
2 scallions, finely shredded

Put rice in a deep, enamelled cast-iron casserole and wash well, changing water several times until water becomes clear. Leave to soak for 1 hour in just enough water to cover rice.

Meanwhile, in a saucepan, mix sake, soy sauce, and sugar over high heat and quickly toss in clams. Skim surface and remove from heat. Pour juice from pan into a liquid measuring cup and keep clams warm in the pan.

Drain rice. Add enough water to measuring cup to total 1 cup and dissolve salt in it. Pour mixture over rice, cover, and place on high heat. Bring to a boil and cook 7 or 8 minutes or until it sizzles, then lower heat and simmer 10 minutes. Place clams and scallions on top. Cover and cook over high heat 2 seconds. Remove from heat and let stand 10 to 15 minutes. Gently mix clams and scallions into rice. Serve in rice bowls.

Makes 4 to 6 servings.

TEMPURA RICE BOWL

3 cups Japanese rice
12 raw jumbo shrimp
12 okra, trimmed
1 egg
1 cup all-purpose flour
vegetable oil for deep-frying
TARE SAUCE:
2 tablespoons sugar
3 tablespoons soy sauce
½ cup dashi (see page 29)

Boil rice (see page 209) and keep warm. Peel shrimp, retaining tail, and devein. Make a slit along the belly to prevent curling.

To make tare sauce, dissolve sugar with soy sauce and dashi in a saucepan over medium heat and set aside. Beat egg in a liquid measuring cup and add enough water to make 1 cup. Add flour to cup and gently fold in a few times. Do not stir, as the batter should be lumpy. Heat oil in a wok or deep skillet to 340°F. Plunge shrimp and okra, one or two at a time, into batter and deep-fry until light golden. Drain on absorbent paper towels.

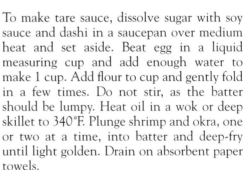

Divide rice between 4 large individual bowls. Pour about 1 tablespoon of tare sauce over each portion. Arrange 3 shrimp and 3 okra on top of each portion of rice and pour remaining tare sauce on top. Serve hot.

Makes 4 servings.

Note: Cold leftover tempura (see page 92) can be used for this dish. Gently reheat tempura in tare sauce before placing it on top of boiled rice.

NOODLES

NOODLES WITH CHOP SUEY

1 tablespoon peanut oil
2 cloves garlic, finely chopped
1 green bell pepper, thinly sliced
1 red bell pepper, thinly sliced
13 shallots, chopped
2 small zucchini, cut into matchstick strips
2 large carrots, cut into matchstick strips
1 cup bean sprouts
2 teaspoons sugar
2 tablespoons light soy sauce
¼ cup Chinese Vegetable Stock (see page 17)
salt and freshly ground pepper
4 nests dried egg noodles

Heat oil in a wok and stir-fry garlic, green and red bell peppers, shallots, zucchini, and carrots 2 or 3 minutes or until just softened. Add bean sprouts, sugar, soy sauce, stock, and salt and pepper. Bring to a boil, reduce heat, and simmer 6 or 7 minutes.

Meanwhile, bring a large saucepan of water to a boil, add noodles, and cook 5 minutes or until just tender. Drain well and transfer to warmed serving plates. Top with vegetable mixture and serve.

Makes 4 servings.

SHRIMP NOODLES

8 oz. rice vermicelli
1 oz. dried Chinese mushrooms, soaked in hot water 20 minutes
2 teaspoons chili oil
4 scallions, shredded
8 oz. cooked, peeled large shrimp, thawed and dried if frozen
1½ cups frozen green peas
1 tablespoon oyster sauce
grated zest of 1 lemon
1 egg, lightly beaten

Bring a large saucepan of water to a boil. Turn off heat and add noodles. Loosen with 2 forks and let soak 3 minutes.

Drain noodles well and rinse in cold water. Drain mushrooms and squeeze out excess water. Discard stems and slice caps. Heat half of chili oil in a wok and stir-fry mushrooms, scallions, shrimp, and peas 2 minutes. Add oyster sauce, lemon zest, and noodles, and stir-fry 2 minutes. Keep warm.

Heat remaining oil in a small nonstick skillet and cook egg 1 or 2 minutes on each side or until set. Slide onto a plate, roll up, and cut into thin slices. Garnish noodles with egg and serve immediately.

Makes 4 servings.

FRIED RICE NOODLES

8 oz. dried rice noodles, ½ in. wide
2 tablespoons vegetable oil
3 small onions, sliced into thin rings
2 cloves garlic, finely chopped
3 fresh red chilies, seeded, cored, and finely chopped
3 Chinese pork sausages, total weight about 6 oz.,
   thinly sliced diagonally
8 oz. raw tiger shrimp, peeled and deveined
2 eggs, beaten
1 cup bean sprouts
3 tablespoons light soy sauce
¼ cup chicken stock
2 scallions, including some green parts, cut
   diagonally into ¼-in. pieces

In a bowl, soak rice vermicelli in hot water 30 minutes or until softened. Drain well. In a wok or sauté pan, heat oil over medium-high heat. Add onions and stir-fry 3 or 4 minutes or until starting to brown. Add garlic, chilies, and Chinese sausage, and stir-fry about 30 seconds until fragrant. Add shrimp and stir-fry 1 or 2 minutes or until they just turn pink.

Increase heat to high. Quickly stir in eggs, then add bean sprouts, rice noodles, soy sauce, and stock. Stir about 1 minute. Serve sprinkled with scallions.

Makes 4 servings.

NOODLES WITH PEANUT SAUCE

8 oz. fresh thin egg noodles
2 tablespoons sesame oil
¼ cup unsalted roasted peanuts
1 clove garlic, crushed
1 tablespoon light soy sauce
2 teaspoons Chinese black vinegar
1 teaspoon light brown sugar
1 tablespoon peanut oil
few drops hot chili oil
white part scallion, thinly sliced, to garnish
fresh red chili, very thinly sliced, to garnish

Bring a large saucepan of water to a boil. Add noodles, return to boil, stir, then cover pan and boil until just tender.

Drain well and tip into a serving bowl. Toss with 1 tablespoon sesame oil. Set aside. In a blender or a spice grinder, or using a mortar and pestle, crush 1 tablespoon peanuts. Set aside. Put remaining peanuts and sesame oil, garlic, soy sauce, vinegar, sugar, and peanut oil in a blender. Add ¼ cup water. Mix to a smooth paste. Add chili oil to taste.

To serve, pour peanut sauce over noodles. Toss to mix. Sprinkle crushed peanuts on top and garnish with scallion and chili slices.

Makes 3 or 4 servings as a side dish.

NOODLES WITH BEAN SPROUTS

8 oz. fresh thin egg noodles
2 tablespoons sesame oil
1 clove garlic, finely crushed
3 tablespoons light soy sauce
1 tablespoon rice vinegar
½ teaspoon light brown sugar
½ fresh red chili, cored, seeded, and finely chopped
1 cup bean sprouts
4 crisp inner romaine lettuce leaves, shredded

Bring a large saucepan of water to a boil. Add noodles, return to boil, stir, then cover and boil according to package directions, until just tender.

Drain well and tip into a warm serving bowl. Toss with 1 tablespoon sesame oil. Set aside. Put remaining sesame oil, garlic, soy sauce, vinegar, sugar, and chili in a blender. Mix together.

Sprinkle bean sprouts and lettuce shreds over noodles. Stir sesame oil dressing and pour over noodles and vegetables. Transfer to serving dish, toss, and serve.

Makes 3 or 4 servings as a side dish.

CHICKEN & SHRIMP NOODLES

8 oz. chicken fillets, very thinly sliced
8 oz. raw shrimp, peeled and deveined
⅓ cup peanut oil
1 tablespoon sesame oil
1 teaspoon ground coriander
pinch Chinese five-spice powder
2 nests dried thin egg noodles
2 oz. snow peas
2 oz. green beans, halved
2 cloves garlic, finely crushed
1½ teaspoons grated fresh ginger
2 fresh red chilies, cored, seeded, and finely chopped
1 tablespoon dark soy sauce
1 tablespoon lime juice
2 tablespoons chopped cilantro leaves
toasted candlenuts or cashews

Put chicken and shrimp into a nonreactive bowl. Stir together 1 tablespoon peanut oil, 1 teaspoon sesame oil, ground coriander, and five-spice powder. Pour over chicken and shrimp. Stir until evenly coated. Cook noodles according to package directions. Meanwhile, in a wok or sauté pan, heat 2 tablespoons peanut oil. Add chicken and shrimp and stir-fry 2 minutes. Using a slotted spoon, transfer to absorbent paper towels to drain. Add snow peas and green beans to pan and stir-fry 1 minute.

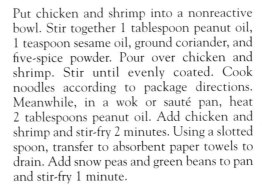

Transfer chicken and shrimp to serving bowl. Keep warm. In a small pan, heat remaining peanut oil and sesame oil. Add garlic, ginger, and chilies, and fry gently 4 or 5 minutes or until softened but not colored. Whisk in soy sauce, lime juice, and 2 tablespoons water. Bring to a boil, then remove from heat. Drain noodles and quickly toss with chicken and garlic mixtures. Serve warm or cold sprinkled with chopped cilantro and toasted nuts.

Makes 4 servings.

NOODLES WITH FISH

3 tablespoons tamarind
8 oz. rice vermicelli
12 oz. mixed white fish and snapper, salmon, or
    trout fillets
4 fresh red chilies, cored, seeded, and finely chopped
1 stalk lemongrass, crushed and thinly sliced
8 scallions, thinly sliced
1½ teaspoons shrimp paste, roasted (see page 11)
6 oz. peeled, raw medium shrimp
4 nests dried medium egg noodles
1 tablespoon light brown sugar
¼ teaspoon ground turmeric
6 shallots, very thinly sliced
leaves from small bunch mixed basil and mint

NOODLES WITH TOFU

3 nests dried thin egg noodles
2 tablespoons vegetable oil
6 shallots, finely chopped
3 cloves garlic, finely crushed
2 fresh red chilies, cored, seeded, and chopped
5 eggs
8 oz. firm tofu, cut into thin strips
2 tablespoons soy sauce
¼ cup rice vinegar
1½ tablespoons light brown sugar
salt
grated zest of ½ lime
2 scallions, white and green parts, thinly sliced
3 tablespoons chopped cilantro leaves
1 cup bean sprouts

Soak tamarind in 3 tablespoons boiling water 3 hours. Strain through cheesecloth and set aside. Soak rice sticks in boiling water until softened. Put fish, chilies, lemongrass, scallions, and shrimp paste in a saucepan. Add 7½ cups water. Bring to a boil. Add shrimp and poach until fish just flakes and shrimp turn pink. Remove fish and shrimp and keep warm.

Cook noodles according to package directions. Meanwhile, in a wok or sauté pan over medium heat, heat oil. Add shallots, garlic, and chilies, and stir-fry until shallots are lightly browned.

Bring fish stock to a boil, then simmer 5 minutes. Add egg noodles. Stir, then boil, uncovered, until just tender. Cut fish into bite-size pieces. Drain both types of noodles. Add sugar and turmeric to stock and return to a simmer. Divide noodles between 6 warm bowls. Top with fish, shrimp, and shallots. Strain over enough stock to moisten well. Add mint and basil leaves. Serve tamarind juice separately or sprinkle over noodles before serving.

Makes 6 servings.

Break all eggs into the pan. Stir 1 minute, breaking up yolks. Add tofu, soy sauce, vinegar, sugar, and salt to taste. Toss ingredients together until eggs are set. Drain noodles. Toss with egg and tofu mixture, lime zest, scallions, and cilantro. Sprinkle bean sprouts on top.

Makes 4 servings.

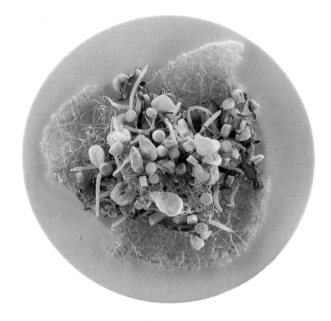

CRISPY NOODLES

6 oz. rice vermicelli
6 pieces dried Chinese black mushrooms
4 oz. lean pork
4 oz. boneless, skinless chicken fillets
vegetable oil for deep-frying
2 eggs
4 cloves garlic, finely chopped
3 shallots, thinly sliced
1 fresh red chili, seeded and sliced
1 fresh green chili, seeded and sliced
⅓ cup lime juice
1 tablespoon fish sauce
1 tablespoon crushed palm sugar
1½ oz. cooked peeled shrimp
1 cup bean sprouts
3 scallions, thickly sliced

Soak vermicelli in water 20 minutes, then drain and set aside. Soak mushrooms in water 20 minutes, then drain, chop, and set aside. Cut pork and chicken into 1-in. strips or small dice. Set aside.

For garnish, heat 2 tablespoons oil in a wok. In a small bowl, beat eggs with 2 tablespoons water, then drip small amounts in batches in tear shapes onto wok. Cook 1½ or 2 minutes or until set. Remove using a fish slice or thin spatula. Set aside.

Add more oil to wok until there is a sufficient amount for deep-frying. Heat to 375°F. Add rice vermicelli in batches and fry until puffed, light golden, and crisp. Transfer to absorbent paper towels. Set aside.

Pour off oil, leaving 3 tablespoons. Add garlic and shallots and cook, stirring occasionally, until lightly browned. Add pork, stir-fry 1 minute, then mix in chicken and stir 2 minutes. Stir in chilies, mushrooms, lime juice, fish sauce, and sugar.

Bubble until liquid becomes very lightly syrupy. Add shrimp, bean sprouts, and noodles, tossing to coat with sauce without breaking up noodles. Serve sprinkled with scallions and garnished with egg "tears."

Makes 4 servings.

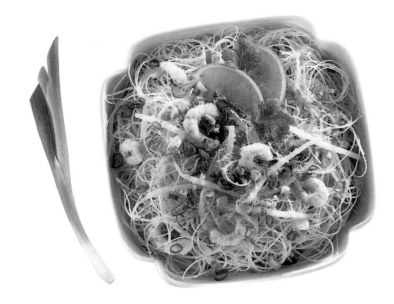

THAI FRIED NOODLES

NOODLES & THAI HERB SAUCE

3 tablespoons vegetable oil
4 cloves garlic, crushed
1 tablespoon fish sauce
3 or 4 tablespoons lime juice
1 teaspoon crushed palm sugar
2 eggs, beaten
12 oz. rice vermicelli, soaked in water 20 minutes,
    then drained
4 oz. cooked peeled shrimp
1 cup bean sprouts
4 scallions, sliced
2 tablespoons ground dried shrimp, finely chopped
    roasted peanuts, cilantro leaves, and lime slices,
    to garnish

⅓ cup vegetable oil
2 tablespoons raw shelled peanuts
1 small fresh green chili, seeded and sliced
¾-in. piece galangal, chopped
2 large cloves garlic, chopped
leaves from bunch of Thai holy basil (about 90)
leaves from small bunch of Thai mint (about 30)
leaves from small bunch of cilantro (about 45)
2 tablespoons lime juice
1 teaspoon fish sauce
6 to 8 nests dried egg noodles, soaked for
    5 to 10 minutes

In a wok, heat oil, add garlic, and cook, stirring occasionally, until golden. Stir in fish sauce, lime juice, and sugar until sugar has dissolved. Quickly stir in eggs and cook a few seconds. Stir in vermicelli to coat with garlic and egg, then add shrimp, ¾ cup bean sprouts, and half of the chopped scallions.

Over a high heat, heat oil in a wok, add peanuts, and cook, stirring, about 2 minutes or until browned. Using a slotted spoon, transfer nuts to absorbent paper towels to drain; reserve oil.

When noodles are tender, transfer contents of wok to a warmed serving dish. Garnish with remaining bean sprouts and scallions, dried shrimp, peanuts, cilantro leaves, and lime slices.

Makes 4 servings.

Using a small blender, roughly grind nuts. Add chili, galangal, and garlic. Mix briefly. Add basil, mint, cilantro, lime juice, fish sauce, and reserved oil. Drain noodles, shake loose, then cook in a pan of boiling salted water 2 minutes or until soft. Drain well, turn into a warmed dish, and toss with sauce.

Makes 4 servings.

CRAB & EGGPLANT NOODLES

8 oz. brown and white crabmeat
3 nests dried egg thread noodles
3 tablespoons vegetable oil
1 eggplant, weighing about 8 oz., cut into
  2 x ¼-in. strips
2 cloves garlic, very finely chopped
½-in. slice galangal, finely chopped
1 fresh green chili, seeded and finely chopped
6 scallions, sliced
1 tablespoon fish sauce
2 teaspoons lime juice
1½ tablespoons chopped cilantro leaves

In a bowl, thoroughly mash brown crabmeat and roughly mash white crabmeat. Set aside.

Add noodles to a saucepan of boiling salted water and cook about 4 minutes or until just tender. Drain well. Meanwhile, in a wok, heat 2 tablespoons oil, add eggplant, and stir-fry about 5 minutes or until evenly and well colored. Using a slotted spoon, transfer to absorbent paper towels and set aside.

Add remaining oil to wok, heat, then one by one stir in garlic, galangal, chili, and scallions. Add noodles, toss together for 1 minute, then toss in crabmeat and eggplant. Sprinkle with fish sauce, lime juice, and cilantro, and toss to mix.

Makes 3 servings.

NOODLES WITH BROCCOLI

1 lb. wet rice noodles
½ medium head broccoli
2 tablespoons vegetable oil
3 cloves garlic, finely chopped
8 oz. lean pork, finely chopped
¼ cup roasted peanuts, chopped
2 teaspoons fish sauce
½ teaspoon crushed palm sugar
1 fresh red chili, seeded and cut into thin slivers,
  to garnish

Remove wrapping from noodles and immediately cut into ½-in. strips; set aside. Cut broccoli diagonally into pieces 2 in. wide and cook in a saucepan of boiling salted water 2 minutes. Drain, rinse under cold running water, and drain well; set aside.

In a wok, heat oil, add garlic, and fry, stirring occasionally, until golden. Using a slotted spoon, transfer to absorbent paper towels; set aside. Add pork to wok and stir-fry 2 minutes. Add noodles, stir quickly, then add broccoli and peanuts and stir-fry 2 minutes. Stir in fish sauce, sugar, and 3 tablespoons water. Stir briefly and serve garnished with reserved garlic and chili slivers.

Makes 4 servings.

VEGETARIAN FRIED NOODLES

2 tablespoons vegetable oil
1 clove garlic, chopped
1 onion, sliced
2 or 3 small red chilies, seeded and shredded
1 carrot, thinly shredded
2 cups bean sprouts
salt and freshly ground black pepper
8 oz. rice vermicelli, soaked in hot water 5 minutes,
   then drained and cut into short lengths
2 tablespoons soy sauce
shredded scallions, to garnish

Heat oil in a wok or skillet and stir-fry garlic and onion 1 minute until opaque.

Add chilies and carrot shreds, continue stirring 2 minutes, then add bean sprouts with salt and pepper. Blend well and stir-fry an additional 2 minutes.

Add rice vermicelli with soy sauce, mix and toss, then cook 2 or 3 minutes. Garnish with shredded scallions and serve at once.

Makes 4 servings.

Note: Serve this dish with chili sauce or Spicy Fish Sauce (see page 233), if desired.

SPICY COLD NOODLES

8 oz. rice vermicelli
3 tablespoons vegetable oil
2 eggs, beaten
1 clove garlic, finely chopped
2 shallots, chopped
4 oz. pork, shredded
4 oz. peeled raw shrimp
1 tablespoon dried shrimp, soaked
1 or 2 tablespoons vegetables chow-chow, chopped
½ cup bean sprouts
2 small red chilies, seeded and chopped
salt and freshly ground black pepper
2 tablespoons fish sauce
3 tablespoons crushed peanuts
2 or 3 scallions, shredded
cilantro sprigs, to garnish

Cook vermicelli in boiling water 5 minutes; drain, rinse, and set aside. Heat about 1 tablespoon oil in a wok or pan and scramble eggs until just set, then break up into small pieces and remove. Heat remaining oil and stir-fry garlic and shallots about 30 seconds. Add pork and shrimp and continue stir-frying 1 or 2 minutes. Add dried shrimp, vegetables chow-chow, bean sprouts, scrambled eggs, chilies, salt, pepper, and fish sauce. Blend well to make a dressing and stir-fry 2 or 3 minutes. Set aside.

Place vermicelli on a large serving dish or plate and add spicy dressing with a mound of crushed peanuts and scallions on top. Serve garnished with cilantro.

Makes 4 servings.

Note: Serve with chili sauce and/or Spicy Fish Sauce (see page 233), if desired.

BEEF & RICE NOODLE SOUP

3 lbs. oxtail, cut into pieces
2 stalks lemongrass, chopped
1 large piece fresh ginger, peeled
1 onion, sliced
5 or 6 whole star anise
6 cloves
1 cinnamon stick (optional)
1 tablespoon sugar
1 teaspoon salt
2 tablespoons fish sauce
1 lb. flat rice noodles, soaked in hot water
   10 minutes, then drained
8 to 10 oz. sirloin beefsteak, cut into small,
   paper-thin slices

SOUP ACCOMPANIMENTS
1 cup bean sprouts
½ cucumber, thinly shredded
4 or 5 lettuce leaves, shredded
1 onion, thinly sliced
4 small red chilies, seeded and chopped
2 limes, cut into wedges
fresh mint, basil, and cilantro leaves
chili sauce

Trim off as much excess fat from oxtail as possible. Place pieces in a large pot, add lemongrass, ginger, onion, star anise, cloves, and cinnamon stick, if using. Add 9 cups water and bring to a boil. Reduce heat and simmer oxtail at least 2½ hours, skimming the surface occasionally to remove film.

Arrange accompaniments on a serving platter. Place a portion of rice noodles in each of 4 to 6 large individual serving bowls.

Bring beef broth to a rolling boil. Place a few slices of beefsteak on top of noodles and pour in boiling broth to fill the bowls about three-quarters full. Bring them to the table.

Strain stock and discard oxtail and flavoring ingredients (the meat from the bones can be used for another dish). Add sugar, salt, and fish sauce to clear stock, bring back to a boil, and simmer 2 or 3 minutes. (At this stage, stock can be cooled and refrigerated 1 or 2 days, if desired. Fat can be removed from surface and stock reheated, ready for use.)

Each person takes a small amount of bean sprouts, cucumber, lettuce, onion, chilies, and herbs, and places them on top of the noodles, with a squeeze of lime and more seasonings as desired.

Makes 4 to 6 servings.

Note: This is almost a meal on its own, and traditionally may be eaten as breakfast, lunch, or as a snack at any time of day.

SOY SAUCE RAMEN WITH PORK

POT-COOKED UDON

1 lb. 2 oz. egg noodles
⅓ cup soy sauce
3 tablespoons sake
9 oz. pork, shredded
3 oz. fine green beans, trimmed and halved
2 cups bean sprouts, trimmed
vegetable oil for frying
salt and freshly ground pepper
BROTH:
1-in. piece fresh ginger, peeled
2 cloves garlic
2 scallions
6 cups chicken stock
2 teaspoons salt

4 fresh or dried shiitake or any mushrooms, stalks
  removed, plus sugar and soy sauce if using dried
  shiitake
2 lbs. fresh cooked udon noodles or 14 oz. dried
  uncooked udon noodles
4 eggs
4 raw jumbo shrimp, peeled and deveined.
4 fish balls or cakes (optional)
½ cup watercress
BROTH:
6 cups second dashi (see page 29), or water and
  2 teaspoons dashi-no-moto
1½ teaspoons salt
¼ cup soy sauce
1 tablespoon sugar
2 tablespoons mirin

To make broth, roughly chop ginger, garlic, and scallions, and add to chicken stock. Bring to a boil over medium heat and simmer, half-covered, 30 minutes. Meanwhile, cook noodles in plenty of boiling water, following package directions. Wash away starch and drain. Sprinkle 1 tablespoon sake and 2 tablespoons soy sauce over pork and set aside. Parboil beans, then drain. Stir-fry bean sprouts in a little oil over high heat 1 minute. Add beans and stir-fry 1 or 2 minutes. Season with salt and pepper and remove to a plate.

Make a cross slit on top of fresh shiitake caps. If using dried ones, soak in warm water with a pinch of sugar about 1 hour, then cook in mixture of ½ cup soaking water and 2 tablespoons each sugar and soy sauce. Meanwhile, if using dried udon noodles, cook them in plenty of boiling water until tender, following package directions. Wash away starch from noodles under running water and drain. To make broth, in a saucepan over medium heat, put second dashi, salt, soy sauce, sugar, and mirin. Keep at a gentle simmer.

Add pork to pan and stir-fry 5 or 6 minutes or until well cooked. Strain broth into another pan, discarding ginger, garlic, and scallions. Season with remaining soy sauce and sake, salt, and pepper. Bring to a boil, add noodles, and cook over medium heat for 1 minute. Divide noodles between 4 individual noodle bowls, keeping broth at a gentle simmer. Divide cooked ingredients between bowls. Pour broth over them and serve garnished with chili oil, if desired.

Lightly poach eggs. Place noodles in an earthenware pot or cast-iron casserole and add mushrooms, shrimp, fish balls or cakes (if using), and watercress. Place poached eggs on top. Ladle in enough broth to just cover ingredients, then bring to a boil, covered, over medium heat, and simmer an additional 4 or 5 minutes or until all ingredients are hot and cooked. Serve at once in noodle bowls.

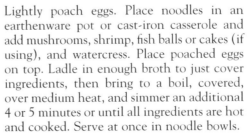

Makes 4 servings.

Makes 4 servings.

MISO RAMEN WITH CHICKEN

2 boneless, skinless chicken fillets
1-in. piece fresh ginger, peeled and grated
3 to 4 tablespoons soy sauce
1 lb. 2 oz. egg noodles
1¼ cups bean sprouts, trimmed
vegetable oil for frying
salt and freshly ground black pepper
½ cup cooked corn kernels
1 cup spinach leaves, trimmed
BROTH:
6 cups chicken stock
1-in. piece fresh ginger, peeled and sliced
2 cloves garlic
2 scallions, each cut into thirds
½ cup miso (white, if available)
2 tablespoons each soy sauce and sake

To make broth, put stock in a saucepan with sliced ginger, garlic, and scallions. Bring to a boil and simmer over medium heat for 30 minutes. Slice chicken into ¼-in.-thick, bite-size pieces. Spread pieces on a large plate, add the grated ginger and 3 to 4 tablespoons soy sauce, and marinate for 10 minutes. Cook noodles following package directions and wash off any starch. Stir-fry bean sprouts in a little oil 1 or 2 minutes, season with salt and pepper, and remove to a plate. Drain chicken and fry in a little oil until all sides are golden brown.

Blanch corn in boiling water 1 minute; drain. Cook spinach in lightly salted water 1 or 2 minutes, drain, squeeze out water, and cut into 1-in. pieces. Strain broth into a large pan, discarding ginger, garlic, and onions; bring to a boil. Add 2 tablespoons soy sauce and sake and miso diluted with a little broth. Add noodles, bring to a boil, and simmer 2 minutes. Remove noodles to individual bowls, put remaining ingredients on top, and pour hot broth into the bowls.

Makes 4 servings.

SOBA WITH DIPPING SAUCE

1 lb. dried soba (buckwheat) noodles
1 sheet nori (wafer-thin dried seaweed)
3 or 4 teaspoons wasabi paste or powder
2 scallions, finely chopped
DIPPING SAUCE:
2 cups second dashi (see page 29), or water and 1
   teaspoon dashi-no-moto (freeze-dried dashi powder)
½ cup soy sauce
¼ cup mirin
1 teaspoon sugar

Cook noodles in plenty of boiling water, following package directions. Wash away starch under running water and drain.

Lightly toast both sides of nori sheet over low heat and crush into pieces in absorbent paper towels or cut into 1-in.-long shreds with kitchen scissors. If using wasabi powder, make a paste by mixing it with the same amount of water. To make dipping sauce, mix together second dashi, soy sauce, mirin, and sugar in a saucepan and simmer over medium heat until sugar has dissolved. Half-fill 4 small individual bowls or teacups with sauce and put remaining sauce in a glass container.

Rinse noodles under cold running water for a second and arrange a quarter on each of 4 individual bamboo mats placed on large plates, or directly onto plates. Sprinkle nori on top. Serve with small plates of chopped scallion and wasabi paste and sauce. Diners dip some noodles into their own sauce mixed with condiments.

Makes 4 servings.

DIPS, SAUCES, CURRY PASTES, & PICKLES

SPICE MIXES & COCONUT MILK

NUT MASALA
2 tablespoons vegetable oil
1 teaspoon cumin seeds
1 teaspoon cardamom seeds
1 tablespoon poppy seeds
1 teaspoon black peppercorns
2 cloves garlic, crushed
1-in. piece fresh ginger, grated
⅓ cup blanched almonds or unsalted cashews, chopped
⅓ cup boiling water

Heat oil in a heavy-bottomed skillet, add cumin, cardamom, and poppy seeds and black peppercorns, and fry over a medium heat 5 to 10 minutes, until golden brown, stirring constantly. Add garlic and ginger and cook an additional 2 minutes, then let cool. Put spice mixture in a blender or food processor fitted with a metal blade. Add almonds or cashews and water and grind to a smooth paste. Cover tightly and store in a cool place up to 1 week.

MURGHAL MASALA
seeds from 1 cup green cardamom pods
two 3-in. cinnamon sticks, crushed
1 tablespoon whole cloves
1 tablespoon black peppercorns
1 teaspoon grated nutmeg

Grind spices to a fine powder using a coffee grinder or mortar and pestle. Store in a small, airtight jar up to 2 months.

GARAM MASALA
4 teaspoons cardamom seeds
3-in. cinnamon stick, crushed
2 teaspoons whole cloves
4 teaspoons black peppercorns
3 tablespoons cumin seeds
3 tablespoons coriander seeds

Put spices in a heavy-bottomed skillet and fry over medium heat 5 to 10 minutes, until browned, stirring. Cool, then grind to a fine powder. Store up to 2 months.

HOT SPICE MIX
¼ cup cumin seeds
8 dried red chilies
1 tablespoon black peppercorns
1 tablespoon cardamom seeds
3-in. cinnamon stick, crushed
4 teaspoons black mustard seeds
1 tablespoon fenugreek seeds

Prepare as Garam Masala (above). Store in an airtight jar up to 2 months.

COCONUT MILK
1 cup dried, fresh, or creamed coconut
2 cups hot water

Put coconut and water in a blender or food processor fitted with a metal blade; process 1 minute. Strain through a nylon sieve, squeezing out liquid, then discard coconut. (There is no need to sieve creamed coconut.)

Makes about 2 cups.

FRESH MANGO CHUTNEY

2 mangoes
1 red chili, seeded and finely sliced
¼ cup cashews, chopped
2½ tablespoons raisins
2 tablespoons chopped fresh mint
pinch asafoetida
½ teaspoon ground cumin
¼ teaspoon cayenne pepper
½ teaspoon ground coriander
mint sprigs, to garnish

Peel and pit mangoes, then very thinly slice flesh.

Put mango slices in a bowl with chili, cashews, raisins, and mint, and stir gently. In a small bowl, mix asafoetida, cumin, cayenne, and cilantro together, then sprinkle over mango mixture.

Stir gently to coat mango mixture in spices, then cover and chill 2 hours. Serve chilled, garnished with mint sprigs.

Makes about 1 cup.

LIME PICKLE

12 limes
¼ cup coarse sea salt
1 tablespoon fenugreek seeds
1 tablespoon mustard seeds
2 tablespoons chili powder
1 tablespoon ground turmeric
1 cup vegetable oil, such as sunflower or peanut
cilantro sprigs, to garnish

Cut each lime lengthwise into 8 thin wedges. Place in a large sterilized bowl, sprinkle with salt, and set aside.

Put fenugreek and mustard seeds in a skillet and dry roast over a medium heat 1 or 2 minutes, until they begin to pop. Put them in a mortar and grind them to a fine powder with a pestle.

Add chili powder and turmeric and mix well. Sprinkle spice mixture over limes and stir. Pour over oil and cover with a dry cloth. Leave in a sunny place 10 to 12 days, until softened. Pack into sterilized jars, then seal and store in a cool, dark place. It can be kept 1 to 2 weeks. Serve at room temperature, garnished with cilantro.

Makes about 3½ lbs.

Variation: Substitute 8 lemons for limes to make Lemon Pickle.

CUCUMBER RAITA

⅓ cucumber
1 cup plain yogurt
1 tablespoon chopped cilantro leaves
1 tablespoon chopped fresh mint
1 green chili, seeded and finely chopped
salt
1 teaspoon cumin seeds
1 teaspoon mustard seeds
cilantro or mint leaves, to garnish

Cut cucumber into ⅛ x ½-in. sticks and place in a bowl.

Add yogurt, cilantro, mint, and chili, and stir gently to mix. Season with salt. Chill for 30 minutes.

Meanwhile, put cumin and mustard seeds in a skillet and dry roast over a medium heat 1 or 2 minutes, until they begin to pop. Let cool, then sprinkle over yogurt mixture. Serve chilled, garnished with cilantro or mint leaves.

Makes about 1½ cups.

CARROT & PISTACHIO RAITA

¼ cup coarsely chopped pistachio nuts
⅓ cup raisins
⅓ cup boiling water
4 carrots, coarsely shredded
¾ cup plain yogurt
1 tablespoon chopped fresh mint
½ teaspoon chili powder
½ teaspoon cardamom seeds, crushed
½ teaspoon ground cumin

Put pistachio nuts and raisins in a small bowl and pour over boiling water. Leave to soak 30 minutes, then drain and pat dry with absorbent paper towels.

Put carrots, yogurt, chopped mint, chili powder, cardamom seeds, and cumin in a bowl, season with salt, and stir to mix.

Chill 30 minutes. Stir all but 2 tablespoons pistachio nuts and raisins into yogurt, then sprinkle remainder on top. Serve raita chilled.

Makes about 1½ cups.

Variation: Substitute chopped blanched almonds for pistachio nuts.

MALAYSIAN SAUCES

SATAY SAUCE

DIPPING SAUCE:
1 clove garlic, crushed
¼ cup light soy sauce
2½ tablespoons lime juice
1 tablespoon very finely sliced scallion
1 teaspoon light brown sugar
1 or 2 drops chili sauce

Mash garlic with a very small pinch of salt. In a small dish, put garlic, soy sauce, lime juice, scallion, and sugar. Add chili sauce to taste. Stir before serving.

Makes 4 servings.

SPICY SAUCE:
4 dried red chilies, cored, seeded, and chopped
⅓ cup peanut oil
4 shallots, finely chopped
8 cloves garlic, finely chopped
2 small ripe tomatoes, coarsely chopped
1 teaspoon ground coriander seeds
1 teaspoon ground cumin seeds
1 teaspoon light brown sugar

In a bowl, soak chilies in 3 tablespoons hot water 15 minutes. Drain and reserve. Heat oil in a skillet over medium-low heat. Add shallots and fry until softened.

Add garlic, tomato, coriander seeds, cumin seeds, and sugar to skillet. Bring to a boil, then simmer 3 or 4 minutes. Pour into a fine sieve placed over a bowl. Press through as much of the contents of sieve as possible. Cover and keep in a cool place until required.

Makes 6 servings.

½ cup roasted peanuts
1 fresh red chili, cored, seeded, and chopped
1 clove garlic, chopped
¼ cup red curry paste
1⅔ cups coconut milk
squeeze of lime juice
2 tablespoons light brown sugar

Put peanuts, chili, and garlic in a blender. Mix together, then add curry paste, 2 tablespoons of coconut milk, and a squeeze of lime juice. Mix to blend evenly.

Pour mixture into a saucepan. Stir in remaining coconut milk and sugar. Bring to a boil, stirring, then boil 2 minutes.

Lower heat and simmer 10 minutes, stirring occasionally. Add a little water if sauce becomes too thick.

Makes 6 servings.

SHRIMP PASTE RELISH

8 fresh red chilies, cored, seeded, and chopped
1 tablespoon shrimp paste, roasted (see page 11)
2½ tablespoons lime juice

In a mortar or small bowl, pound chilies with a pestle or end of a rolling pin. Add shrimp paste and pound thoroughly.

Gradually add lime juice, using pestle or end of rolling pin to work lime juice into pounded chilies.

Serve relish in a nonreactive bowl, or store in a covered glass jar.

Makes 4 to 6 servings.

COCONUT SAMBAL

2 oz. dried shrimp
2 cups dried coconut
2 fresh red chilies, cored, seeded, and chopped
1 small onion, chopped
2 cloves garlic, crushed
1 stalk lemongrass, chopped
3 tablespoons vegetable oil

In a mortar or small bowl, pound shrimp with a pestle or end of a rolling pin until fairly fine. Add coconut and work in lightly.

Put chilies, onion, garlic, and lemongrass in a blender. Mix to a paste.

Heat oil in a wok or small skillet over medium heat. Add spice paste and fry, stirring, about 3 minutes or until very fragrant. Add coconut mixture and fry until coconut is crisp and golden. Transfer to a small serving bowl and leave until cold. Store in a covered glass jar in the refrigerator.

Makes 6 servings.

FRESH MINT SAMBAL

2 cups mint leaves
½-in. piece fresh ginger, coarsely chopped
1 small onion, coarsely chopped
¼ cup lime juice
salt

Put mint, ginger, onion, and lime juice in a blender. Mix to a paste. Season with salt to taste.

Transfer sambal to a small serving bowl. Serve sambal with curries or Curry Puffs (see page 40).

Makes about 1 cup.

QUICK MIXED PICKLE

2 fresh red chilies, cored, seeded, and chopped
7 shallots, 5 chopped, 2 left whole
6 cloves garlic, 3 chopped, 3 left whole
1½-in. piece fresh ginger, grated
½ cup cauliflower florets
4 small carrots, cut into fine sticks
1 small unpeeled cucumber, cut into fine sticks
3 tablespoons vegetable oil
1 tablespoon curry powder
½ teaspoon black mustard seeds
½ teaspoon ground turmeric
2 teaspoons light brown sugar
¼ cup rice vinegar
salt
1 tablespoon sesame oil
1 tablespoon toasted sesame seeds

Put chilies, chopped shallots and garlic, and three-quarters of the ginger in a blender. Add 1 tablespoon water and mix to a paste. Bring a large saucepan of water to a boil. Add cauliflower and carrots. Quickly return to a boil. After 30 seconds, add cucumber and boil about 3 seconds. Tip into a colander and rinse under running cold water.

Heat oil in a large saucepan. Add spice paste and fry 1 minute. Add whole shallots and whole garlic and remaining ginger. Stir-fry 30 seconds. Reduce heat to medium-low. Stir in curry powder, mustard seeds, turmeric, and sugar. Add vinegar, blanched vegetables, and 1½ teaspoons salt. Bring to a boil. Remove from heat and stir in sesame oil and sesame seeds. Cool, then ladle into a warm jar and cover with a nonreactive lid. Refrigerate when cold.

Makes 4 cups.

GREEN CURRY PASTE

2 teaspoons coriander seeds
1 teaspoon cumin seeds
1 teaspoon black peppercorns
8 fresh green chilies, seeded and chopped
3 shallots, chopped
4 cloves garlic, crushed
3 cilantro roots, chopped
1-in. piece galangal, chopped
2 stalks lemongrass, chopped
2 kaffir lime leaves, chopped
2 teaspoons shrimp paste
2 tablespoons chopped cilantro leaves

Heat a wok, add cilantro and cumin seeds, and heat until aroma rises.

Using a mortar and pestle or small blender, crush cilantro and cumin seeds with peppercorns.

Add chilies, shallots, garlic, cilantro roots, galangal, lemongrass, lime leaves, shrimp paste, and chopped cilantro, and pound or mix to a smooth paste. Store in an airtight jar in the refrigerator up to 4 weeks.

Makes about 1 cup.

Note: Yield and heat of this paste will vary according to size and heat of chilies.

RED CURRY PASTE

1 tablespoon coriander seeds
1 teaspoon cumin seeds
1 teaspoon black peppercorns
4 cloves garlic, chopped
3 cilantro roots, chopped
8 dried red chilies, seeded and chopped
2 stalks lemongrass, chopped
grated zest of ½ kaffir lime
1¼-in. piece galangal, chopped
2 teaspoons shrimp paste

Heat a wok, add cilantro and cumin seeds, and heat until aroma rises. Using a mortar and pestle or small blender, crush cilantro and cumin seeds with peppercorns.

Add garlic, cilantro roots, chilies, lemongrass, lime zest, galangal, and shrimp paste, and pound or mix to a smooth paste. Store in an airtight jar in the refrigerator up to 4 weeks.

Makes about ¼ cup.

Note: Yield and heat of this paste will vary according to size and heat of chilies.

FRAGRANT CURRY PASTE

2 cloves garlic, chopped
1 shallot, chopped
4 dried red chilies, seeded and chopped
1 thick stalk lemongrass, chopped
3 cilantro roots, chopped
finely grated zest of 2 kaffir limes
1 kaffir lime leaf, torn
4 black peppercorns, cracked
½ teaspoon shrimp paste

Using a mortar and pestle or small blender, pound or mix together garlic, shallot, chilies, lemongrass, and cilantro roots.

Add lime zest, lime leaf, peppercorns, and shrimp paste, and pound or mix to a smooth paste. Store in an airtight jar in the refrigerator up to 4 weeks.

Makes about ¼ cup.

THAI DIPPING SAUCE 1

1 cup tamarind water (see page 11)
½ or ¾ tablespoon crushed palm sugar
1 or 2 drops fish sauce
½ teaspoon very finely chopped scallion
½ teaspoon very finely chopped garlic
½ teaspoon finely chopped fresh red chili

In a small saucepan, gently heat tamarind water and sugar until sugar has dissolved.

Remove pan from heat and add fish sauce. Stir in scallion, garlic, and chili. Pour into a small serving bowl and let cool.

Makes 4 servings.

THAI DIPPING SAUCE 2

NAM PRIK

⅓ cup lime juice
1½ or 2 teaspoons crushed palm sugar
½ teaspoon fish sauce
½ teaspoon very finely chopped red shallot
½ teaspoon very finely chopped fresh green chili
½ teaspoon finely chopped fresh red chili

1 tablespoon fish sauce
about 22 whole dried shrimp, chopped
3 cloves garlic, chopped
4 dried red chilies with seeds, chopped
2 tablespoons lime juice
1 fresh red or green chili, seeded and chopped
about 1 tablespoon pea eggplants, chopped (optional)

Using a mortar and pestle or small blender, pound or mix fish sauce, shrimp, garlic, dried chilies, and lime juice to a paste.

In a small bowl, stir together lime juice and sugar until sugar has dissolved. Adjust amount of sugar, if desired.

Stir in fresh red or green chili and pea eggplants, if using. Transfer paste to a small bowl.

Stir in fish sauce, shallot, and chilies. Pour into a small serving bowl. Serve with deep-fried fish, fish fritters, wontons, or spring rolls.

Makes 4 servings.

Serve with a selection of raw vegetables. Store in a covered jar in the refrigerator several weeks.

Makes 6 to 8 servings.

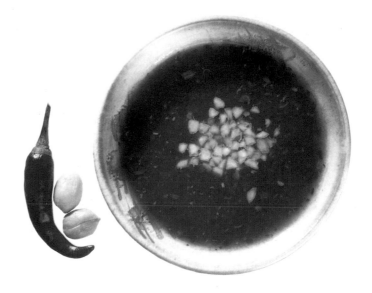

SPICY FISH SAUCE

2 cloves garlic
2 small red or green chilies, seeded and chopped
1 tablespoon sugar
2 tablespoons lime juice
2 tablespoons fish sauce

VEGETARIAN DIPPING SAUCE

1 tablespoon sugar
2 tablespoons chili sauce
2 or 3 tablespoons water
1 small red or green chili, seeded and chopped
1 tablespoon roasted peanuts, coarsely chopped

Using a mortar and pestle, pound garlic and chilies until finely ground. If you do not have a mortar and pestle, just finely mince garlic and chilies.

In a small bowl, mix sugar with chili sauce and water.

Place mixture in a bowl and add sugar, lime juice, fish sauce, and 2 or 3 tablespoons water. Blend well. Serve in small dipping saucers.

Makes 4 servings.

Note: This sauce is known as *nuoc cham*. You can make a large quantity of the base for later use by boiling lime juice, fish sauce, and water with sugar in a pan. It will keep months in a tightly sealed jar or bottle in the refrigerator. Add freshly crushed garlic and chilies when serving.

Add chopped chili and transfer sauce to 4 individual saucers to serve. Sprinkle chopped peanuts over the top as a garnish.

Makes 4 servings.

Note: This sauce is known as *nuoc leo*. The liquid base can be made in advance; add freshly chopped chili and peanuts just before serving.

SWEET & SOUR SAUCE

2 tablespoons vegetable oil
1 clove garlic, chopped
2 shallots or ½ onion, chopped
1 teaspoon chili sauce
2 tablespoons tomato ketchup
2 tablespoons soy sauce
i tablespoon fish sauce
2 tablespoons sugar
2 tablespoons red rice vinegar
about ½ cup chicken stock
2 tablespoons cornstarch

Heat oil in a medium saucepan and gently stir-fry garlic and shallots or onion until golden but not brown.

Add chili sauce, tomato ketchup, soy and fish sauces, sugar, and vinegar. Stir to blend well, then add stock and bring to a boil, stirring continuously.

Taste sauce to check sweet and sour balance and adjust seasoning if necessary. Mix cornstarch with 2 or 3 tablespoons water and add to sauce, stirring until smooth, then remove from heat and serve.

Makes about 2 cups.

Note: This sauce is traditionally used for fried or broiled dishes, or it can be used as a dip at the table.

VIETNAMESE HOT SAUCE

1 clove garlic, chopped
2 small red or green chilies, seeded and chopped
1 teaspoon finely chopped fresh ginger
1 tablespoon chili sauce
2 stalks lemongrass, peeled and chopped
2 tablespoons vegetable oil
2 tablespoons soy sauce
1 tablespoon fish sauce
2 tablespoons sugar
2 tablespoons lime juice with pulp
4 to 6 tablespoons chicken stock or water
2 tablespoons chopped cilantro leaves
1 tablespoon cornstarch

Using a mortar and pestle, pound garlic, chilies, ginger, chili sauce, and lemongrass to a paste. Heat oil in a medium saucepan and gently stir-fry paste with soy sauce, fish sauce, sugar, lime juice, and stock or water, then bring to a boil.

Blend in chopped cilantro. Mix cornstarch with 2 tablespoons water and stir paste into sauce to thicken it. Remove from heat and serve.

Makes about 1½ cups.

Note: This highly spiced sauce goes well with all sorts of meat or fish dishes—it can form the base for curry sauce, or it can be served as a dip.

DESSERTS

FRITTERS & FRAGRANT SYRUP

2 cups superfine granulated sugar
5 green cardamom pods, bruised
1 teaspoon rosewater
pinch saffron threads
1 cup all-purpose flour
1 tablespoon baking powder
2½ cups low-fat milk powder
1 tablespoon butter, melted
⅔ cup plain yogurt
about ½ cup milk
⅓ cup raisins
vegetable oil for frying
rose petals, to decorate (optional)

Put sugar and 2 cups water in a heavy-bottomed pan and heat gently, stirring occasionally, until sugar dissolves. Bring to a boil, then boil about 5 minutes or until thickened and syrupy. Stir in cardamom pods, rosewater, and saffron threads, and keep warm. Meanwhile, sift flour and baking powder together into a mixing bowl and stir in milk powder. Mix in butter and yogurt and enough milk to make a soft dough.

With floured hands, divide the dough into 24 pieces. Make a depression in center of each and press in 2 or 3 raisins. Cover raisins with dough and roll into balls. Half-fill a deep-fat pan or fryer with oil and heat to 375°F. Fry 4 or 5 balls at a time, 3 to 5 minutes, until a deep golden brown. Drain on absorbent paper towels, then add to syrup. Serve hot, decorated with rose petals, if desired.

Makes 4 to 6 servings.

CARDAMOM & NUT ICE CREAM

8 cups milk
12 green cardamom pods, bruised
⅓ cup superfine granulated sugar
⅓ cup chopped blanched almonds, toasted
⅓ cup chopped pistachio nuts
mint sprigs, to decorate

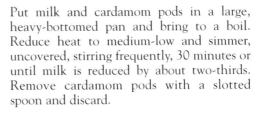

Put milk and cardamom pods in a large, heavy-bottomed pan and bring to a boil. Reduce heat to medium-low and simmer, uncovered, stirring frequently, 30 minutes or until milk is reduced by about two-thirds. Remove cardamom pods with a slotted spoon and discard.

Stir in sugar, almonds, and half the pistachio nuts, and simmer an additional 5 minutes. Let cool. Pour reduced milk into a plastic container, cover, and freeze 2 to 3 hours, until frozen around edge. Spoon into a food processor fitted with a metal blade and process, or whisk with an electric hand whisk, until smooth and light. Return to container, cover, and freeze 1 hour. Meanwhile, put 6 individual ¾-cup molds into freezer to chill.

Spoon semifrozen mixture into molds, pressing down firmly. Cover and freeze 2 to 3 hours, until solid. To serve, dip molds in hot water a few seconds and turn out onto plates. Serve at once, sprinkled with remaining pistachio nuts and decorated with mint sprigs.

Makes 6 servings.

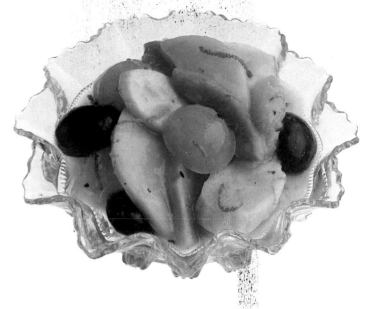

SAFFRON YOGURT

2½ cups plain yogurt
pinch saffron threads
2 tablespoons boiling water
seeds from 6 cardamom pods
3 tablespoons superfine granulated sugar
lemon zest and cardamom seeds, to decorate

Pour yogurt into a nylon sieve lined with cheesecloth and leave in refrigerator overnight to drain.

Put saffron and water in a small bowl and let soak 30 minutes. Tip drained yogurt into a bowl and stir in saffron and its soaking liquid.

Put cardamom seeds in a mortar and crush lightly with a pestle. Stir into yogurt with sugar. Serve chilled, decorated with lemon zest and cardamom seeds.

Makes 4 to 6 servings.

INDIAN FRUIT SALAD

2 mangoes
2 bananas
2 oranges
⅓ cup black grapes
⅓ cup green grapes
1 papaya
grated zest and juice of 1 lime
¼ cup superfine granulated sugar
freshly ground black pepper
plain yogurt, to serve

Peel and pit mangoes and cut flesh into thin slices, reserving any scraps. Peel and diagonally slice bananas.

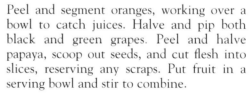

Peel and segment oranges, working over a bowl to catch juices. Halve and pip both black and green grapes. Peel and halve papaya, scoop out seeds, and cut flesh into slices, reserving any scraps. Put fruit in a serving bowl and stir to combine.

Put orange juice, lime juice, sugar, and scraps of mango and papaya in a blender or food processor fitted with a metal blade and process until smooth. Add lime zest and pepper. Pour over fruit and chill at least 1 hour before serving with yogurt.

Makes 4 to 6 servings.

Variation: Use other fruits, such as melon, guava, or pineapple, if preferred.

GOLDEN SEMOLINA PUDDING

½ cup superfine granulated sugar
3 tablespoons butter or ghee
¾ cup semolina
seeds from 3 cardamom pods
2½ tablespoons raisins
⅓ cup slivered almonds, toasted
plain yogurt, to serve (optional)

Put sugar in a heavy-bottomed saucepan with ⅔ cup water. Cook over a low heat, stirring occasionally, until sugar has dissolved. Bring to a boil and boil 1 minute, then remove from heat and set aside.

Melt butter or ghee in a large, heavy-bottomed skillet, add semolina, and cook 8 to 10 minutes over a medium heat, stirring constantly, until semolina turns golden brown.

Remove from heat and let cool slightly, then stir in sugar syrup and cardamom seeds. Cook over a low heat 3 to 5 minutes, stirring frequently, until thick. Stir in half the raisins and almonds. Serve warm, decorated with remaining raisins and almonds, and with plain yogurt, if desired.

Makes 4 to 6 servings.

COCONUT LAYER CAKE

½ cup all-purpose flour
1¾ cups coconut milk (see page 224)
6 egg yolks, beaten
½ cup superfine granulated sugar
seeds from 4 green cardamom pods, crushed
pinch of freshly grated nutmeg
½ cup butter, melted
plain yogurt and banana slices, to serve

Put flour in a mixing bowl, whisk in coconut milk, egg yolks, sugar, cardamom seeds, and nutmeg, then leave batter to stand for 30 minutes.

Preheat oven to 425°F. Butter and line the bottom of a 6-in. soufflé dish. Add 1 tablespoon butter to dish and heat in oven 5 minutes. Pour in ⅓ cup batter and bake 10 to 15 minutes, until firm to touch and lightly browned. Continue adding another 3 layers, brushing cooked layer with butter before adding batter, then cooking each layer 10 to 15 minutes.

Put soufflé dish in a baking pan half-filled with boiling water, then continue adding final 3 layers in same way as before. When last layer is cooked, remove dish from oven and let cool. Run a knife around edge of dish to loosen cake and turn out onto a serving plate. Serve warm, with yogurt and sliced bananas.

Makes 4 to 6 servings.

APRICOT DESSERT

2 cups ready-to-eat dried apricots
1 cup superfine granulated sugar
1 cup whipping cream
⅓ cup blanched almonds, chopped and toasted

Put apricots in a saucepan with 1 cup water and bring to a boil, then simmer, covered, about 25 minutes or until very soft.

Meanwhile, put sugar and 2 cups water in a heavy-bottomed saucepan and heat gently, stirring occasionally, until sugar has dissolved. Bring to a boil and boil 3 minutes or until syrupy. Drain apricots and purée in a blender or food processor fitted with a metal blade. Add syrup and process again.

Pour mixture into a bowl and let cool, then chill at least 1 hour. Whip cream until holding soft peaks, fold half into apricot purée, leaving it slightly marbled, and spoon into serving dishes. Chill 30 minutes, then top with remaining cream and sprinkle with chopped almonds.

Makes 4 to 6 servings.

PISTACHIO HALVA

1⅓ cups shelled pistachio nuts
1 cup boiling water
2 tablespoons milk
½ cup sugar
2 tablespoons butter or ghee
few drops of vanilla extract

Put pistachio nuts in a bowl, add boiling water, and let soak 30 minutes. Grease and line the bottom of a 7-in. square pan.

Drain pistachio nuts thoroughly and put in a blender or food processor fitted with a metal blade. Add milk and process until finely chopped, scraping mixture down from sides once or twice. Stir in sugar. Heat a large nonstick skillet, add butter or ghee, and melt over a low to medium heat. Add nut paste and cook about 15 minutes, stirring constantly, until mixture is very thick.

Stir in vanilla extract, then spoon into prepared pan and spread evenly. Let cool completely, then cut into 20 squares using a sharp knife.

Makes about 20 squares.

Note: This halva will keep 2 to 3 weeks when stored in the refrigerator.

TOASTED ALMOND TOFFEE

2 cups sugar
2 cups low-fat milk powder
few drops of vanilla extract
¼ cup slivered almonds, toasted

Grease and line the bottom of a 7-in. square pan. Put sugar in a large, heavy-bottomed saucepan with 1 cup water and heat gently, stirring occasionally, until sugar is dissolved.

Bring to a boil, then boil over a medium-high heat until a few drops of mixture will form a soft ball in cold water. Stir in milk powder and cook an additional 3 or 4 minutes, stirring constantly, until mixture begins to dry on spoon. Stir in vanilla.

Pour into prepared pan and spread evenly. Sprinkle almonds on top and press into surface. Let cool slightly, then cut into 25 squares with a sharp knife while still warm. Leave in pan until cool and firm.

Makes 25 squares.

CASHEW FUDGE

1½ cups unsalted cashews
1½ cups boiling water
2 tablespoons milk
⅔ cup sugar
1 tablespoon butter or ghee
few drops of vanilla extract
few sheets of silver leaf (see page 161)

Put cashews in a bowl, add boiling water, and let soak 1 hour. Grease and line the bottom of a 7-in. square pan.

Drain cashews thoroughly and put in a blender or food processor fitted with a metal blade. Add milk and process until smooth, scraping mixture down from sides once or twice. Stir in sugar. Heat a large, nonstick skillet, add butter or ghee, and melt over a low to medium heat. Add nut paste and cook about 20 minutes, stirring constantly, until mixture is very thick.

Stir in vanilla extract, then spoon into prepared pan and spread evenly. Let cool completely, then press silver leaf onto surface. Cut fudge into about 25 diamond shapes using a wet, sharp knife.

Makes about 25 pieces.

Note: This fudge will keep 2 to 3 weeks if stored in an airtight container.

PEKING APPLES

1 egg, beaten
1 cup all-purpose flour
4 crisp eating apples
SYRUP:
1 tablespoon vegetable oil
⅓ cup brown sugar
2 tablespoons light corn syrup
iced water, to set

In a large bowl, stir egg and ½ cup water into flour to make a thick batter. Peel, core, and thickly slice apples. Dip each apple slice in batter to evenly coat, allowing excess to drain off.

In a wok, heat oil until smoking. Add apple pieces in batches and deep-fry 3 minutes or until golden brown. Using a slotted spoon, remove to absorbent paper towels to drain.

To make syrup, in a small saucepan, gently heat oil, sugar, and 2 tablespoons water, stirring until sugar has dissolved. Simmer 5 minutes, stirring. Stir in light corn syrup and boil 5 to 10 minutes or until hard and stringy. Reduce heat to very low. Dip each piece of apple into syrup to coat, then place in ice-cold water a few seconds to set syrup. Remove to a serving dish. Repeat with remaining apple. Serve immediately.

Makes 4 servings.

CHINESE FRUIT SOUP

½ cup rice wine or dry sherry
juice and zest of 2 limes
3½ cups water
1 cup granulated sugar
1 piece lemongrass
4 whole cloves
2-in. stick cinnamon
1 vanilla pod, split
pinch of ground nutmeg
1 teaspoon coriander seeds, lightly crushed
1½-oz. piece fresh ginger, peeled and thinly sliced
2½ tablespoons raisins
1 lb. (about 2½ cups) prepared sweet fruits, e.g.
  mango, strawberries, lychees, star fruit, kiwi fruit

In a saucepan, place rice wine or dry sherry, lime juice and zest, water, sugar, lemongrass, cloves, cinnamon, vanilla, nutmeg, coriander seeds, and ginger. Heat gently, stirring until sugar dissolves, then bring to a boil. Reduce heat and simmer 5 minutes. Let cool, then strain into a bowl. Add raisins, then chill in refrigerator.

Arrange a selection of prepared fruit in 4 individual serving dishes and spoon syrup on top.

Makes 4 servings.

GREEN TEA FRUIT SALAD

4 teaspoons jasmine tea leaves
2 tablespoons dry sherry
2 tablespoons sugar
1 lime
2 kiwi fruit
8 oz. fresh lychees
¼ honeydew melon
¾ cup seedless green grapes
lime slices, to decorate

Place tea leaves in a small bowl and add 1¼ cups boiling water. Leave to steep 5 minutes. Strain through a sieve into a saucepan.

Stir in sherry and sugar. Using a vegetable peeler, pare zest from lime and add to pan. Squeeze juice from lime and add juice to pan. Bring to a boil, reduce heat, and simmer 5 minutes. Let cool, then discard lime zest.

Peel and thinly slice kiwi fruit. Peel, halve, and pit lychees. Peel melon and slice thinly. Arrange prepared fruits and grapes in small clusters on serving plates. Spoon cooled tea syrup over fruit, decorate, and serve.

Makes 4 servings.

CARAMEL SESAME BANANAS

4 bananas
juice of 1 lemon
½ cup sugar
2 tablespoons sesame seeds
mint sprigs and lemon slices, to decorate

Peel bananas and cut into 2-in. pieces. Place in a bowl, add lemon juice, and stir to coat.

Place sugar and ¼ cup water in a saucepan and heat gently, stirring, until sugar dissolves. Bring to a boil and cook 5 or 6 minutes or until mixture caramelizes and turns golden brown. Drain bananas well and arrange on nonstick baking parchment.

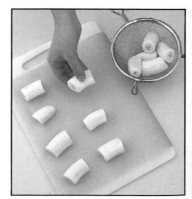

Drizzle caramel over bananas, working quickly, as the caramel sets within a few seconds. Sprinkle with sesame seeds. Let cool 5 minutes, then carefully peel away from paper, decorate, and serve.

Makes 4 servings.

Note: Tossing banana in lemon juice keeps it from turning brown.

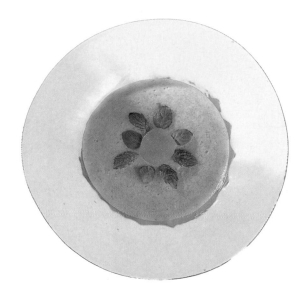

LYCHEE & GINGER MOUSSE

FRUIT-FILLED WHITE CRÊPES

12 oz. fresh lychees, peeled and pitted
½ teaspoon ground ginger
3 tablespoons sweet sherry
2 pieces candied ginger in syrup, chopped
¼ cup ground almonds
2 teaspoons powdered gelatin dissolved in
   2 tablespoons boiling water
2 egg whites
sliced candied ginger and mint leaves, to decorate

3 egg whites, lightly beaten
¼ cup cornstarch
1 teaspoon sunflower oil
mint sprigs, to decorate
FILLING:
4 slices fresh pineapple, chopped
2 kiwi fruit, peeled and quartered
½ mango, peeled, pitted, and sliced
½ papaya, peeled, seeded, and chopped
2 tablespoons dry sherry
1 tablespoon brown sugar
1 whole cinnamon stick, broken
2 star anise

Put lychees in a food processor with ground ginger, sherry, and chopped ginger. Blend until smooth. Transfer to a small bowl and stir in ground almonds and gelatin mixture.

Chill 30 to 40 minutes or until beginning to set. In a large, grease-free bowl, whisk egg whites until very stiff. Using a large metal spoon, carefully fold in lychee mixture.

Place all filling ingredients in a wok and mix gently. Bring to a boil, reduce heat, and simmer very gently 10 minutes. Remove and discard cinnamon stick and star anise. Set aside. Meanwhile, make crêpes. Put egg whites and cornstarch in a bowl and stir in 3 tablespoons water, mixing well to form a smooth paste.

Divide mixture among 4 sundae glasses or dishes and chill 1 hour or until set. Decorate with candied ginger and mint leaves and serve.

Makes 4 servings.

Brush a nonstick or well-seasoned crêpe pan with a little oil, and heat. Pour in a quarter of the mixture, tilting pan to cover the bottom. Cook 1 minute on one side only, until set. Drain on absorbent paper towels, layer with waxed paper, and keep warm while making remaining 3 crêpes. Lay crêpes cooked-side up, fill with fruit, and fold crêpes over filling. Decorate and serve.

Makes 4 servings.

STUFFED RAMBUTANS

1 small banana, chopped
grated zest and juice of 1 lime
16 rambutans
12 pitted dates, chopped
1 papaya, peeled, seeded, and chopped
strips of lime zest, to decorate

Mix banana with lime zest and juice and set aside. Slice top off rambutans, exposing tip of pit. Using a sharp, small-bladed knife, carefully slice down around pit, loosening flesh away from pit.

Peel away skin and slice lengthwise through flesh at quarterly intervals. Gently pull down flesh to expose pit and carefully cut away pit. The flesh should now resemble a four-petalled flower.

In a food processor or blender, blend banana and dates until smooth. Place a teaspoon of filling in the center of each rambutan and bring up sides to enclose filling. Cover and chill 30 minutes. Blend papaya in a food processor or blender until smooth, pass through a sieve and spoon onto 4 serving plates. Top with rambutans, decorate with strips of lime zest, and serve.

Makes 4 servings.

STEAMED FRUIT DUMPLINGS

1 small banana, chopped
grated zest and juice of 1 small lemon
¼ cup dried mango or dried apricots, chopped
8 pitted dates, chopped
¼ cup ground almonds
large pinch of ground cinnamon
12 round wonton skins
1 egg white, lightly beaten
2 teaspoons confectioners' sugar
strips of dried mango, and date and mint sprigs, to decorate

Place banana, lemon zest and juice, mango, dates, almonds, and cinnamon in a food processor and blend until smooth.

Divide fruit mixture among wonton skins, placing it in the center of each one. Brush edges of wonton skins with egg white, fold in half to form crescent shapes, and press edges together to seal.

Bring a wok or large saucepan of water to a boil. Place dumplings on a sheet of nonstick baking parchment in a steamer and place over water. Cover and steam 10 minutes or until soft. Dust with confectioners' sugar, decorate, and serve.

Makes 4 servings.

COCONUT CUSTARDS

1 pandan leaf (optional)
2½ cups coconut milk
3 whole eggs
3 egg yolks
⅓ cup superfine granulated sugar
½ cup light cream

Run tines of a fork through pandan leaf, if using. Tie in a knot. Pour coconut milk into a nonstick saucepan, add pandan leaf, and bring to just below a simmer. Remove from heat, cover, and leave 20 minutes. Discard pandan leaf.

Preheat oven to 350°F. Reheat coconut milk to a boil. In a bowl, whisk together eggs, egg yolks, and sugar until evenly blended. Slowly pour in coconut milk, whisking constantly. Stir in cream.

Strain into a pot and pour into 8 ramekin dishes. Set ramekins in a baking pan and pour boiling water into pan to come halfway up sides of ramekins. Cook in the oven 20 to 25 minutes or until a skewer inserted in the center comes out clean. Remove ramekins from pan and let cool. Chill until needed.

Makes 8 servings.

PINEAPPLE WITH COCONUT

½ cup superfine granulated sugar
1½-in. piece fresh ginger, grated
½ cup light brown sugar
12 thin slices fresh pineapple
3 or 4 tablespoons toasted coconut flakes

Put superfine granulated sugar, ginger, and light brown sugar in a heavy-bottomed saucepan. Stir in 1⅔ cups water. Heat gently, stirring with a wooden spoon, until sugars have melted. Bring to a boil. Simmer until reduced by about a third.

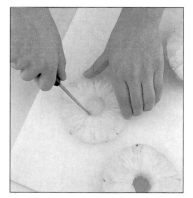

Remove cores from slices of pineapple using a small, sharp knife or a small pastry cutter. Strain syrup over pineapple rings and let cool. Cover and chill.

To serve, lay 2 pineapple rings on each plate. Spoon some of the syrup on top and sprinkle with toasted coconut flakes.

Makes 6 servings.

MALAYSIAN FRUIT SALAD

⅓ cup light brown sugar
grated zest and juice of 1 lime
1 small pineapple, peeled, cored, and cubed
1½ lbs. lychees, peeled, halved, and pitted
3 ripe mangoes, peeled, pitted, and chopped
1 papaya, peeled, seeded, and chopped

Put sugar, lime zest and juice, and ⅔ cup water in a saucepan. Heat gently, stirring with a wooden spoon, until sugar has dissolved.

Heat syrup to boiling point, then simmer 1 minute. Remove from heat and let cool.

Put pineapple, lychees, mangoes, and papaya in a serving dish. Pour cool syrup on top. Cover dish with plastic wrap and put in the refrigerator to chill.

Makes 4 servings.

SAGO PUDDING

2 cups milk or water
6 oz. sago, rinsed
1½ cups coconut milk
¼ cup light cream
SYRUP:
¾ cup palm sugar or brown sugar
small piece fresh ginger or lemongrass
1 pandan leaf (optional)

In a saucepan, bring milk or water to a boil. Add sago, stir, and simmer 10 to 15 minutes, stirring occasionally, until tender. Cool slightly and spoon into individual glass dishes. Cool completely, then refrigerate.

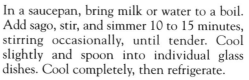

To make syrup, in a saucepan, gently heat sugar with ¾ cup water, ginger or lemongrass, and pandan leaf, if using, stirring with a wooden spoon until sugar has dissolved. Bring to a boil. Simmer a few minutes or until syrup thickens. Strain and let cool.

Mix together coconut milk and cream, then chill. To serve, pour creamy coconut milk around edges of sago puddings. Make a well in the center of the puddings and pour in some of the syrup.

Makes 6 servings.

MANGO WITH STICKY RICE

1¼ cups sticky rice, soaked overnight in cold water
1 cup coconut milk
pinch salt
2 to 4 tablespoons sugar, to taste
2 large ripe mangoes, peeled and halved
3 tablespoons coconut cream (see page 8)
mint leaves, to decorate

Drain and rinse rice thoroughly. Place in a steaming basket lined with a double thickness of cheesecloth. Steam over simmering water 30 minutes. Remove from heat.

In a bowl, stir together coconut milk, salt, and sugar to taste until sugar has dissolved. Stir in warm rice. Set aside 30 minutes.

Thinly slice mangoes by cutting lengthwise through flesh to the pit. Discard pits. Spoon rice into a mound in center of serving plates and arrange mango slices around edge. Pour coconut cream over rice. Decorate with mint leaves.

Makes 4 servings.

COCONUT PANCAKES

⅔ cup rice flour
⅓ cup superfine granulated sugar
pinch salt
1 cup dried coconut
2 eggs, beaten
2½ cups coconut milk
green and red food coloring (optional)
vegetable oil for frying
mandarin segments, to serve (optional)

In a bowl, stir together rice flour, sugar, salt, and coconut.

Form a well in the center, add egg, then gradually fold in flour, slowly pouring in coconut milk at same time, to make a smooth batter. If desired, divide batter evenly between 3 bowls; stir green food coloring into one bowl to color batter pale green; color another batch pink and leave remaining batch plain. Heat a 6-in. crêpe or omelette pan over a moderate heat, swirl around a little oil, then pour off excess. Stir batter well, then add 2 or 3 spoonfuls to pan.

Rotate to cover bottom, then cook over moderate heat about 4 minutes or until lightly browned underneath and quite firmly set. Carefully turn over and cook briefly on the other side. Transfer to a warmed plate and keep warm while cooking remaining batter. Serve rolled up with mandarin segments, if desired.

Makes about 10 pancakes.

Note: The mixture is quite delicate and the first few pancakes may be difficult to make.

GREEN & WHITE JELLIES

1 tablespoon powdered gelatin
scant 1 cup coconut milk
⅓ cup superfine granulated sugar
⅓ cup coconut cream (see page 8)
2 pieces pandanus leaf, each 3 in. long,
  or ¾ to 1 teaspoon kewra water
green food coloring

Sprinkle 1½ teaspoons of gelatin over 1½ tablespoons water in a small bowl and let soften 5 minutes. Stand bowl in a small saucepan of hot water and stir until dissolved. Remove from heat.

Put coconut milk and half the sugar into a medium saucepan and heat gently, stirring until sugar has dissolved. Remove from heat and stir in coconut cream.

Stir a little into dissolved gelatin, then stir back into medium pan. Divide between 4 or 6 individual molds. Place in refrigerator to set.

Put remaining sugar in a medium saucepan with 1¼ cups water and pandanus leaf or kewra water. Heat gently, stirring, until sugar dissolves. Bring to a boil, simmer 2 or 3 minutes, cover, and remove from the heat. Set aside 15 minutes, then remove pandanus leaf, if used.

Dissolve remaining gelatin in the same way as first half. Stir in a little pandanus liquid, then stir back into medium pan. Add green food coloring to color.

Set aside until cold but not set, then pour over set coconut mixture. Place in a refrigerator to set. Dip molds into hot water 1 or 2 seconds, then turn out onto cold plates.

Makes 4 to 6 servings.

Note: If pandanus leaf or kewra water are unavailable, flavor with rosewater and color pink with red food coloring to make Pink & White Jellies.

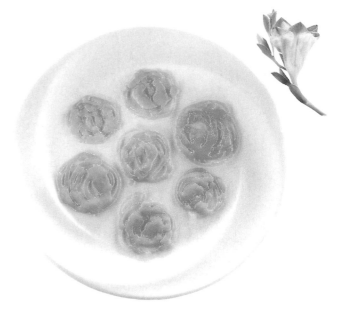

LYCHEES & COCONUT CUSTARD

3 egg yolks
3 or 4 tablespoons superfine granulated sugar
scant 1 cup coconut milk
⅓ cup coconut cream (see page 8)
about 1 tablespoon triple-distilled rosewater
red food coloring
about 16 fresh lychees, peeled, halved, and pitted
rose petals, to decorate

In a bowl, whisk together egg yolks and sugar.

In a medium-size, nonstick saucepan, heat coconut milk to just below boiling point, then slowly stir into egg yolk and sugar mixture. Return to pan and cook very gently, stirring with a wooden spoon, until custard coats the back of the spoon.

Remove from heat and stir in coconut cream, rosewater to taste, and sufficient red food coloring to color pale pink. Leave until cold, stirring occasionally. Spoon a thin layer of rose-flavored custard into 4 small serving bowls. Arrange lychees on custard. Decorate with rose petals. Serve remaining custard separately to pour over lychees.

Makes 4 servings.

GOLDEN THREADS

6 egg yolks
1 teaspoon egg white
2 cups sugar
few drops of jasmine extract

Strain egg yolks through cheesecloth into a small bowl. Beat lightly with egg white. In a saucepan, gently heat sugar, jasmine extract, and 1 cup water, stirring until sugar dissolves, then boil until thickened slightly. Adjust heat so syrup is hot but not moving.

Spoon a small amount of egg yolk into a piping bag fitted with a very fine nozzle or a cone of waxed paper with very small hole in pointed end. Using a circular movement, carefully dribble a trail into syrup, making swirls about 1½ to 2 in. in diameter with a small hole in center. Make a few at a time, cooking each briefly until set.

Using a skewer inserted in hole in center of spiral, transfer each nest to a plate. Continue making similar nests with remaining egg yolks. When nests are cool, arrange on a serving plate.

Makes 4 servings.

LYCHEE SORBET

1 lb. fresh lychees in their shells,
    or 6 oz. canned lychees
about ½ cup syrup (see opposite)
fresh mint sprigs, to decorate

Peel fresh lychees and pit them. Place lychees in a food processor or blender with syrup and process to a smooth purée.

Pour purée into a freezerproof container and place in the freezer about 2 hours until almost set.

Break up iced mixture and whip until smooth. Return mixture to the freezer 30 to 45 minutes to set until solid. Serve sorbet decorated with mint leaves.

Makes 4 to 6 servings.

Variation: 2 teaspoons grated fresh ginger can be added to sorbet mixture before blending, if desired.

VIETNAMESE FRUIT SALAD

⅔ cup rock candy or crystal sugar
about 1½ cups boiling water
½ small watermelon or a whole honeydew melon
4 or 5 different fruits (fresh or canned), such as
    pineapple, grapes, lychees, rambutan, banana,
    papaya, mango, or kiwi fruit
crushed ice cubes

Make a syrup by dissolving rock candy in boiling water, then let cool.

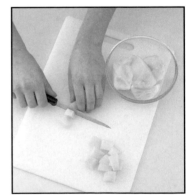

Slice about 3 in. from top of melon, scoop out flesh, discarding seeds, and cut flesh into small chunks. Prepare all other fruits by cutting them into small chunks the same size as the melon chunks.

Fill melon shell with fruit and syrup. Cover with plastic wrap and chill in the refrigerator at least 2 to 3 hours. Serve on a bed of crushed ice.

Makes 4 to 6 servings.

Note: If using canned fruit with syrup or natural juice, you can use this instead of making syrup for the dessert.

FRUIT SALAD WITH KANTEN

⅔ oz. dried kanten (agar-agar)
2 tablespoons sugar
1 small red apple, cut into 6 wedges and cored
salt
11-oz. can mandarin oranges, syrup reserved
4 canned pear quarters, sliced in half
20 green grapes, cut in half and seeded
strawberries, hulled, to decorate
light cream and 4 oz. sweet azuki (red bean) paste,
  to serve
SYRUP:
4 or 5 tablespoons pouring sugar syrup
1 cup syrup from canned tangerines or satsumas

Rinse kanten and soak in water 30 to 60 minutes, then squeeze out water and tear kanten into small pieces. Put in a saucepan with scant 1 cup water and cook over moderate heat until kanten has dissolved. Stir in sugar and, when it has dissolved, strain. Put liquid back into the pan and continue to cook, stirring, for another 3 minutes. Pour into a wet square mold, let cool, then chill in the refrigerator. To make dressing, dissolve sugar syrup in mandarin orange syrup and chill in the refrigerator.

Slice apple wedges into thin, half-open, fan-shaped pieces and plunge into salted water to prevent discoloration. Drain and pat dry. Cut hardened kanten into ⅔-in. dice. Put all fruits and kanten in a large salad bowl, pour syrup dressing over them, and fold in. Decorate with strawberries and serve with cream and sweet azuki (red bean) paste.

Makes 4 to 6 servings.

PANCAKES & RED BEAN PASTE

3 eggs, beaten
⅔ cup sugar
1 tablespoon pouring sugar syrup
1½ cups all-purpose flour
1 teaspoon baking powder
vegetable oil for frying
9 or 10 oz. sweet azuki (red bean) paste

In a mixing bowl, mix eggs, sugar, and syrup. Using a whisk, beat until sugar has dissolved and mixture has a smooth consistency. Add flour, a little at a time, and mix well.

Dissolve baking powder in ⅔ cup water and slowly stir into batter. Beat well. Place a small skillet over medium heat and when hot, wipe bottom with oil-soaked absorbent paper towels. Reduce heat to lowest setting and slowly ladle batter into center of skillet. The size of the ladle determines the size of the "gong" pancake, which should be about 5 in. in diameter. Cook about 3 minutes; when bubbles appear on the surface, turn pancake over and cook other side about 2 minutes. Remove to a plate.

Repeat process of oiling and baking until remaining batter is used up. As the skillet gets hotter, gradually reduce the cooking time by 1 minute on each side. Spread about 2 tablespoons sweet azuki (red bean) paste in the center of a pancake and cover with another pancake to make a "gong." Alternatively, make a half-gong by folding 1 pancake with 1 tablespoonful of paste inside. Serve hot or cold, accompanied by Japanese green tea, if desired.

Makes 6 to 8 gongs or 12 to 16 half-gongs.

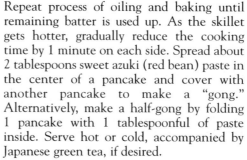